Jeremiah

INTERPRETATION
A Bible Commentary for Teaching and Preaching

INTERPRETATION

A BIBLE COMMENTARY FOR TEACHING AND PREACHING

James Luther Mays, *Editor*
Patrick D. Miller, Jr., *Old Testament Editor*
Paul J. Achtemeier, *New Testament Editor*

R. E. CLEMENTS

222

Jeremiah

INTERPRETATION

A Bible Commentary
for Teaching and Preaching

John Knox Press
ATLANTA

Library of Congress Cataloging-in-Publication Data
Clements, R. E. (Ronald Ernest), 1929–
  Jeremiah.

  (Interpretation, a Bible commentary for teaching and preaching)
    Bibliography: p.
    1. Bible. O.T. Jeremiah—Commentaries.
I. Title. II. Series.
BS1525.3.C57   1988   224′.207   88-9339
ISBN 0-8042-3127-3

© copyright John Knox Press 1988
10 9 8 7 6 5 4 3 2 1
Printed in the United States of America
John Knox Press
Atlanta, Georgia 30365

SERIES PREFACE

This series of commentaries offers an interpretation of the books of the Bible. It is designed to meet the need of students, teachers, ministers, and priests for a contemporary expository commentary. These volumes will not replace the historical critical commentary or homiletical aids to preaching. The purpose of this series is rather to provide a third kind of resource, a commentary which presents the integrated result of historical and theological work with the biblical text.

An interpretation in the full sense of the term involves a text, an interpreter, and someone for whom the interpretation is made. Here, the text is what stands written in the Bible in its full identity as literature from the time of "the prophets and apostles," the literature which is read to inform, inspire, and guide the life of faith. The interpreters are scholars who seek to create an interpretation which is both faithful to the text and useful to the church. The series is written for those who teach, preach, and study the Bible in the community of faith.

The comment generally takes the form of expository essays. It is planned and written in the light of the needs and questions which arise in the use of the Bible as Holy Scripture. The insights and results of contemporary scholarly research are used for the sake of the exposition. The commentators write as exegetes and theologians. The task which they undertake is both to deal with what the texts say and to discern their meaning for faith and life. The exposition is the unified work of one interpreter.

The text on which the comment is based is the Revised Standard Version of the Bible. The general availability of this translation makes the printing of a translation unnecessary and saves the space for comment. The text is divided into sections appropriate to the particular book; comment deals with passages as a whole, rather than proceeding word by word, or verse by verse.

Writers have planned their volumes in light of the requirements set by the exposition of the book assigned to them. Biblical books differ in character, content, and arrangement. They also differ in the way they have been and are used in the liturgy, thought, and devotion of the church. The distinctiveness and use of particular books have been taken into account in decisions about the approach, emphasis, and use of space in the commentaries. The goal has been to allow writers to develop the format which provides for the best presentation of their interpretation.

The result, writers and editors hope, is a commentary which both explains and applies, an interpretation which deals with both the meaning and the significance of biblical texts. Each commentary reflects, of course, the writer's own approach and perception of the church and world. It could and should not be otherwise. Every interpretation of any kind is individual in that sense; it is one reading of the text. But all who work at the interpretation of Scripture in the church need the help and stimulation of a colleague's reading and understanding of the text. If these volumes serve and encourage interpretation in that way, their preparation and publication will realize their purpose.

The Editors

PREFACE

The suggestion that I might write this commentary on the Book of Jeremiah came at a time when I was deeply committed to examining the problems of the Book of Isaiah, which eventually resulted in the publication of my commentary on Isaiah 1—39 for the New Century Bible (1980). At that time it appeared that very little recent commentary work had been undertaken on the Book of Jeremiah. This has now been remedied with the valuable works from J.A. Thompson and R.P. Carroll on the whole book and those of W.L. Holladay and W. McKane on Jeremiah 1—25. The first fascicle of S. Herrmann's major work in German has also recently appeared. All of these studies have appeared too late for me to give their detailed contents the attention they deserve in my own study. However, much of the preliminary work for these major commentaries has been discussed and given expression in many articles and special studies, which I have consulted with profit. I hope therefore that the exposition set out here will not appear indifferent to the issues that these larger commentaries have raised. The Book of Jeremiah is a complex literary composition, as are all of the prophetic writings of the Old Testament. Only now, after a century and a half of critical examination, are these works beginning to yield more of their secrets concerning their origin.

At one time the task of the commentator appeared to be that of the expert guide whose goal it was to enable the modern reader to hear again the authentic voice of the prophet publicly declaring his message to ancient men and women. Although clearly the prophet was a preacher, rather than a writer, that goal has seemed to me unrealizable and probably mistaken. On the basis of what the prophet had preached, a book intended to be read by persons in ancient times of recorded sayings, reminiscences, and reflections has been compiled. Their needs were not those of the original hearers and much of what they had experienced since the prophet first preached was viewed in light of the prophet's message. My aim therefore has been to try to enable the modern reader to sense how this remarkable book would have been read in ancient Israel and to discern the situation to which it was addressed. In many respects the question of who read this book is as important to understanding it as is the question of who wrote it. Neither question is wholly answerable, but neither should we be too pessimistic or negative in making intelligent reconstructions over such issues.

That I have left many of the technical literary and textual questions to the larger commentaries will be abundantly clear to the modern reader, and this is in line with the purpose of the series. I hope very much that the commentary will prove readable and that it will open up some fresh insight into and understanding of the worth and richness of this book of prophecy.

My indebtedness to other commentators and researchers will already be abundantly evident. I am especially grateful to Professor Patrick D. Miller, Jr., and to Professor James L. Mays for their patience in waiting for this text and for their expert advice and help in its production.

R.E. Clements
King's College
University of London

CONTENTS

Introduction

The Book of the Prophet Jeremiah

The Old Testament prophets were preachers rather than writers and the nature of prophecy is generally that of an orally proclaimed message to a circle of listeners. We read of prophets like this in the Old Testament and in reports of prophetic activity from outside the Bible. We should have been able, in any case, to deduce this from the character and content of the prophecies we have in written form, because the style and forms of speech betray all the characteristics of public proclamation. Prophecy in ancient Israel acquired a written form through its development, and that written form eventually took on a distinctive quality and importance, that of canonical status. Written prophecy made further prophetic interpretations possible and a more connected and coordinated presentation of the message of prophecy was formulated. The transition from oral to written prophecy had far-reaching significance and was eventually to have major implications, not only for understanding prophecy but also in bringing about change in the use and function of prophecy in Israelite-Jewish religion.

The earliest prophetic records in the Old Testament are found in narratives dealing with matters of wide national and political character. Despite the very substantial connections between the figures of Elijah and Elisha and the larger religious needs of Israel, we learn only little of what these prophets actually said. Not until the time of Amos, a century later (ca. 760–750 B.C.), do we have an extensive written collection of prophetic sayings from one individual. This makes it evident that written preservation of what had earlier been spoken in public represents a secondary stage of the prophetic activity. As a consequence of the effort to preserve prophetic messages in writing, which began at this time and continued until the close of the eighth century, we have books of prophecies from Hosea, Isaiah, and Micah.

1

The work of Jeremiah opens up a new phase of written prophecy around the end of the seventh century B.C. If we allow that an extensive literary effort in editing the prophecies of Isaiah and Micah took place, it is likely that such a gap is more apparent than real. It is important for us to recognize that the transition from oral to written prophecy was not a simple evolutionary development from within but that it occurred in response to certain outstanding events.

From the middle of the eighth century the Northern Kingdom was seriously threatened, internally from political unrest and factions and externally from Assyria. By the end of the century it had been wholly absorbed into the Assyrian imperial system. As a result of these political pressures it never afterwards recovered its unity and sense of national identity; whereas Judah, which also suffered imperial domination by Assyria, retained more of its sense of individual national identity. It was able to reassert itself when Assyrian control collapsed during the final two decades of the seventh century B.C. Shortly afterwards however a further century of Mesopotamian interference and political domination over Judah reappeared through Babylonian imperial expansion.

The primary reason for recording and preserving Israelite prophecy in literary form is not to be sought in prophecy itself but in the momentous events to which it bore witness. These events overwhelmed both Israel and Judah, threatening the complete destruction of their national institutions and their religion. These events were destroying the very fabric of their national identity. The preaching of the great prophets, beginning with Amos, supplied a kind of God-given commentary on the events that took place: forewarning that they would happen, offering reasons why they must happen, and seeing in them the judgment of God upon a sinful people. Alongside this threatening and forewarning activity, however, the prophets also had provided Israel and Judah with a message of hope, looking beyond the defeat and national humiliation to eventual renewal and restoration. Prophecy, therefore, can be adequately understood and interpreted only in relation to the events to which it was first addressed. Yet, once it had written form, it took on a more timeless and enduring significance and meaning.

2

The main body of the prophetic literature of the Old Testament relates either to the period of the onset of Assyrian domination in the eighth century (Amos, Hosea, Isaiah, Micah) or to that of Babylonian control at the close of the seventh and the first half of the sixth centuries B.C. The Book of Jeremiah belongs to this latter period as does that of Ezekiel, his contemporary. Other prophecies from Nahum, Habakkuk, and Zephaniah also belong to this era. Jeremiah lived through the time when Assyrian control over Judah fell into decline and eventually collapsed. After a brief respite, hopes in Judah for a new period of national recovery and greatness appeared justifiable and were extensively canvassed until the Babylonian power asserted its will over Judah (from 605 B.C.).

The transfer of allegiance to a new Mesopotamian imperial ruler appeared to pass peacefully, but after an early rebellion among the western territories in which Judah took part, harsh punitive measures were inflicted upon the kingdom. Further rebellion brought almost complete ruination. Of all this Jeremiah was a witness, and many of the more tragic and ruinous events of the period were the subject of specific prophecies from him. His book is commentary upon the most disastrous episodes of Judah's history to which the Old Testament bears witness, both in their religious and political consequences.

Predominantly, however, Jeremiah's book contains a message of hope. This message of hope, set against the background of political disaster and immense human suffering that accompanied it, gives the book its essential character (cf. R.E. Clements, "Jeremiah. Prophet of Hope," pp. 345ff.). This element of hope pervading the message of a prophet who lived through such tragic times is not in any way out of place or difficult to understand. From the perspective of the readers the book envisages, these political, religious, and military disasters were now events of the past. Nothing could be done to turn back the clock or to prevent from happening what had so painfully and tragically taken place. In preserving the record of Jeremiah's prophecies, the unknown scribes and compilers have done so with a view to assisting men and women overtaken by these tragedies to face them, to respond courageously to them, and to look in hope beyond them. Although many of the prophecies necessarily look back upon events belonging to an irreversible past, they did so in a manner designed to promote a deep and certain hope in the future and in the eventual restoration of Israel.

3

The Chronology of Jeremiah's Activity

The superscription (1:1–3) reports that Jeremiah first began to prophesy in the thirteenth year of king Josiah (639–609 B.C.), which points to the year 627–626 B.C. This means that he would have been prophesying for five years by the time the major religious and political reform took place in Jerusalem in the eighteenth year of Josiah's reign (II Kings 22:3). The fundamental presupposition of this reform was the weakening and eventual collapse of Assyrian imperial control over Judah during this decade. In the east Assyria maintained itself for another ten years, until the Babylonian armies overran Nineveh in 612 and defeated the last remnants of the Assyrian forces at Haran in 609 B.C. In that year king Josiah of Judah was killed attempting to prevent the Egyptian Pharaoh Necho from marching through Judah to render assistance to the Assyrians (II Chron. 35:20–24). For three months Jehoahaz (Shallum) reigned in Jerusalem until he was deposed by the Egyptian king in favor of his older brother Eliakim (Jehoiakim). II Kings 23:31–37 records these events which brought about a brief period when Judah was under the control of Egypt.

The circumstances of Josiah's untimely death indicate clearly that Judah had had ample reason to fear the growing interference of Egypt in its affairs during the preceding years. The existence of this Egyptian threat is important for understanding the background of Jeremiah's early prophesying. Since there are almost no surviving prophecies from Jeremiah that can be dated with confidence to these years between 626 and 609 B.C., many scholars have entertained serious doubts concerning the accuracy of the date given for the commencement of his ministry. J.P. Hyatt (*Jeremiah,* pp. 779, 798) regarded 626 as more probably the date of Jeremiah's birth, so that he would then have begun to prophesy soon after 609 B.C. Alternatively, it has been suggested that an error in transmission has occurred and the correct date for Jeremiah's call should be regarded as the twenty-third year of Josiah's reign (617/616 B.C.). Neither of these hypotheses are necessary however and we may assume that the date given in Jeremiah 1:2 is correct.

The fact that we do not have more than a brief outline sketch of Jeremiah's preaching before the time of Josiah's death has confused the issue. Jeremiah 36 contains a report of how a scroll of prophetic oracles from Jeremiah came to be written in the fourth year of Jehoiakim (605 B.C.). There is no reason for doubting that this year marked the beginning of the preservation in writing of a collection of Jeremiah's prophecies. Although we cannot know precisely what was included in this scroll, it appears highly probable that its contents have been incorporated into chapters 1—25 of the extant book (C. Rietzschel, pp. 127ff.). The reason for the concern to preserve Jeremiah's prophecies in writing taking place so late after his call must lie in the changed political situation that occurred in 605–604 B.C., the year Judah came within the orbit of Babylonian imperial control. The beginning of Jeremiah's work as a prophet therefore was not conterminous with the concern to preserve a record of his prophecies on a scroll.

The subsequent framework of political events which determined the fate of Judah and provided the background for Jeremiah's preaching is clear in its major features. In 601 B.C. Jehoiakim was persuaded to withhold tribute from Babylon and to align his people with a revolt against its imperial will. The Babylonian ruler Nebuchadnezzar reacted firmly and marched against Judah and Jerusalem. The city fell and Babylonian rule was reimposed (598 B.C.). During the siege Jehoiakim died and was succeeded by his son Jehoiachin, who was then deposed and taken as a prisoner to Babylon. His uncle (Mattaniah) was made king in his place, bearing the royal name Zedekiah (II Kings 24:8–17). Within a few years Zedekiah was induced to join a number of neighboring states in planning further rebellion against Babylon. The initial scheme apparently foundered but was quickly followed by another, which brought Judah once again into conflict with Babylon. Following a long siege, the city of Jerusalem fell to the Babylonians in the summer of 587 B.C. Zedekiah was forced to witness the death of his sons and was himself then blinded and taken as a prisoner to Babylon. In Jerusalem the palace area and the temple were systematically burned (II Kings 25:8–17).

The Babylonian authorities appointed Gedaliah to be governor in Judah, with his administrative center at Mizpah. Along with Zedekiah a substantial number of leading citizens were deported to Babylon, joining those who had already been taken in 598 B.C. Jeremiah would have been among them, but he was singled out and allowed to remain in the city because of his prophetic preaching and his advocating surrender to Zedekiah and all the citizenry of Jerusalem. Thereafter he stayed with the survivors in Judah until Gedaliah was assassinated. In fear of reprisals for this action many of the leaders in Jerusalem, against Jeremiah's advice, fled to Egypt, compelling Jeremiah to accompany them. The last picture given to us of Jeremiah (chap. 44) is that of the prophet condemning the idolatry of his fellow Judeans in Egypt. Presumably he died there, *circa* 580 B.C.

From this outline sketch of the main political background to Jeremiah's work, it is evident that Judah and the city of Jerusalem, brought under Babylonian rule after 605 B.C., witnessed in this period their most deeply wounding events. Moreover the collapse of resistance in Jerusalem in 587 led to two events that had immense repercussions upon the religious life of the nation. The temple, built under Solomon in Jerusalem, was destroyed and the Davidic dynasty ceased to reign in Jerusalem. This brought an end to the family line of Davidic kings that had survived in Judah for four centuries. It brought an end to kingship as a political office and left the heirs of the Davidic family out of office and uncertain of regaining it. Kingship itself was not restored to Judah for several centuries, and then in the hands of a non-Davidic family (the Hasmoneans).

At one stroke the year 587 witnessed the removal of the two institutions—the temple and the Davidic kingship—which had stood as symbolic assurances of God's election of Israel. Their loss was far greater than a loss of national prestige and left the entire understanding of Israel's special relationship to Yahweh its God in question. What had happened demanded a total reappraisal and rethinking of Israel's self-understanding as the People of God.

We must furthermore recognize that, although the consequences could not have been foreseen at the time, the deportations of Judah's leading citizens into exile in Babylon marked the first step in what we have come to know as the Diaspora. It is true that earlier, under Assyrian rule after 722 B.C., many of the citizens of the Northern Kingdom had suffered enforced removal to other regions of the Assyrian Empire (II Kings 17:6). Other citizens from Judah fled to Egypt, as we learn from the Book of Jeremiah (chaps. 42—44).

However, the Babylonian deportees of 598 and 587 B.C. from Judah formed the nucleus of the exiles whose descendants subsequently emerged as the leading element of the Diaspora. Jeremiah's prophetic ministry therefore took place during the years the state of Judah suffered the political collapse from which it did not recover for centuries. Out of this collapse the first elements of the scattered Jewish communities living among foreign host nations emerged, which resulted eventually in the experience of dispersion becoming the fundamental feature of Jewish life and religion. The Book of Jeremiah therefore provides us with an irreplaceable insight into the ideas, attitudes, and experiences relating to these formative events.

The Structure and Character of the Book

We have already pointed out that first and foremost Jeremiah was a prophetic preacher rather than a writer and the preservation of his messages in written form represents a secondary stage in their history. The prophet's use of Baruch the son of Neriah as a scribe to set down his messages in writing (36:4) strongly suggests that Baruch may have possessed special qualifications as a scribe-secretary; but the book indicates that his relationship to Jeremiah was closer and more intense than would have been the case for one simply employed to write. We must conclude that somewhere among the chapters of the present Book of Jeremiah the contents of Baruch's second scroll (36:32) are preserved. Although we can confidently assume that this material is within chapters 1—25 of the present book, it cannot be identified with any one part of this section. The evidence of subsequent rearrangement, supplementation, and further development of prophetic themes is too strongly marked for us to make any such conclusion. The importance of chapter 36 then is what it has to tell us concerning the time and circumstances of the writing down of Jeremiah's prophecies, rather than which part of the present book was written first.

So far as the structure of the book is concerned, we can readily detect a major distinction between the prophetic messages in chapters 1—25 and the series of narratives describing the experiences and activities of Jeremiah now located in chapters 26—29, 32, 34—45. This narrative material is too selective for it to be properly described as a prophetic biography. Although Baruch must have had some share in the recording of the events covered, the present form of these narratives cannot be ascribed to him. Marks of later narrative and theological interests are too clearly present for this to have been the case. Nevertheless, the conclusion of this section with a personal prophecy addressed to Baruch (chap. 45) confirms the conviction that he was an important link in the chain of preservation.

7

Chapter 1 contains an account of Jeremiah's call to be a prophet, and the prophecies that follow in chapters 2—25 are, with few exceptions, undated. There are indications that a loose chronological sequence has been maintained for several of them. So also the narratives of 26—45 preserve some chronological sequence, although it is evident that the pivotal events surrounding the siege and capture of Jerusalem, with all their tragic consequences, occupy the center of interest. A collection of prophecies dealing with the last kings of Judah is to be found in 22:1—23:7. Overall, we are compelled to conclude that no one characteristic explains the present shape of the book. This, in any case, appears somewhat differently in the ancient Greek translation (the Septuagint). There are powerful reasons for believing that the Septuagint rests on a form of the book that was also at one time current in Hebrew. Our present book is undoubtedly the product of a relatively long period of editorial collection and shaping. Its overall form has undergone changes; a prominent feature of this concerns the prophecies against foreign nations. In the Hebrew text they appear in chapters 46—51 and are to be found as 25:14—31:44 in the ancient Greek version (see further below under Textual and Literary Questions).

From this review of the contents of the book we see that no evaluation of the material can apply equally to all its parts. In the narrative episodes circumstantial detail is recorded that offers us a convincing and reliable picture of what happened to Jerusalem when it was besieged and captured by the Babylonians in 588–587 B.C. Over against this, only the barest sketch of the situation in Judah is available from the time of Jeremiah's call in 627/626 B.C. until Josiah's death and the accession of Jehoiakim after Shallum's (Jehoahaz) deposition in 609 B.C.

A further point can be readily observed. The revelation of how a message of hope came to Jeremiah in the period of Jereusalem's siege (chap. 32) has clearly provided a point of attachment for a larger series of hopeful prophecies in chapters 30—33. These are frequently referred to as "The Little Book of Consolation." Whether they all date from 587 B.C. and immediately afterwards is not made clear. This probably is not too important a consideration. The message of hope set out most strikingly in chapters 30—33 now forms the pivotal center for the entire book. Until the time Jeremiah received this word of hope while Jerusalem was under siege for the second time his message had predominantly been one of warning and threat. Then, when disaster had become inevitable, Jeremiah held out the word of assurance and hope from God concerning a new beginning for Israel.

This awareness that Jeremiah held out hope to those who were plunged into despair in Judah accounts for a distinctive aspect of the theological character of the book. Those who had listened to Jeremiah preach during the forty-year period from his call (627 B.C.) until Jerusalem was facing imminent destruction (587 B.C.) had listened to fearful warnings that sought to shake them out of their complacency. When disaster was about to strike, complacency had turned to despair and a feeling of disillusion and hopelessness had emerged. It was to this mood of despair and disillusionment that Jeremiah's words of hope had been addressed. Those intended to read the book were undoubtedly to be found among those who had been plunged into despair; as a consequence the theme of hope pervades the entire book. The past was past and could in no way be reversed. All that could be hoped for was that out of the ruins of the past a new Israel could come to birth and become the heir to all the ancient, but previously frustrated, promises of God. In this sense the shadow of the events of 587 B.C. covers the entire Book of Jeremiah, in much the same way as the shadow of the crucifixion rests over the whole of Mark's Gospel.

This is to draw attention to the point that besides a certain literary structure to the Book of Jeremiah there exists also a theological structure. This prophet had forewarned of a grave political danger which took shape in the arrival of Babylonian armies in Judah. Such warnings had at first been greeted with derision by men and women who felt confident that Mesopotamian interference in Judah's affairs was coming to an end. They had been proved wrong and Jeremiah's words had been proved a more trustworthy interpretation of affairs. It was important therefore to remember and ponder Jeremiah's words of warning, even after their terrifying message had been fulfilled. They made it plain that what had happened did not lie outside the sphere of God's control. In this way their explanations of a tragic past were inseparable from the message of hope concerning Judah's future. They pointed to the righteous wrath of the holy and gracious God whose love had not ceased. As God had punished an erring people, so as surely he both could and would raise them up again. As he had uprooted and

9

pulled down, so also would there be a time for building and planting again (1:10).

Textual and Literary Questions

From the point of view of the textual critic the Book of Jeremiah must undoubtedly be reckoned one of the most interesting and challenging subjects among the prophetic writings of the Old Testament. This is because the Greek (Septuagint) translation of the book differs substantially from that of the Hebrew (Massoretic) text. The most striking feature of this is that the Greek is approximately three thousand words shorter. We have already noted that, along with this divergence, the "foreign nation" prophecies are located differently in the Greek translation (see Structure and Character of the Book). Various theories have been proposed to account for these differences. Several scholars have claimed that the Greek translator(s) abbreviated the text, either deliberately or inadvertently. This may account for some of the divergence, but it does not account for all. Strengthened by the evidence of some fragments of Hebrew text found at Qumran, the conviction has grown recently that the Greek translator(s) worked from a Hebrew text that was much shorter than our present one.

If this is the case, as is strongly supported by the arguments of J.G. Janzen, then this sheds valuable light on the stages through which the composition of the book passed. The Greek represents at many points (not necessarily in all) an earlier stage in the formation of the book. A guide by which the non-specialist in textual criticism can perceive the differences is to be found in L. Stulman. Evidence of the growth of the book in at least two distinct forms points to the fact that there were several stages in its composition. How long the process took to make a collection of prophecies into a "book" is not clear, but it must have taken several decades. Since the prophecies against Babylon in chapters 50—51 imply that the downfall of that great empire was still awaited in the future, it indicates a time around 550 B.C. for the Hebrew text to have reached the form we are familiar with. If Jeremiah died in Egypt *circa* 580 B.C., then we can conclude that the book was in process of formation during 605–550 B.C.

10

There are two other points of major importance regarding the literary character and background of the book. The first of these is the evidence of substantial connections in religious language, style, and basic themes between the narratives set within Jeremiah 26—45 and the editorial interests of the historians who composed Joshua—Second Kings (usually referred to as the Deuteronomistic History because of its concern with the law-book of Deuteronomy). A detailed study of these similarities has been made by W. Thiel (1981) and such connections are also demonstrated in P. Diepold. Since it can be said that the Jeremiah narratives demonstrate a "Deuteronomistic" character, the editors of the prophecies of Jeremiah would probably be found among the same circles of scribes who were responsible for composing the law-book of Deuteronomy, the history of Joshua—Second Kings, as well as this major prophetic work. It is often helpful to compare the development of a number of major religious themes in all three writings; for example, covenant, land, law, disloyalty to God.

This leads us to consider what has become one of the most widely debated issues in Jeremiah studies during this century. In chapters 1—25, alongside the poetically formulated prophecies ascribed to Jeremiah, there appear a number of sermon-like addresses (prose discourses). These are untypical of most prophecy and are closely akin to the hortatory addresses in the law-book of Deuteronomy and in the Deuteronomistic History. The extent to which they are firmly "Jeremianic" (so W. L. Holladay) or are "Deuteronomistic" (so W. Thiel [1973]) has been extensively debated. The view presented in this commentary is that these prose discourses are not directly the work of the prophet Jeremiah but are based on words, themes, and situations authentic to the prophet. They represent a form of "developmental interpretation" important to the preservation and interpretation of written prophecy, parallel examples are also evident in the Books of Isaiah and Ezekiel. From the perspective of the exposition presented here, it is important to bear in mind that these prose discourses originated at a late stage in the book's composition and are among those parts which reveal most clearly a consciousness of the aftermath of 587 B.C. To this extent these discourses are especially admonitory about the past and hopeful about the future.

The bringing together of most of the prophecies of hope into a single block in chapters 30—33 and the collection of "foreign nation" prophecies in chapters 46—51 marks a consequence of a planned editorial process. Basically the book consists of prophecies from Jeremiah and narratives in which the prophet's activities figure significantly, or which concern events directly linked to the prophet's warnings. It is not the prophet himself, nor even his close associate Baruch, however, who has been responsible for shaping the present book. This has taken place in a circle of interpreters and scribes whose thinking and aims were closely, but not wholly, related to those of the Deuteronomistic school. By this "school" we refer to a body of thoughtful and intensely loyal Israelites who strove energetically to promote the true worship of Yahweh and to eradicate traces of the old Canaanite Baal religion in the period between 650 and 550 B.C. In many ways their work provides a center and foundation for both the Pentateuch and the prophetic literature of the Old Testament (cf. S. Herrmann).

PART ONE

God's Messenger of Doom
JEREMIAH 1—10

Jeremiah 1
Superscription and Call

As we should expect, the book commences with a first-person narrative account of how Jeremiah received his call and commissioning from God (vv. 4–10). This is preceded by a more general prefatory heading in third-person form explaining who Jeremiah was, when his call to prophesy came to him, and for how long it continued (vv. 1–3). This type of superscription compares closely with those in other prophetic collections (cf. Isa. 1:1; Ezek. 1:1–3; Hosea 1:1; Amos 1:1; and Micah 1:1). It is clear the editors of the prophetic literature recognized the importance of knowing the particular historical setting to which the prophecies that follow belong. This introduction to Jeremiah also provides a kind of total picture of the prophet's preaching. It conveys the idea that the work of a prophet, once set down in writing, offered a kind of divine overview upon the events to which the prophecies contained in the book were originally related. In this way the superscription implies that the word of prophecy may provide an interpretation of an entire age. As the sequence of prophecies unfolds, it becomes much clearer that this age had been one of momentous significance for the nation of Israel.

The superscription also clarifies that the audience to whom the prophecies were addressed was the nation of Judah as a whole and not just the smaller groups who had heard Jeremiah preach on specific occasions. In a deeply felt sense, it is evident that the intended readers of the Book of Jeremiah were

13

survivors of this nation of Judah. They in turn were merely a part of what was once the larger nation of Israel. A desire to publicize these prophecies for those who would have had no opportunity to hear them was a fundamental reason for writing them down. More significantly, however, those for whom this book of prophecies was intended were those who found themselves, as a result of what had taken place in the life of the nation, victims and survivors of events to which the prophet's words had been addressed. Their personal histories and misfortunes, recalled and illuminated by the prophecies of Jeremiah, provide the spiritual background of the book. The superscription makes unmistakably clear that these events have happened and cannot now be reversed. All that may be hoped for is that the men and women for whom this remarkable compilation of prophetic words and sayings was put together might gain some understanding of why they were suffering as they undoubtedly were. Prophecy is the divine word of hope and explanation, which is the antidote to human despair.

Nor is there any room for doubt or uncertainty concerning the horrifying catastrophe through which these people had passed. It left them bewildered, shocked, and deeply disillusioned with their world. (See Introduction: The Chronology of Jeremiah's Activity.) A cynical response to the events of Judah's downfall might have concluded that such gods as there were were cruel and despotic, paying no heed to human misery and grief. Another perspective would have been to think of one God alone as the ruler of the universe, but as a being so remote and detached from human affairs as to play no effective part in them. It would then have been appropriate to lay all the blame for what had taken place upon the politicians and false prophets who had encouraged Judah to embark upon such disastrous policies. Prophecy shared neither of these views, at least in the authentic form of prophecy which had been communicated through Jeremiah. Here was a man who had held himself aloof from the headstrong currents of popular opinion, often isolated and alone, as the speaker and interpreter of God. Setting down in writing what this prophet had said and experienced, based on records which he himself and his disciple Baruch had left, has provided for us a message of faith. This faith was big enough and bold enough to embrace the whole tragic sense of human history and to see that God had been fully involved in it. Such a prophetic faith recognized the reality of human freedom, the stark and inevitable consequences that pertain to human

14

choices, and the fact that men and women may, in spite of every God-given warning, choose what is evil and spurn what is good. They will then have to bear the consequence of their own decisions, experiencing all its pain and suffering.

Such faith is also a conviction that God is more than the fair and just arbiter of human deserts. His love for his creatures remains real, patient, and searching. Such love ultimately spells hope and the possibility of a new beginning. The surest sign that such love and hope do belong to the reality of God is to be found in the way in which God had, through the prophet Jeremiah, consistently and repeatedly warned and admonished the people of Judah of the dangers facing them. Faithfulness did not begin when human resources were at an end but had been demonstrated time and again through a long succession of prophetic warnings and admonitions. Jeremiah was then to be seen as the vindicator of the truth about God. His prophecies were to be read as a meaningful interpretation of the events which had brought tragedy and disaster upon Judah.

The period of Jeremiah's early activity as a spokesman for God (627–626 B.C.) was one in which a very strong national revival was taking place in Judah. This national revival, with a great deal of heady optimism, was a result of the ending of the century-long control of Assyria. This had drained the nation of its economic wealth, compromised its political rulers, and prejudiced its religious heritage. By way of reaction it had also reawakened a sense of the oneness of Israel and Judah as the Chosen People of Yahweh their God. It had also led a significant section of the nation to reaffirm with greater intensity than ever their determination to be loyal to Yahweh as God. Jeremiah must have embarked upon his prophetic activity with divided feelings about the changes he saw taking place in the life of his nation. On the one hand he can only have welcomed the spirit and aims of those who had encouraged and revitalized Judah's religious life. Over against this, we can discern throughout his early prophecies a deep suspicion that hope and optimism were easily slipping into complacency and an almost irrational belief that God could be relied upon to guard and protect Judah no matter how the people conducted their affairs. It was this complacent optimism which proved to be Judah's downfall; but before the full extent of this was felt, Jeremiah had to spend forty years as an isolated and derided prophet warning against its folly.

15

The account of Jeremiah's call (1:4–10) must, in company with other such prophetic call-narratives, have been composed at some interval after the event. The most likely suggestion is that it was itself composed to provide an introduction to a written collection of his prophecies. In this case almost two decades would have passed since he had first experienced this sense of a divine commissioning. The interval of time, however, makes little difference as to how it is to be understood. It reveals a sense of divine authority, compulsion, and empowering which had remained with Jeremiah throughout his prophetic ministry and upon which he must certainly have reflected many times as the years had passed.

Most strikingly, the book goes on to show how this sense of divine call and empowering had been tested, almost to the breaking point at a number of crisis-points in his work. The prophet could never have known at the time when he had first responded to God's call what it would truly mean. Nor could he have known how heavy and almost unbearable would be the strains it would put upon him. It was long after the first bold words of prophetic utterance from his lips had been given that he discovered how hard the task was to be that he had undertaken and how hopelessly weak and inadequate were his own human resources to cope with its demands.

The sense of call, with all that this meant by way of reliance upon God and the stripping away of all other social and personal supports, was something that was taking shape over a long and difficult period of time. It had begun for Jeremiah at a specific moment in his personal life and had continued. The experience of inner self-discovery had not ceased since that first day. The sense of call belonged too to his private inner world as a part of his personal understanding of God. Yet it had to be a public and openly declared part of his self-understanding, since it alone could explain his declarations and his perceived authority to declare them. No one could confirm or deny that he possessed this calling; it was between himself and God. Just as certainly however no one could prove or disprove the truth of his prophecies save the events themselves about which they testified. It was a supremely private event to Jeremiah, while at the same time public, national, and ultimately international in its significance and consequences (cf. 1:5,10).

16

Jeremiah's family background from among the priests "who were in Anathoth in the land of Benjamin" (1:1) is of great interest. It is unlikely that the youthful Jeremiah would have already begun to officiate in the sanctuary at Anathoth, just a few miles north of Jerusalem. He would certainly have undergone the training and preparation for such a task. Moreover Anathoth was the shrine to which Abiathar, the priest and close associate of David, had been banished when Solomon came to the throne (I Kings 2:26–27). As worship in the temple built by Solomon greatly enriched Jerusalem, as befitted the national royal capital, Anathoth must have accordingly declined in prestige. Nor would its situation amid the territory of Benjamin have helped in any way to alleviate the tensions and grievances of Abiathar's descendants at their deprivation from serving in the great religious center of the nation. The dynasty of Saul, although brief and unsuccessful, had been eclipsed in the struggle for Israel's throne by the dynasty of David. Saul was of the tribe of Benjamin, whereas David had sprung from the tribe of Judah. Just how extensively such inter-tribal rivalry had played a part in the political life of the kingdoms of Israel and Judah has been variously estimated. No doubt it would be easy to exaggerate; yet there is enough evidence to suggest that a strong and vigorous tradition of religious, political, and social opposition had lived on in the towns of Benjamin which had fallen under the jurisdiction of Judah. Although Anathoth belonged to Judah, there are grounds for thinking that many of its loyalties and traditions of religious allegiance were those of the northern tribes associated with the names of Ephraim and Israel.

This tradition of rivalry and bitterness would have been familiar to Jeremiah from his earliest days: the strong atmosphere of faith and loyalty which could not regard the political decisions nor the impressive ceremonies of Jerusalem as the unquestioned expressions of a divinely given right and privilege. Jeremiah would have been accustomed to look beneath the surface of the contemporary religious and political scene. He would have tested its validity and its veracity against the insights and principles of the older traditions of the nation's beginnings in the days of Moses and the Exodus.

Jeremiah's readiness to criticize and oppose the politics of the royal house of David and the claims and pretensions of the Jerusalem temple would lead him to positions of an extreme and radical nature. He could never have discerned this at the moment of his call. Yet he was convinced that from the moment of his being conceived he was divinely destined to be a prophet to Israel and the nations:

> "Before I formed you in the womb I knew you,
> and before you were born I consecrated you;
> I appointed you a prophet to the nations" (1:5).

With such words from God to him, Jeremiah sensed that he could not be and never could have been other than a prophet to declare God's word to his entire nation. At the same time he was to be a messenger to those other nations who also found themselves caught up in the web of events which had their origin in the impress of Babylonian imperialism upon the coastlands of the eastern Mediterranean. In a practical and relevant fashion Jeremiah's birth among the priests of Anathoth in the territory of Benjamin was to prove to be a significant aspect of this divine fore-ordaining to such a task.

The dialogue that embodied for Jeremiah his sense of a divine call and commissioning follows a relatively well-established pattern. Jeremiah protested to God his unreadiness and unfitness for such a high responsibility. As a youth still in his teen-age years, how could he command the respect and elicit the response of kings and counselors? Yet he ultimately and unflinchingly fulfilled these tasks through his sense that God had not only commanded him to prophesy but had empowered him to do so. Had not the prophets who had gone before Jeremiah experienced the same divine empowering? Had the same experience not been true even before them in the charismatic leadership shown by the tribal judges in the days before the monarchy? Strikingly the sense of an inner exchange of words between himself and God took on a reality so sure and certain for Jeremiah that it could almost be seen and felt. So he describes the experience in visual and tangible terms: "Then the Lord put forth his hand and touched my mouth; and the Lord said to me, . . ." (1:9).

How far this reflects a genuine vision of God's presence and how far it expresses images and feelings hidden within his own mind has been an issue commentators have frequently discussed but it has not been resolved. In any case it is a point of psychological interest only and has no bearing on the spiritual and personal sense of a transforming gift of power from God that came to the prophet. Looking back after years of testing prophetic utterance and experienced opposition, such as Jere-

18

miah's record of his call must undoubtedly reflect, this account of the experience has suppressed all the irrelevancies to concentrate upon the one utterly clear and totally relevant feature: God had given him the authority and strength to be a prophet.

In the concluding words of his commission the prophet reveals the two-sided nature of his task:

> "Behold, I have put my words in your mouth.
> See, I have set you this day over nations and over kingdoms,
> to pluck up and to break down,
> to destroy and to overthrow,
> to build and to plant" (1:9–10).

With exceptional boldness such words regard the prophet's pronouncements about God's intentions as passing over inexorably into stark facts and realities. Words of judgment become messengers of doom and destruction which bring to ruin nations and kingdoms, like battering-rams smashing down a city's wall of defense. Words of hope and assurance, conversely, become messengers of renewal and rebirth, like seeds planted in the soil to await the life-giving spring rains.

Two visions providing vivid summary insights into the character of his prophetic preaching during his early years follow the account of Jeremiah's call. The first is of the shoot of an almond tree, springing up and waiting to blossom forth as the first harbinger of spring. The second is of a cooking-pot, with the flames that burn under it to heat its contents fanned by a wind from the north. Just when these particular visions occurred for Jeremiah, whether as the immediate sequel to his experience of call or at some interval of time afterwards, is not made clear. Most probably Jeremiah's editors have placed them here, out of a feeling of their general appropriateness and probably also out of a feeling that truths seen in vision convey a note of special realism and authority. At any rate these two visions express truths about the divine intentions towards Israel which remained valid and secure for almost twenty years of the prophet's ministry. Not until the fateful year of 605 B.C., when Nebuchadnezzar came to power, did their full meaning become clear. At that time Egypt suffered defeat, leaving Judah at the mercy of Babylon and giving a new urgency to warnings regarding the renewal of a threat to Judah from Mesopotamia.

One feature is striking in respect to both visions, the almond-twig (1:11–12) and the cooking-pot (1:13–15). They relate to objects the prophet had seen. These provided him with a theme through a verbal or mental image conveyed by the object. We should probably draw the conclusion that Jeremiah actually saw these objects. As a result of the mental associations brought on by this experience, he interpreted their meaning in relation to God and his people. The almond twig was the harbinger of spring, but this was not the warmly reassuring sense of hope that such a sight conveyed. Rather the name of the almond tree (Heb. *shaqed*) suggested that God was watching (Heb. *shoqed*) over his word (of threat and warning) to fulfill it. The people's natural eagerness for the beginning of spring failed to reveal to them, as it did to Jeremiah, the note of danger and of imminent threat. God was watching over his word; he would not be indifferent to whether men and women listened to him, as would those who regarded every spring as the "play-time" of the year.

The second vision, the cooking-pot facing away from the north, has occasioned some difficulties for commentators in that the text does not make clear how the pot is placed in relation to the north. Its message, however, is made completely explicit through the interpretation that Jeremiah has placed upon what he has seen (1:14–15).

The implications of the prophetic message are clear, but one feature of it has occasioned a good deal of discussion and requires separate attention. Jerusalem, and the kingdom of Judah as a whole, was to be subjected to military attack and the city would be placed under siege. The precise outcome of this siege is not elaborated upon, but there are powerful hints that it would result in defeat and physical ruination for the city. This is suggested by the accusation that the people of Judah have forsaken God, so these impending events will serve as punishment. The picture of the kings of each of the kingdoms of the north sitting upon a throne outside a city under siege appears rather forced, yet we know from Assyrian portrayals of siege-warfare that this is precisely how an attacking commander would establish himself to handle the situation, especially in determining the fate of the inhabitants after a city's surrender. Why, however, does Jeremiah declare that this foe will come "from the north"? One view that was once widely popularized must now be dismissed altogether: that the prophet had in mind at this time an invasion, otherwise unrecorded in the Old Testament books, of marauding bands of Asiatic tribesmen (the

Scythians). Yet no really firm evidence exists to substantiate that Judah was threatened by bands of Scythians at this time.

A more plausible explanation combining a knowledge of Judah's earlier history with some elements of a more mythological nature has been proposed. During the century and a half in which Judah and Israel had been subjected to the imperial control of Assyria, the most humiliating defeats and the most serious threats had consistently come from the north-easterly routes linking Judah with Syria and Mesopotamia. Furthermore in the old Canaanite mythology the north as the location of the dwelling-place of the God Baal could have acquired a certain sinister and threatening connotation. Possibly, therefore, in affirming that Jerusalem and Judah were threatened "out of the north," Jeremiah was basing his portrayal on a combination of previous historical experience and certain overtones of a religious and mythological nature.

There is, however, a far more straightforward and convincing explanation for Jeremiah's insistence upon turning the attention of his people to the dangers that threatened them from the north. He was challenging the excessive enthusiasm with which his compatriots were celebrating the waning of Assyrian influence in Judah's affairs. Many believed that this was the last time they would see Mesopotamian military might parading across their land and pillaging its towns and cities. Jeremiah was warning against such premature and ill-judged complacency. Furthermore, from the perspective of the editors of the book, and by implication in the minds and understanding of its intended readers, the question of the identity of the "foe" was never in doubt; it was Babylon, as events had incontrovertibly made plain! Just how early Jeremiah himself had narrowed down the identity of the enemy to Babylon is less clear; probably not until after Nebuchadnezzar had risen to the throne and siezed control over Judah from the Egyptians in the year 605/604 B.C. This would not rule out but rather would confirm the view that the enemy Jeremiah had at first described vaguely as coming "from the north" should subsequently have become more narrowly identified as Babylon, or more explicitly, the neo-Babylonian empire that gained the upper hand in Mesopotamia after the collapse of Assyria.

Therefore there is no difficulty in recognizing that Jeremiah's deeply religious and fervently spiritual prophetic thinking and language was through and through imbued with a

21

political relevance. Politics and religion were not two separate spheres in Judah. We can readily see that Josiah's achievements, during whose reign Jeremiah began to preach, had had equally strong political and religious aims.

The narrative concerning Jeremiah's call to be a prophet and the account of the two visions which summarize the character and content of his early prophesying conclude with a personal injunction from God to the prophet himself (1:17–19). This clearly is not intended as simply sound advice and an assurance to Jeremiah concerning the expected nature of his career but was also a considered preface to the book. Jeremiah, beleaguered and threatened by his own people, was to stand like a city surrounded by its attackers. Against him would be ranged virtually the entire leadership of his nation: "the kings of Judah, its princes, its priests, and the people of the land" (v.18). They would fight against Jeremiah when they discovered that his words sounded a strident note of opposition to their own positions and policies. It would be Jeremiah's words that would prevail, however, not theirs! When ruin and disaster struck, as the book's readers knew only too well was to be the story that would unfold, it would be Jeremiah's words that could bring light and understanding. When events revealed the foolishness of the plausible, yet complacent, attitudes displayed by the nation's leaders—kings, princes, priests, and even prophets—then Jeremiah's words alone would retain their credibility as God's revealed truth to the nation. The tragedy would be in discovering how few had listened to such a prophet, how grievous and painful the sufferings he had had to bear for no other reason than that he had possessed the courage to tell the truth as God had revealed it to him!

Jeremiah 2
The Indictment of Israel

After the report of Jeremiah's call in the first chapter, 2:1–2 recounts how the prophet was commanded to "Go and proclaim in the hearing of Jerusalem" (2:2). It becomes clear, however, that the message in 2:2—3:5 was addressed to the people of Israel as a whole. Because it was "holy to the Lord," Israel was

22

a unique people, implying a relationship to God comparable to that of the firstfruits of the harvest (v.3), which were to be given over wholly to God (cf. Exod. 22:29). The invitation given in verse 4 to "Hear the word of the Lord" is explicitly addressed to "all the families of the house of Israel." From the broad and general nature of the indictment of Israel's sin in 2:5–37 it becomes evident that this was directed at the entire people in all its politically and geographically separated parts. Such a comprehensive condemnation of Israel stretched laterally across separated communities and extended vertically through Israel's history, going back to the nation's beginning in the wilderness.

The indictment proper extends as far as 3:5, whereupon the sections 3:6–14, 19–20, 21–25 reach their climax in a call to repentance in 4:1–2. These sections are addressed to the "forgotten communities," those remnants of the old Northern Kingdom of Israel (Ephraim) that had lost their political identity under Assyrian imperial control after the fall of Samaria in 722 B.C. These seemingly incidental forms of address alert the reader to the fact that the message of Jeremiah concerned all Israel, not simply the primary locations of Jeremiah's preaching ministry in Judah and Jerusalem. The message of hope for the future interjected in 3:15–18 is also addressed to all Israel.

These features concerning the understanding of Israel are central to the interpretation of the Book of Jeremiah. As far as the book's readers were concerned, the great new fact that had taken place in which their own personal destinies had been so intimately caught up was the scattering of Israel among the nations. Some remained in Judah, some had been deported to Babylon, and some had fled to Egypt. Israel was no longer a "nation" in the self-evident sense that such a word normally conveyed. Yet God had called Israel to be a holy nation (Exod. 19:5–6), covenanted to him to be his own peculiar treasure and witness among the nations of the world. How could Israel enjoy this privilege and fulfill this role when it was no longer a nation? It was therefore a matter of paramount significance that Jeremiah's book be read and understood as a message from God about Israel—its identity; how its unique nationhood was bound to its unique religion; how it had aroused the anger and consequent punishment of Yahweh, its Lord and God; and how it had experienced the resulting forfeiture of its land, royal kingship, and unity.

We have already noted that Jeremiah's place of origin in Anathoth made him particularly sensitive to the divided political, social, and religious loyalties that had so profoundly affected Israel's history. As a prophet of the kingdom of Judah, with its religious loyalties focused on Jerusalem, he was wholly caught up in the economic and political destiny of this small kingdom. But he was a resident in the territory of the tribe of Benjamin; he was a descendant of the priest Abiathar, who had been banished to Anathoth by Solomon; Jeremiah must also have been conscious from his youth of his loyalties to the northern tribes of Israel. These had separated themselves from Judah when they refused to maintain allegiance to the royal house of David after Solomon's death (cf. I Kings 12:16–20). His prophecies show that Jeremiah, like Isaiah before him, was fully alive to the conviction that Israel was essentially one people. The phrase "all the families of the house of Israel" (2:4) was an especially meaningful one for Jeremiah. This was also true for the readers of the book who still felt that they were a part of Israel, even when they had been forced to flee to other lands. Their identity, their sense of a god-given destiny, was inseparably linked to their sense of belonging to Israel.

Understanding Israel in its widest sense as being applicable to the descendants of all twelve tribes of Jacob-Israel, we encounter a major theme of the prophecies and of the Book of Jeremiah. During the century prior to Jeremiah's call a deep sense of crisis arose, occasioned by the imperial expansion of Assyria into the Mediterranean coastlands. As a result the political identity and coherence of the Northern Kingdom had largely disappeared. Many of the population of these territories had been forcibly deported to other parts of the Assyrian empire. All of this had served to reinforce the conviction that the political disunity of Israel and Judah had been a fundamental manifestation of human sinfulness. Examination of the measures taken by Josiah to strengthen and reunite his kingdom shows that underlying these measures was a fundamental desire to establish once again a single, unified Israel on the pattern originally set up by David. Jeremiah and also the editors who compiled the book of his prophecies were deeply concerned to reaffirm the oneness of Israel.

24

By the time Jeremiah began to prophesy in 627/626 B.C., we can recognize that the oneness of Israel had become a major religious and political question. Josiah was only partially successful in restoring Israel to the glory tradition ascribed to it under David and Solomon. Moreover the events following Josiah's untimely death and the first encounter between Judah and Babylon had brought about an even greater scattering of the people of Israel. It cannot be too strongly emphasized that the three phases of deportation to Babylon, recorded in an appendix to the Book of Jeremiah (52:28–34), were to have the most far-reaching and profound impact upon Israel. Exile in Babylon passed slowly, and at times almost imperceptibly, into the experience of diaspora. Judaism became the religion of communities scattered among the nations of the world, yet all were linked by historical and spiritual ties to an understanding of Israel as the covenant People of God.

For the readers of the Book of Jeremiah, the first and most dramatic steps towards this development had taken place. Consequently there is in the book a marked awareness of the fate of those who had been forcibly deported to Babylon (cf. especially 24:4–7; 29:1–14) as well as of the questionable future facing those who had chosen to flee to Egypt, taking Jeremiah with them (chaps. 42–44). This breakup of the political unity of Judah-Israel under Babylonian rule added further to the sense of sinful failure attached to the entire history of Israel. The issues that it raised, the problems that it aroused concerning the possibility of any future for Israel as a people, and the need to reaffirm some sense of corporate identity remained of paramount concern to the book's readers. There are good reasons for asking whether it could be assumed that these readers were still living under Babylonian rule in the old territory of the kingdom of Judah or whether they were now to be found among the exiles deported to Babylon. At least it is clear that the book evidences a marked interest in the hope that attached to these Babylonian deportees and the role they were expected to play in the future restoration of Israel (cf. E.W. Nicholson, pp. 116ff.).

All of this adds up to an awareness that the question of the nature and identity of Israel had become central to the issues facing those for whom Jeremiah's book had been compiled on the basis of his prophecies. It was all the more essential, therefore, to show that Jeremiah's prophecies had been addressed to all Israel. Its indictment of sin applied equally and without distinction to the entire nation; its call to repentance was addressed wholly and unreservedly to all; and for those in Judah

25

who had become accustomed to pointing an accusing finger at the tribes of the Northern Kingdom for their rebellion against the Davidic dynasty, it was important to show that Judah too had become every bit as guilty. "All have sinned" (cf. Rom. 1:18–32) Jeremiah declared, not yet in a universal application to all mankind but decisively and unequivocally in relation to Israel as a people.

With relatively few exceptions the early part of the Book of Jeremiah in chapters 1—25 concerns prophecies from the period of the prophet's call to the time of the rebellion of Jehoiakim against the Babylonian king Nebuchadnezzar in 601–598 B.C. This resulted in humiliating defeat for Judah, the siege and capture of Jerusalem, and the deportation of the new youthful King Jehoiachin (often also called Jeconiah) to Babylon. Jehoiakim, Judah's ruler in rebellion, had died during the time of siege. These events form a constantly presupposed, but usually not explicitly expressed, background to what Jeremiah had to proclaim to the citizens of Judah during these years.

For the first readers of Jeremiah's book all of this was past history, although its consequences were still deeply and painfully felt by them. History could record and describe the events, and this is done succinctly and accurately in II Kings 24—25, but prophecy could interpret and explain the divine meaning hidden within them and the special purposes they fulfilled. For this we must look most directly and explicitly to the prophecies of Jeremiah. Here one word stands out starkly, clearly, and repeatedly: "sin." Closely linked to this are the related terms "guilt," "rebel," "be unfaithful"; yet they all point unmistakably to the same manifestation of disloyalty to and rejection of God.

We might have expected Jeremiah, as was no doubt the case with several of his contemporaries, to concentrate upon the political miscalculations, the dangerously heady patriotism, and the over-optimistic defense alliances that persuaded Jehoiakim to join the rebellion against Babylon. This is not the case. About such matters he says little overtly, although much by implication. Instead he penetrates more deeply into an analysis of the situation and puts his finger directly upon the deceitful waywardness of the human heart. It is not simply the king and his counselors who are to be blamed for what had happened to Judah and Jerusalem but the entire nation. All have sinned!

26

From an outward historical perspective what had happened to the nations surrounding Judah in the Mediterranean coastlands during the transition from Assyrian to Babylonian rule in the region is poetically summed up in words from Jeremiah occurring towards the end of chapters 1—25:

> "Thus says the LORD of hosts:
> Behold, evil is going forth
> from nation to nation,
> and a great tempest is stirring
> from the farthest parts of the earth!" (25:32)

Babylon was the "tempest" called upon by God to be an instrument of punishment to follow that of Assyria, so that it might awaken his people Israel to a knowledge of their sinfulness. Such is the message of the prophecies of Jeremiah set out in chapters 2—25, and these begin in a mood of devastating sharpness in chapter 2.

The make-up of chapter 2 is a series of indictments against Israel, connected by their content rather than by the fact that they originally constituted one single prophecy from Jeremiah. We may cite the literary judgment of the material by J.A. Thompson (p. 160): "The chapter consists of a literary arrangement of several originally independent segments brought together to serve a theological purpose." The arrangement, therefore, is not that of a single prophetic proclamation presented as Jeremiah had once preached it but rather a composition brought together by the editors of the book. They have carefully considered the needs and circumstances of the readers and have consequently established where responsibility for the misfortunes that had overtaken Israel was to be placed. Equally importantly, their formulation of this case, resting securely on what Jeremiah had proclaimed, contained a guideline as to how Israel should respond to the situation in which it now found itself: Israel must repent (cf. 4:1–2)! It cannot be too strongly stressed that although the situation of the first hearers had been different, judgment now had indeed fallen on those who had survived the decades of terror and destruction and could now read the words of Jeremiah. It was no longer a question of whether disaster would strike but rather of how there could be any reasoned hope for the future in the aftermath of national ruination.

The indictment of Israel in chapter 2 falls into four sections:

Verses 4–13: Israel's unfaithfulness towards God goes back to the very beginning of its national existence when its

27

ancestors first entered the land. They abandoned the Lord, the God who had delivered them from Egypt, and worshiped instead the gods of the land—the detested forms of Baal.

Verses 14–19: Instead of recognizing the political misfortune which befell them as punishment for their religious disloyalty, the leaders of Israel had sought to establish their security by political means—through treaties with Egypt—"to drink the waters of the Nile" (v.18)—or with Assyria—"to drink the waters of the Euphrates" (v. 18). Neither course had proved to offer any genuine help and security, and Israel should have recognized the inevitability of this (v. 19).

Verses 20–28: Israel had indeed been disloyal to God and had preferred instead to worship the Baals. Evidence that demonstrated this conclusively was to be seen across the length and breadth of the land. The simple rustic sanctuaries dedicated to the worship of Baal were to be found in profusion in a fertile spot "under every green tree" (v. 20).

Verses 29–37: In the face of such blatant religious apostasy, which the prophet poignantly compares to a wife's disloyalty to her husband (vv. 33–34), shame and humiliation are to be regarded as inevitable (v. 37).

We can appreciate the passionate depth of feeling the prophet brings to his indictment of his compatriots and his intent to exclude no generation since the beginning of Israel's national life. All had sinned against God; the manner and depth of this sin is described by a human analogy focusing centrally upon marital unfaithfulness. Israel is compared to a young bride playing fast and loose with many lovers and scorning any sense of obligation of loyalty to her husband. In ancient Israelite society the enormity of such behavior needed no further word of explanatory condemnation. We must, however, probe behind the metaphors and imagery used by the prophet to see precisely what it was about Israel's national conduct that he so vigorously castigates.

Two features stand out sharply and provide the essential core of his accusations. First, Israel had abandoned the worship of Yahweh and had preferred instead to worship the abundant local manifestations of the god Baal in the land. They had been established there by the earlier political masters of the territory—the peoples of Canaan. Secondly, once this religious apostasy had brought political weakness and failures in the face of other nations, Israel had sought to bolster up its declining strength by making alliances with the great imperial powers, Egypt to the south and Assyria to the north. Neither course had provided any genuine security at all but had brought further tension and decline. Instead of turning to the root cause of its failure—its religious apostasy—and seeking to remedy this by a genuine return to the worship of Yahweh, Israel had sought a vain and worthless remedy for its national ills. In consequence it would find itself rejected and ruined (2:37).

By the portrayal of Israel as a young woman with her hands upon her head (2:37), the prophet is referring to the hapless plight of a prisoner of war, helpless and at the captors' mercy. This was precisely the condition those who now read these words would remember had happened to their compatriots, and in many cases to them. A further point is instructive and worthy of reflection with regard to the long and imaginatively constructed indictment of Israel extending throughout chapter 2. Essentially prophecy consists of sayings of pronouncement declaring what God intends to do, and motives or reasons explaining why the Lord must act in this fashion. When prophecies, as here, are threatening in their character, we find pronouncements of coming ruin and woe explained and backed up by sharp invective showing that punishment is necessary. It is noteworthy here and in many other sections of the first part of the Book of Jeremiah that the element of invective predominates, whereas pronouncement of the threat facing the prophet's audience is surprisingly brief and allusive. The reasons for this are clear; political downfall and national ruination had already stricken Israel by the time these words were being read. The fact of suffering was clear; the fact that this was a divinely imposed punishment was not. More important still was a need for a clear declaration of the sins and offenses that had brought such misfortunes upon the people.

In the eyes of many these tragic events appeared to cast doubt on the reality of God. They set in question whether the Lord, the acknowledged one and only God of Israel, possessed either the power or the will to protect his people. In showing that Israel's failure was not from weakness on God's part, Jeremiah sees it as a sign of the disloyalty and waywardness of the nation. All had sinned—this truth stared accusingly at Israel through the events that had transpired. Yet, even in the light of such events, it was hard to accept.

Scholars have frequently noted how closely the religious

29

accusations raised by Jeremiah against Israel for Baal worship follow earlier condemnations voiced by Hosea (cf. esp. Hosea 2:2–13; 4; 5:13; 7:11). It is hard to avoid the conclusion that Jeremiah was familiar with a collection of Hosea's prophecies and may himself have been a strong and ardent admirer of the earlier prophet. Jeremiah's familiarity with a collection of Hosea's sayings may not be the only link to explain such similarities.

Hosea had been a prophet of the Northern Kingdom and must have preached largely in the vicinity of the sanctuaries of Bethel and Shechem as well as the political capital of Samaria. Jeremiah, although from Judah, had no doubt drunk deeply from the religious feelings and aspirations of the more loyal Israelite elements of the north. Sensitivity to the issue of the rivalry between Yahweh and Baal, confused religious traditions, and conflicting political loyalties all appear to have been factors more keenly felt in the territory of the northern tribes. Judah was more compact than Ephraim in the north and found an all-encompassing influence in the Davidic kingship and the temple of Jerusalem. With Hosea and Jeremiah the Davidic kingship and the temple appear to have been regarded rather negatively. Their strongest denunciations are kept for the wayward and wavering religious affections of the people and the tendency to confuse Yahweh with Baal. Clearly factions existed in the north that even preferred the worship of Baal to that of Yahweh, the Lord God of Israel.

In comparing Israel's worship of Baal to the attitude of a fickle young woman, spurning her husband and resorting to a host of lovers, the prophet was pointing to a prominent feature of the ancient Baal worship. This form of religion practiced sexual immorality in the name of a "fertility ritual." This feature had had a long history in ancient religion and was by no means restricted to Baal worship. Two points are important if this seemingly strange aberration of religious impulses is to be understood. Ancient religion leaned heavily upon the symbolism of actions and gestures. These fulfilled a semi-magical role as imitating, and thereby influencing, the action of a god. Secondly, religion was a means of securing "life" in all its many aspects through the life-giving power of the gods. Such a gift of "life" comprised not simply blessing and vitality as we regard them but also healing, safe childbearing, rich harvests, and ultimately even safe passage to a life beyond death. Although cer-

30

tain forms of ancient Near Eastern and classical Greek religion have often been described as "fertility" rituals, in reality the lines of demarcation between "fertility" and "blessing" were never drawn with any firm clarity, save in the Israelite tradition that emerged within the Old Testament. As a consequence the castigation by Hosea and Jeremiah of the worship of Baal as a manifestation of sexual waywardness had a literal, as well as a metaphorical, significance. The appeal of the worship of Baal was the age-old appeal of unrestrained sexual licentiousness. It was all the more destructive of social stability and dignity because it allowed the name of "god" to be invoked as its justification.

Clearly long before the time of Hosea and Jeremiah, the social havoc and moral insensitivity of such licentious cults was firmly recognized. Religion itself could thereby become a negative and destructive force in society. It could threaten the bonds of marriage and the family, which were the foundation stones upon which the social fabric of every ancient society was built. The importance of the growth of the written prophetic tradition in ancient Israel was the elevation of this issue to a central matter of religious, moral, and social concern and the consequent condemnation of the immoral rites of Baal. Worship of those aspects of life, if untempered and unrestrained by moral awareness, can undermine the bedrock of family life upon which all human society rests. Religion itself then becomes an evil and destructive power. At the very heart of the prophetic tradition lies the recognition that a religion is not necessarily good and beneficial to humankind just because it engages in an ultimate concern with spiritual and transcendent powers. If it is to be worthy of the name, religion must always distinguish between what is true and what is false—what belongs to Baal and what belongs to the Lord God. Unless this is the case, then religion and those for whom it has provided an illusion of life and power must be destroyed. Religion cannot remain true religion if it bypasses genuine moral concern for the welfare of society.

On the one hand Jeremiah raises this powerful and unforgettable indictment of the way of life practiced by his compatriots since their beginning as a nation. They had pursued worthlessness and had become worthless (2:5) by perverting their religious affections to submit themselves to Baal. They had succumbed to a temptation that has persistently reappeared

31

throughout the history of religion. This temptation is to pursue and cultivate a spirituality, and even to create a prosperous and secure society, while remaining indifferent to the claims of morality and the health of the family unit in society. Alongside such powerful and forcefully expressed denunciations Jeremiah sets the accusation that his nation had sought to find security for itself through its external political alliances with Egypt to the south and Assyria to the north. Neither had offered any genuine security at all. Elsewhere in the book we discover how deeply the political dimension enters into the thinking and reckoning of the prophet.

Jeremiah 3:1—4:2
Further Condemnation of Israel

The theme of the sinfulness of Israel, and the consequent responsibility of the entire nation for the disasters that had overtaken it, continues in 3:1—4:2. Here however the message that "all have sinned" is raised afresh directly in relation to the division of the nation that once had been united under David and Solomon. Inevitably the years of separation from each other into what the Old Testament terms two "houses" had raised a good deal of bitterness and recrimination between them. The fact that the Northern Kingdom—the house of Ephraim—had suffered almost complete political eclipse after the fall of Samaria to the Assyrians in 722 B.C. could most readily be interpreted as evidence that the sins of this kingdom were greater than those of Judah. Jeremiah, however, was greatly concerned as a prophetic interpreter of Israel's history to demonstrate that this was a false and selfishly mistaken interpretation of the situation. Because Judah had witnessed the consequences of God's punishment of Ephraim, this amounted to a special call and opportunity to repent. Judah, however, had not interpreted the situation in this fashion. Judah had not repented; instead it arrogantly congratulated itself upon its escape and had begun to behave worse than its sister kingdom (3:8). There is therefore a kind of theme text running through the whole of chapter 3: Faithless Israel (3:11) has shown herself less guilty than false Judah.

Before comparing the experiences and attitudes of the two kingdoms of Israel and Judah, the prophet brings to a climax his highly imaginative presentation of the false and disloyal attitude towards God that the people of both kingdoms have displayed throughout their history. This is in 3:1–5, where almost certainly the original continuation is to be found in verses 19–20. The initial metaphor of the faithless wife, used to convey the prophet's understanding of the wayward and disloyal behavior of the people toward God, is reaffirmed (3:1). In a human situation involving such treacherous and intolerable behavior on the part of a woman would not her husband feel compelled to divorce her. "Of course!" is the unexpressed reply. Would he then, after having divorced her, wish to go back to her. "Of course not!" is the implicit reply to this question. In the case of a woman who had had not one but several other lovers would her husband receive her back at all? The nature of the imagery and the intensity of the human feelings aroused by the situation provide all the answer that is necessary. How monstrous, then, for the people of Israel to seek to return to God without at the same time seeking to reform its conduct. Such would be monstrous conduct because it would lack sincerity or permanence. It would merely demonstrate that Israel's attitude remained frivolous toward God in asking for divine help when it found itself in trouble, as it had been at the start in turning away from him.

We can see in the skillful use of human analogies used here that Jeremiah's purpose is to convey his conviction regarding the essential primary loyalty and sincerity that true religion demands. Israel is doomed; just as marriage and family cannot survive if a wife's pledge of loyalty to her husband is discounted and ignored. In similar fashion the religious relationship of Israel to God demanded comparable standards of loyalty. To appreciate the full vigor and meaning of Jeremiah's language, it is necessary to bear in mind the essential role of marriage, kinship, and the family structure of society in all human experience. The prophet conveys his religious sense by pointing out that the marriage relationship, on which society rests, cannot survive without loyalty, trust, and steadfastness of purpose. It cannot be an occasional affair! The prophet's hearers and readers would have felt sufficiently outraged at the described behavior of the woman for this point to need no additional explanation. Yet what they failed to realize was that the

33

religious relationship binding Israel to God was subject to precisely the same rules of conduct. To have any meaning at all it needed the same steadfastness and loyalty. It too could not be an "occasional affair," which is how so many in the nation had come to regard it. In times of national crisis and temporary emergencies, such as when the vital spring rains failed to come (3:3), special prayers and rites of repentance from the people sought the pity of God. Yet it was all a mockery of true religion, since it lacked the two essentials for any meaningful human relationship—sincerity and loyalty.

Seen in this light, Israel's behavior was all the more an outrage because the people willfully refused to see anything amiss in what they were doing. They had developed "a harlot's brow" of set refusal to admit to wrongdoing. In 3:4–5, 19–20 the prophet extends further his use of imagery drawn from the pattern of human relationships to emphasize that all such relationships demand certain qualities if they are to be real and effective. So fatherhood and friendship, especially friendships fashioned in youth, demand a reciprocal basis of loyalty and trust; religion could be no less dependant upon these values than could human relationships. The prophet argues, however, that Israel's religion had become empty of loyalty and sincerity—virtues indispensable in all other relationships.

The question of the differing past experiences of Israel and Judah is taken up in 3:6–11. This prose section owes its present position to the book's editors. The passage as a whole is located "in the days of king Josiah" (3:6), and the reason for this lies in its special appositeness to the political developments that had taken place in this king's reign. When Assyrian imperial control over Judah had lapsed, Josiah, strongly backed by ardent national feeling in Judah, had endeavored to reclaim a significant part of the old Northern Kingdom. How far he had been able to extend his rule in the north is not specified, but the violent suppression of the religious sanctuary at Bethel (cf. II Kings 23:15–20) was the most forthright expression of his desire to reestablish a single kingdom of Israel.

The condemnation of "faithless Israel" in 3:6–11 has a double purpose. On the one hand it reestablishes the claim that Israel is one people, a conviction that had so powerfully molded the policies of Josiah. Israel must indeed then acknowledge its guilt if it is to become once again a part of a single nation of

God's people. This reaffirmation of the guilt of the Northern Kingdom, however, did not serve to exonerate Judah but to show that Judah had been every whit as faithless as had the sister kingdom in the north.

The indictment is followed in 3:12–14 by an impassioned appeal to the survivors of Ephraim to "return." This verb (Heb. *shub*) covers a wide range of meanings that provide the Book of Jeremiah with one of its central doctrines. The need of the hour is a "return" to God, which denotes an inner repudiation of past disloyalty and a genuine turning back to God in repentance of heart. It also conveys a sense of the returning in political allegiance to one government and nationhood under the rule of Jerusalem. That this might also entail a return to government under the rule of the Davidic dynasty is a more complex question that needs to be considered in regard to the Book of Jeremiah as a whole (see esp. below on chap. 33). The appeal for repentance in verses 12–14 provides a beautifully concise and impressive presentation of the understanding of repentance that colors the whole book.

There is set at the beginning a clear statement of the essential ground on which repentance becomes possible. This lies not in human nature, taken by itself, but in the nature of God: " . . . for I am merciful, says the Lord" (v. 12). Returning to God, however, cannot be the temporary and irresolute turning to God in prayer in times of trouble that had characterized Israel's behavior in the past (cf. 3:3). It must rest on a wholehearted repudiation of the feckless conduct of the past: "Only acknowledge your guilt, that you rebelled against the Lord your God . . ." (v. 13). Without such acknowledgment of the reality of the situation, the notion of repentance would only be the pursuit of an illusion, unable to heal the wounds that Israel had suffered. In many respects the most striking of all the aspects of the prophetic teaching on repentance set out here is to be found in verse 14: "I will take you, one from a city and two from a family, and I will bring you to Zion." The implicit recognition that Israel has become scattered in distinct cities and in small family groups points us to the recognition that these words were formulated after the deportations of 598 and 587 had taken place. Israel was beginning to experience the first stresses and tensions of life in the new world of the dispersion. Loyal citizens of Israel and Judah are here recognized as being scattered in distant lands, but it is also made clear that an effective

35

"returning" to God can be achieved only on a personal and individual basis: "one from a city and two from a family" (3:14).

When we sum up the meaning of 3:6–14 we can see how skillfully its two parts fit together. The first part (vv. 6–11) establishes the truth that all Israel has sinned, both Ephraim and Judah. The second part (vv. 12–14) affirms that it is essential for all to repent in order to return to God. The very confidence that had encouraged Judah to interpret the fate of its sister kingdom in the north as a consequence of religious apostasy had now to be turned into a comparable acknowledgment that its own sins were as great, if not greater. Overall the broad portrayal of Israel's history as a self-condemned history of sinful apostasy, which colors all of 2:1—3:5, is brought to a clear conclusion with 3:12–14. Now all must repent and return to God in their hearts; only by such a movement would an eventual return to Zion be rendered possible. With such a message the Book of Jeremiah is given a thematic framework that conveys to the reader its overall message of hope.

In a slightly untidy fashion the editors of the book have incorporated a number of central points to develop the basic theme. We have noted already that 3:6–18 breaks up the continuity between 3:5 and 3:19–20, its original conclusion. It is evident that the question of the eventual return to Zion (3:14) has raised problems for the readers, who would have been well aware that Jerusalem had suffered massive destruction by the Babylonians in 587 B.C. and that the temple had been destroyed. An interpretative comment regarding this situation and what it meant for the future is set in 3:15–18. Since it particularly concerns the Ark of the Covenant, which had stood in the inner sanctuary of the temple, it may be considered in relation to Jeremiah's concern with the temple (see below on 7:1–15).

A further elaboration of the theme of Israel's repentance is set out in 3:21—4:2. In reality it falls into three separate short units. Verses 21–23 describe Rachel's grief over the sins and disloyalty of her children, which brings out a dialogue between the offended God and his shamed and penitent people. Then Israel's acknowledgment of guilt in verses 24–25 sets out in a kind of litany a full confession. The "shameful thing" that has devoured the people is the worship of other gods besides the Lord, especially the popular god Baal. Further evidence, then, that returning must be a returning to the Lord is given in a

36

concluding affirmation in 4:1–2. This brings the whole series of prophecies that began with 2:1 to its conclusion. Their meaning and significance must not be overlooked. No matter how essential contrition and penitence are seen to be, only the Lord himself can save (4:1). Returning, as an act of inward rethinking and renewing, can lead to a blessed future only if it is a sincere and genuine returning to the Lord. It is not the inner movement of the heart that saves, but such may herald a returning to God, who truly can save.

Woven into the prophetic portrayal of Israel's history in Jeremiah 2—3 is a conviction common to all the Old Testament prophets that requires fuller consideration at this point. The connection between sin and national disaster is one the prophets assume to be valid and demonstrable. The Old Testament prophets perceive a process of retribution to be at work in history. This process brings inevitable ruin and destruction upon those who flout the basic essentials of moral and religious integrity. Those who sow sin and apostasy reap a harvest accordingly. This basic assumption, set out in such a formal and abstract fashion, may in many ways be regarded as even more important than the specific conduct the various prophets single out as manifestations of offense to God. We know that this doctrine itself gave rise later in the Old Testament period to new questions and could not be sustained in all its details.

Before attempting a fuller understanding of these processes of divine retribution at work in history, we do well to draw into the discussion some further points that have a bearing on how we are to understand the prophets of the Old Testament. Towards the close of the second millennium B.C., Israel was one of a number of small nations to emerge in the Levant. Egyptian power had temporarily declined and a reawakened Mesopotamian power had not yet sought to extend its influence as far as the border with Egypt. Economic, cultural, and ideological factors made possible a new kind of nationhood. Out of a number of communities structured in large tribal groups and practicing a form of seminomadic sheep farming, Israel had become a nation. To become such meant fleeing from the slavery of Egypt and holding fast to its God who had been revealed as Israel's deliverer and liberator. Two fundamental threats existed to undermine this vitally important sense of nationhood. The first of these was internal. A disunity from a relapse into inter-tribal rivalries and factional antipathies. The second was from outside: the reawakened imperial ambitions of Egypt and Mesopotamia. Egypt had a continuing ambition to reestablish control over the eastern Mediterranean seaboard, whereas Mesopotamia sought control as far as Egypt's border.

Those nations located between these two great "superpowers" of the Fertile Crescent found themselves inevitably caught up in the political moves of these larger empires. Israel was one such nation. The historical situation reflected by all the great prophets from Amos to Jeremiah was one in which Israel and Judah found themselves successively subjugated by, and subservient to, the rulers of Mesopotamia. These rulers were first Assyrian, who were then replaced by the kings of Babylon. All the while Egypt remained in the south, seen variously as either a potential ally or as a threat. During Jeremiah's lifetime all three powers, Assyria, Egypt, and Babylon, had successively imposed their will upon Judah. It is small wonder then that the citizens of Judah could be compared to a fickle woman, not knowing which lover she should turn to next (2:36).

The break-up of national unity brought about during the days of Saul, David, and Solomon had threatened Israel internally. Its national unity was lost through the backlash aroused by Solomon's oppressive policies. Externally the independence of Israel and Judah was lost to the Assyrians in the middle of the eighth century B.C., never to be regained during the Old Testament period. We might easily secularize the ideas and ideals of the Old Testament by speaking of an Israelite sense of nationhood, threatened by factions within and imperialism from outside. But no such secular reinterpretation was possible during the biblical period. It was faith and trust in the Lord, the God worshiped by Israel, that stood between the nation and the destruction of its national consciousness. The point of utmost importance for the modern interpreter is not that we should attempt to make a secular reinterpretation of the biblical religious ideals but that we should avoid making a falsely "religious" interpretation by denuding them of their true historical context. Jeremiah and the other Old Testament prophets were striving for a deep and genuine recognition that Israel's very being and existence was inseparable from its knowledge and service of the Lord its God. In calling Israel back to a completely sincere and uninhibited loyalty to God, Jeremiah was also calling his people to affirm their own identity. By acknowledging their roots as a people they would be affirming a deter-

38

mination not to allow defeat and dispersal to a faceless existence among other nations to be their end. If that were to happen then Israel would indeed have perished in the ruins of Jerusalem in 587 B.C.

When seen in context, Jeremiah's conviction that Israel's abandonment of the Lord meant abandonment of its own true identity as a people and nation makes excellent sense: conflicting political and religious ideologies left Israel defenseless before a series of imperial powers which were destined to rule the Fertile Crescent for more than a millennium—until in fact the rise of Islam brought a new kind of religious society to the region. The prophet was not applying an abstract and narrowly religious doctrine of retribution to the situation in which he found himself and his country. In facing yet another crisis after more than a century of similar political crises had passed, Jeremiah saw that Israel could not heal its wounds except by a return to the foundations of its own national heritage in the Lord its God. By willfully refusing to do this, the people had thrown away their only hope of salvation. With the evidence of disaster and ruin staring at them from all sides, now those editors who have brought together this rich and poignant collection of Jeremiah's prophecies see in this message alone a genuine hope for the people's future.

Jeremiah 4:3—6:30
The Indictment of Judah and Jerusalem

The further carefully edited section that now begins presents an indictment of Judah and Jerusalem, expressing a firm message of impending doom upon the nation and its capital city. In its essentials it forms the most central and straightforward presentation of Jeremiah's basic message, at least so far as this was formulated in the period extending from the time of his call until the destruction of Jerusalem in 587 B.C. Twin events form the essential background for understanding the entire section: Jerusalem's defeat and surrender in 598, deportation of its king and many of its leading citizens; a second siege followed by destruction of the city in 587 B.C. These events represent a "fulfillment" confirming the truth of the warnings

39

the prophet had given. When his hearers refused to heed his message, then Jeremiah had become powerless to avert disaster. The entire section breathes an atmosphere indicating that these disastrous events had taken place and that those who now read and pondered the prophet's advance warnings had much to learn from them.

Jeremiah had no doubt actually given these warnings many times and over a number of years. Almost forty years from the time of his call to prophesy were to elapse before the final catastrophe overtook Jerusalem. Throughout this time it seems virtually certain that the message had constantly returned to a single basic theme: a hostile nation from a distant land would invade and devastate Judah. That nation would come from "the north" (4:6; 6:1,22). Since the warnings had proved to be valid and sustained by events, those now reading the prophetic message would be most directly concerned with Jeremiah's reasons for such divine punishment. Such reasons now provide the central theme of the various sayings: wicked people abound in the land and are allowed to flourish (5:7–8,26); the people as a whole have become utterly faithless (5:11). Even the possibility that a few within the nation would listen to Jeremiah and amend their ways had become remote in the extreme. They shut their eyes and their ears to God's word (5:21; 6:10). We can regard this message as wholly typical of Jeremiah. Its great significance is not so much the manner in which it highlights certain social and religious ills but in the impressive way it served to interpret the tragic events of Judah's defeats at the hands of the armies of Babylon. These events were known to the reader no longer in a position to avert disaster by giving heed to the prophet's words and turning back to God in repentance. It was too late for that to be an effective option, events had overtaken the prophetic message. Rather, all attention is placed on the reasons for Judah's tragic fate; from these reasons there emerges the basis for understanding the past and for laying new foundations for the future.

This whole section has been structured as a whole but is made up from separate, relatively short prophecies which repeat an identical, or closely similar, message: Jeremiah 4:3–4 offers a general introduction; 5–10 announce the impending invasion from the north; verses 11–18 declare that this will be a scorching word of judgment from God. Verses 19–22 proceed to describe the agony of Judah's downfall, and the terrifying

40

extent of this is affirmed in verses 23–28. Finally verses 29–31 picture Jerusalem in torment. Chapter 5 is then taken up almost completely with the enunciation of reasons for this tragic sequence of events: verses 1–9 describe the wickedness of Jerusalem; verses 10–17 voices, in a rhetorical fashion, the people's denial of guilt. Verses 18–19 are a later prose insertion attempting to soften the note of warning and threat, and the major theme is repeated in verses 20–31. This asserts that God's repeated warnings to Judah and Jerusalem have passed unheeded. Chapter 6 reverts to pronouncements about the coming disaster for the nation by picturing its terrifying nature: verses 1–8 describe Jerusalem under attack; verses 9–15 outline the horrors of war; verses 16–21 offer reasons for Judah's suffering such judgment, and this is clearly an added reflection supplied later. In verses 22–26 the threat of a hostile invasion is reiterated and the whole is brought to a conclusion in verses 27–30 by a reflection upon the role of Jeremiah as the nation's examiner and judge.

The first four sections pronounce the coming doom in an orderly sequence of an invading force moving towards Jerusalem. No indication is given whether the prophecies refer to the situation of 599–598 or 588–587, but this has in any case become irrelevant. Reasons for such a course of events are then spelled out. Overall a careful structure is discernible, although it is probably not one established by the prophet himself. From the perspective of the section as we now have it, the date Jeremiah originally gave the prophecies has ceased to be a matter of great importance. So too has the fact that Jeremiah's anonymously described "foe from the north" has taken on the real-life form of the armies of Babylon. No reader could seriously doubt that this was the enemy to whom Jeremiah's prophecies referred. Jeremiah's interpretation of the military threat from Babylon as an act of divine punishment upon Judah and Jerusalem establishes the spiritual foundation of the entire book. With the exception of the late reflective comment in 5:18–19 all the sayings appear to have come from Jeremiah himself.

A number of important questions about the prophecies remain unanswered and are now probably unanswerable. Perhaps the most prominent of these concerns the broad way in which the people's sins are claimed to have made them ripe for judgment. They are accused of forsaking God's law (5:4); no one seeks truth and justice (5:1); they commit adultery and turn to

41

prostitutes (5:7). Such broad condemnation could undoubtedly have been addressed to many communities at any time in ancient Israel's history, but nothing is said to explain why Jeremiah's age had come to feel these moral issues with such acuteness.

Even more noticeable, and lacking clear explanation, is Jeremiah's insistence that a deep and demonstrable connection existed between the moral insensitivity of the people and the invasion and destruction which they were about to suffer. No clear condemnation is made concerning the political misjudgments of the king and his advisers, the headstrong and willful patriotism of the people who had eagerly embraced the opportunity to rebel against Babylon, or their refusal to contemplate any other outcome to their actions than a complete victory. Jeremiah appears to have addressed a people who were so self-assured in the rightness of their cause, and in the backing that God must give to it, that they had discounted the serious possibility of harsh Babylonian reprisals being taken against them. So Jeremiah stands as a starkly religious and moral prophet. He refuses to countenance any explanation for the defeat and sufferings he had foreseen for Judah other than that the people had deeply offended God. He accuses the people of moral obtuseness and gross self-indulgence and allows no room for a heroic patriotism. Nor does Jeremiah give room to support what must have been the popular belief: God would intervene directly to save Israel since it was a divinely elect nation. The prophetic message from Jeremiah is unremittingly personal and inward-looking in its uncovering of the personal and individual nature of sin. At the same time it maintains a markedly unsophisticated and almost bland indifference to political exigencies and the prevalence of national ambition and ideology. The prophet thereby sets a value on the lives and welfare of individuals above those of military heroism and national freedom. Consistently and understandably his modern interpreters have found this aspect of Jeremiah's prophetic message to be dangerous, and even at times shocking, in its indifference to a wider range of social and patriotic virtues.

Most probably the concern of modern interpreters to find in Jeremiah's prophecies a simple, complete, and self-contained system of morality and spirituality is itself mistaken. He was a figure of a particular time who proclaimed his prophetic message with great poetic skill and intensity to a profoundly hostile and unsympathetic audience. His words were remembered and preserved for posterity because his interpretation of Israel's greatest crisis in the Old Testament period proved itself to be a surer and more convincing guide to the nature of historical reality than did the complacent insensitivity to truth of his hearers. As a "true" prophet he had to do battle with many "false" ones whose words could more easily be attuned to what the men and women of Jerusalem were eager to hear. Moreover there are firm signs that the past two centuries of history had bred in Judah a complacent feeling of assurance that whatever may have been the fate of the sister kingdom of Israel at the hands of the Assyrians Judah would remain secure.

Judah's and Jerusalem's survival from the threat posed by Sennacherib at the close of the eighth century had encouraged the conviction that God remained unshakable in his promise to uphold and preserve the Davidic dynasty upon the throne of Judah. This combined with the belief in the divine presence in the temple in Jerusalem (see below on 7:1–15) had encouraged among the people a fatal complacency (cf. Lam. 4:12). It fed on the natural human instinct to believe that somehow God would ensure that events turned out favorably for Judah. In the minds of his hearers, Jeremiah was clearly regarded as the religious innovator, ignoring what they believed to be well tried and self-evidently true doctrines about the nature of divine providence. The one feature that they were not inclined to attach much weight to was the importance of moral rectitude and spiritual loyalty in the accounting of God. It was Jeremiah's insistence that the account books of Judah's dealings on these matters should be opened and examined that led him to refute the spiritual over-assurance that he found. He insisted that the one thing the people of Judah and Jerusalem believed would not happen to them, defeat in battle against a distant Mesopotamian enemy, would be the very fate that God had in store.

Jeremiah 7:1—15
Concerning the Temple of Jerusalem

43

Beginning with 7:1 and extending down to 10:25, we come to a collection of prophecies about true and false forms of worship and the true and false conceptions of God underlying them. The foremost unit in this collection is to be found in 7:1—8:3, which begins in 7:1–15 with what is usually entitled Jeremiah's "temple sermon." This great temple address given in the court area of the temple itself on the occasion of a major public festival is further recounted in chapter 26. There it marks the beginning of the long sequence of narratives dealing with Jeremiah's personal fortunes, particularly the rejection and suffering he had experienced. Placing the report of the temple sermon and its consequences for Jeremiah and the people as a kind of prefatory opening to much larger literary units represents an important editorial procedure by the compilers of the book. The destruction of the temple by the armies of Nebuchadrezzar and the removal of the Davidic kingship hover like a cloud over the entire collection. These had been symbol's of Israel's statehood, the surviving vestiges of the divine calling and destiny of the nation Israel. Hitherto they had remained intact during the years of Assyrian control. Now they too had been brought to an end by the Babylonian armies in such a way as to suggest to the undiscerning observer that the God of Israel had been powerless to defend his people and their ancient institutions in the hour of crisis.

To gain an adequate awareness of the depth of feeling and anguish inflicted upon Judah as a result of these events, it is necessary to consider the depth of popular commitment to the belief that God's very presence was to be found in the temple of Jerusalem.

The main body of Jeremiah's temple sermon is set out in 7:1–15, now formulated in the prose style typical of such discourses. The occasion for Jeremiah's making such a public address must undoubtedly be the same as that reflected in chapter 26. Several features of it must be borne in mind to sense its theological impact. No more precise date is given for it than "the beginning of the reign of Jehoiakim" (26:1). Evidently it could have belonged to virtually any period of Jeremiah's ministry up until 587 B.C. when the temple was destroyed. It makes points of deep theological relevance pertinent to all ages. In this sense it possesses a timeless quality. The elevated prose of the discourses shows that these are not Jeremiah's own words; they have passed through the minds of editors with close Deuteronomic affiliations. Jeremiah's words regarding the temple have been remembered and amplified in the light of events that

44

occurred after he proclaimed them and that so decisively bore relationship to their claim to truth.

Whether Jeremiah had actually foretold the inevitability of the destruction of the temple in the unequivocal fashion now reported of him may be an unresolvable question (cf. 7:14–15). The certainty of the temple's destruction, however, does not control the theological movement of the prophetic sermon; rather it is the false religious attitude. This attitude rendered the removal of the temple an essential divine action in Israel's spiritual education. The theme lies clearly and firmly enunciated: "Do not trust in these deceptive words: 'This is the temple of the LORD, . . .'" (7:4). Ezekiel, Jeremiah's contemporary, later declared in a visionary insight that judgment was to begin at the sanctuary of God (Ezek. 9:6); so Jeremiah perceived the foremost institution of religion as the greatest obstacle to spiritual realism.

The element of popular "deception" arises in Israel's nursing of the conviction that the presence of the temple in Jerusalem would ensure their welfare and protection in time of war. Only God himself could offer such an assurance and this necessarily entailed a right relationship with him. Such a relationship is morally conditioned to exclude anyone who is guilty of theft, murder, adultery, or false testimony in a legal assembly (7:9). This was not how the populace generally regarded the temple and the religion practiced there. Undoubtedly the religion of Israel had embodied a positive moral element since its inception. But it was contained within and at times overlaid by very ancient and deep-rooted assumptions about the efficacy of religious rites and observances. Central to these was the notion of divine blessing (cf. J. Scharbert, pp. 279–308). Such blessing was regarded in the popular thought of Israel as a kind of life force flowing out into the land and enriching the life of the people. Blessing comprised vitality, prosperity, and protection against death and defeat. The popular mind, not only of ancient Israel but throughout the history of all religion, has too readily regarded such "religious" benefits as available to men and women apart from and regardless of the moral sincerity and integrity displayed by them. Jeremiah's temple sermon insists that this is never the case, and to believe that it could be so is to trust in deceptive words. Ultimately this deception lies in the belief **45** that the visible institutions of religion, in this case the temple of Jerusalem, can function in a mechanical fashion. The symbol of trust becomes identified with the object of that faith and trust and thereby distorts and ultimately falsifies the very nature of faith itself.

Almost certainly the remarkable way in which Judah and Jerusalem had survived in the face of the Assyrian threat posed by Sennacherib in 701 B.C.—(II Kings 18:13—19:37; cf. Clements, *Isaiah and the Deliverance of Jerusalem*, pp. 52ff.) had done much to intensify the special regard for Jerusalem and its temple by the time of Jeremiah. As a consequence, the destruction of it in 587 B.C. came to appear as an event that challenged the very foundations of faith in God. Something unthinkable had happened! God had disowned his own sanctuary!

The extremely controversial nature of what had taken place in 587 B.C. and the shocking idea that the Lord might destroy his own dwelling-place has called forth the reference to the historical precedent of the sanctuary at Shiloh (7:12; cf. I Sam. 4). This had been destroyed by the Philistines, even though it was the place where the holy Ark, the most sacred symbol of God's presence, had been housed. Only special circumstances had brought about the preservation of the Ark.

The account of Jeremiah's temple sermon in chapter 26 recalls an earlier prophecy concerning the fate of Shiloh from Micah, who announced that the temple would be destroyed (26:18; cf. Micah 3:12). What is at stake is the fundamental principle that God is necessarily greater than any symbol set on earth as a manifestation of his presence. So it is not a question of an inspired prophetic foretelling of the fate of the temple that is set in the forefront; it is the deeper theological point concerning the nature of the relationship that exists between God and all those religious institutions through which he may be approached by human beings.

Jeremiah 7:16—8:3
The Contrast Between True and False Worship

46

The temple sermon proper in 7:1–15 is followed by a section drawing attention to the sharp contrast between the true forms of worship and unacceptable forms that must inevitably inflict harm and hurt upon those who pursue them. The first of these contrasts in verses 16–20 points to the prevalence of a simple, popular ritual practice in Judah of making cakes devoted to "the queen of heaven" (v. 18). Entire families were involved in this activity, the children collecting wood and their fathers making the sticks into a fire. The women then made dough for the cakes, almost certainly bearing some symbolic marking (possibly crudely sexual in character) to indicate that they were eating in honor of the goddess to whom the title "the queen of heaven" is given. Probably the goddess Anat, who appears in Canaanite tradition as the consort of Baal and as rescuer from the power of "Death," is being referred to here. The title and the ritual activities linked with it, however, belonged primarily to the Mesopotamian goddess Ishtar. Most likely the title was popularly applied to various goddesses who fulfilled the role of mother-goddess and protectress against death (cf. further 44:17). It has been used here, not out of a deliberate desire for vagueness, but out of a realization that this type of worship had continued long after the time of Jeremiah's original temple sermon. Most probably the destruction of the temple in 587 B.C. had encouraged a revival in this popular and seductive form of religion. All the greater importance, therefore, was attached to emphasizing Jeremiah's outright condemnation of it.

The apparently innocent sounding activity of making cakes for the queen of heaven certainly would have contained links with deeply detested forms of fertility ritual, even if only by association. Such associations had shown themselves time and again in Israel's history to lead to ritual activities of a crudely sexual kind. The semi-magical expectations of engaging in ritual to induce life and fertility had, in reality, only led to the confusion and destruction of life within the family group. Religion had in fact been used to promote immorality. Through the pages of the Old Testament no other single issue concerning the right understanding of religion is given greater emphasis than this repudiation of the Baalistic sexual rituals. Time and again the linking together of the ideas of life, blessing, and fertility had led to a relapse into sexual immorality as a misguided means of promoting "life." The religious conflict and rivalry between the Lord God of Israel and Baal, whose sister-consort Anat was, derived from conflicting ideas of religion. One essentially moral and protective of the family social order

47

and the other essentially the pursuit of a semi-magical life-force through rituals involving sexual acts disguised in the mythology of death and rebirth.

This conflict certainly had not come to an end once the temple of Jerusalem had been destroyed, and probably rather a reverse effect had taken place. Spurning belief in a God who had allowed his sanctuary to be destroyed, many had turned back to the worship of "the queen of heaven," since it had ancient roots and had been practiced in the most simple and unpretentious "high-places" of the land.

The popularity of worshiping the figure of the mother-goddess throughout a long history points to the insincerity of the people's claim that they had trusted in the Lord as God. Having drawn attention to this contrast between a false form of worship and a true one in verses 16–20, the prophet then goes on to make a further contrast of a similar nature in verses 21–28. This concerned the passionate performing of rituals involving offering of sacrifices to God with no accompanying sense of wrong over their misconduct. They pleased themselves in their behavior, flouting the basic commandments of God (vv. 23–24). They went on in the expectation that God would be very pleased with them for their careful attention in bringing burnt offerings and sacrifices. Performing acts of worship in honor of an alien deity, which would be bound to threaten the claims to offer an exclusive loyalty to the Lord as God, was not the central issue. Rather there existed a confusion in the basic understanding of the nature of religion. Rendering burnt offerings and sacrifices to God appeared to represent actions that were bound to secure divine favor. It meant giving back to the divine Giver, from whom all life-giving power derived, something of that which his blessing had bestowed. In this way the cycle of life-giving power could be expected to continue flowing through the land and the life of the community. By depriving themselves of part of the benefit that God's bounty had given, men and women felt sure that he would respond favorably to them. They did not reckon at all with the wider aspects of their daily conduct.

We can find in these strictures the uncovering of what has been a perennial temptation in religions of all types: A set program of religious rites appeared to be more pleasing to God than the observance of the basic requirements of social responsibility. The duties of religion seemed deserving of greater attention than the fulfillment of duties to one's neighbor. Yet the prophetic admonition insists that this is entirely contrary to the priorities laid down by the Mosaic law since the Exodus (7:25). The popular mind reversed the priorities God had ordained, placing sacrifice ahead of obedience. Thereby the entire form of religion, so patiently and eagerly practiced in the temple of Jerusalem, had become a perversion of truth.

For this reason, Jeremiah's editors have linked this sharp repudiation of false religion with the warning about the destruction of the temple (7:1–15). This tragic eventuality became a necessary verdict from a patient and long-suffering deity who had borne the misrepresentations and abuses of his people long enough (vv. 27–28). Instead of expressing surprise and shock that the central symbol and focus of their religion had been taken from them by the armies of Babylon, the people needed to look to themselves and their ancestors and to experience grief and penitence over their endless perversions and misrepresentations of the essential truths of religion. They had to face, amidst the sad truths that they could not understand, the one truth that they had willfully refused to understand: they deserved the fate that had befallen their nation; the removal of its centers of false religion had become inevitable. Destruction of these centers amounted to a richly valuable opportunity to set in their place the great truths of faith (7:28). For such a people even the prophet Jeremiah had been commanded to desist from the simplest and most elementary of all religious activities—that of offering prayers of intercession (7:16). Such a simple plea to God would merely serve to hide still further from the people the misdirections of their own religious life.

The overall condemnation of false religion that follows the warning concerning the temple's destruction is brought to a fitting conclusion in 7:29—8:3 with a summons to lamentation. The "deceptive words" of the popular trust in the protective power of the temple were based upon a false understanding of God. The prophet therefore calls upon his hearers to perform the customary rite of cutting off the hair as a sign of mourning for the dead (v. 29). The theme of death is then amplified to illustrate the declaration that the Lord has "rejected and forsaken the generation of his wrath." Those who had died, whose corpses evidenced the grim tragedies that had taken place, are then listed in three categories. First to be noted are the corpses of the place of Topheth in the southwestern corner of Jerusalem. Here some form of infant sacrifice had at times been practiced (v. 31). Second, and as a direct consequence of such a gross

49

misrepresentation of the nature and demands of God, there is a warning given of the large number of Jerusalem's citizens who were destined to die in siege and battle (v. 33). This then leads on to the third group of corpses of the dead which the prophet names—those of the priests, prophets, and other leading citizens of Jerusalem who had so fearfully misled the people (8:1). These, upon whom the greatest blame rests, are to suffer the ultimate shame and abuse; their unburied corpses would be spread out for all to see as a continuing witness to their responsibility in bringing death upon the nation. Finally, and as if all the horrors described in the preceding verses are insufficient to express the awfulness of the ruin brought upon Israel, the unit concludes that even the remnant that survives these disasters will choose death for themselves and their families rather than face the unbearable future left to them (8:3).

The succession of images, beginning with the accusation that many of the people have so grossly misrepresented the nature of God as to offer their own sons and daughters in sacrifice at the high-place of Topheth (7:31), possesses a kind of hidden poetic and religious logic. The whole character and aim of the popular religion of pre-exilic Israel had been directed towards the achievement of life. It was to this end that its sexual rites were performed; it was to perpetuate the cycle of life in flocks and herds that firstling sacrifices were offered. It was even an extension of this regard for life in the giving of the firstborn back to God that had served to provide some putative justification for the offering of human firstborn children to God (cf. Exod. 22:29–30). It was the continued cry of both popular priest and prophet "Do this and you will live (have fuller life)." In reality however this semi-magical pursuit of the force of life through religion would achieve only one end—death! The ultimate deception of which the citizens of Israel had been guilty was to believe that life, as the unique gift of God himself, could be obtained by the precise performance of fixed and demanding rituals. The truth, however, was that life was the gift of God alone, whose will was moral and whose demands were loving and gracious. He had revealed through Moses the nature of the response that he demanded of his people. In a pathetic irony all those measures that appeared so certain of promoting and securing life would lead instead only to death. This included the death of the innocent victims who were sacrificed, the death of Jerusalem's citizens in battle, and the death of those leaders

50

whose misrepresentations of God lay behind the catastrophe that was to befall Judah and Jerusalem.

The question of the historical reality and basis of the practice of human sacrifice in antiquity generally, and in Israel in particular, has been much discussed with meagre results (cf. R. de Vaux, pp. 63ff.). Probably such rituals were not as widely practiced in the region as was at one time believed, although there is firm evidence of the belief that they had been practiced in the vicinity of Jerusalem. Most probably this would have been intended as an extension of the conviction that all first-born domestic animals, like the first-fruits of the harvest, belonged especially to God (cf. Exod. 22:30). Even sporadic instances of such a practice would have sufficed to draw out the sharp prophetic denunciations that we find (cf. also Ezek. 20: 25–26). Belief in the currency of such a terrifying practice, however motivated, provided the fullest and clearest demonstration of the point that Jeremiah was concerned to stress: false religion ultimately derives from a false understanding of God.

Once a clear and firm idea of the nature of God and of the moral nature of his holiness is allowed to lapse, then religion itself becomes the ultimate perversion. The formal practice of religion may become the most crude and blatant obstacle to the right service of God, as the prophet here insists it had for Israel. Nor could men and women suppose that the costliness of their ritual actions and gifts were sufficient proof that God's favor and protection would be granted. All too easily there has arisen in religion a popular and repeated fallacy: the greater the pain and self-deprivation borne by men and women, the greater the value attached to such actions by God. So we may recognize a plethora of examples which fall into such a category of misunderstanding: the painful pilgrimages performed barefoot, and sometimes even on hands and knees; the flagellation and self-inflicted wounds; and as here, the surrender of even the costliest and dearest offerings to God in one's own offspring. Yet all such actions denied the essential nature of God as gracious and loving. What he demanded of men and women was the pursuit of justice and mercy—the virtues which belonged to his own essential nature—rather than the surrender of material gifts, which were themselves the product of divine giving to humankind.

51

In the section 7:30—8:3 Jeremiah affirms the central role that must be played by a right understanding of God if religion is to be honoring to him. Far from theology as the doctrine of the nature and attributes of God being a superficial and unimportant extra to the right performance of religion, it forms its essential basis. Judah found itself enveloped by the horror and tragedy of death. Yet they had pursued their religion with the object of securing life; through their misrepresentations of how such life could be secured, they had come to a point where the death they had sought to avoid appeared preferable to the terror they had brought upon themselves (8:3).

Jeremiah 8:4—9:9
The Inescapable Fate of the People

We have already noted that reasons which led to the ordering and shaping of the separate units of material in the book are not always clearly discernible. Earlier commentators have often assumed that there is no form intention in the way prophecies have been brought together. Often it may be no more than a loose chronological association, or it may be that the present form of the book was accidental. There are however many indications that more than this was intended and that a measure of planned and ordered interconnection was being presented by conjoining one prophecy with another. One group of pronouncements or admonitions could shed light and meaning upon others. This undoubtedly is the case with the sequence of prophetic sayings and warnings in 8:4—10:25. With only minor exceptions all of them possess a sharply threatening and admonitory character, interspersed with brief comments upon the nature of divine wisdom and the depth of insight and wonder that belongs to God's actions. We may note then that the entire section from 8:4—10:25 forms a larger whole and possesses a central overall message. This concerns the awful and inevitable fate that awaits Jerusalem. The message is spelled out clearly and forcefully at a number of points: "Therefore I will give their wives to others and their fields to conquerors" (8:10). "They (the enemy) come and devour the land and all that fills it, the city and those who dwell in it" (8:16). "I will make Jerusalem a heap of ruins, a lair of jackals; and I will make the cities of Judah a desolation, without inhabitant" (9:11). "Thus says the Lord

52

'dead bodies of men shall fall like dung upon the open field, like sheaves after the reaper, and none shall gather them' " (9:22).

The import of this message is unmistakably clear, even though no precise identification of the enemy is made nor time given in which they will come. Such prophecies must belong to the years of Jehoiakim's reign and point to a Mesopotamian enemy attacking from the north (cf. the reference to the city of Dan in 8:16), which materialized in the form of the armies of Babylon under the rule of Nebuchadnezzar. What is lacking in the way in which these prophecies have been preserved is any detail of their exact date, or more importantly any indication of the political insights and reasonings leading the prophet to make such dire and confident warnings of coming doom. It must be borne in mind nevertheless that such pronouncements concerning coming events constituted the essential bedrock of prophetic utterance. These sayings, together with the poetic contexts of invective to which they are connected, are the central core of the entire section 8:4—10:25. This has been further amplified with admonitory comments and elaborations that clearly did not all stem directly from Jeremiah, as its prose formulation strongly indicates. It is the work of later editors who were concerned to provide a larger background of interpretation against which the prophet's warnings were to be understood.

Bearing these points in mind we can recognize once more the significance of the contention that the situation of the prophet's original hearers was very different from that which now presented itself to the readers of the book. What separated the former from the latter was the inescapable knowledge that doom and disaster had come. This difference imposes a considerable shift of emphasis from the prophet to that of his editors. With all the skill and passion his prophetic skill could employ, the prophet foretold that Judah and Jerusalem were facing doom and destruction; for the readers, who knew these events had been realized, the question was more deeply felt: "How can the Lord be God, if he allows such things to happen?" This is well brought out by the citing of the prophet's own rhetorical question: "Is the Lord not in Zion? Is her king not in her?" (8:19). This was precisely the kind of self-assured aphorism, echoed in the psalms of the temple (cf. Ps. 48:3), with which the people had comforted themselves and rejected the prophet's words when the possibility of averting disaster had still existed.

Now that it was too late it was all the more necessary to make absolutely clear to the readers of the book why the prophet's words had gone unheeded.

A further point is also of great significance for the student of prophecy. The early prophetic sayings that have come down to us from Jeremiah appear to have been strikingly a-political. Not until later in the period of his activity do we discover the more daring and remarkable features of his political outbursts (see below on Jer. 37:1—38:28). Yet we know that in a very direct way the collapse of the kingdom of Judah was brought about by the ill-considered and foolhardy attempt of Jehoiakim to withhold from Nebuchadnezzar his allegiance. Jehoiakim's rebellion sealed Judah's fate (601–598 B.C.). Then the subsequent rebellion of Zedekiah (590–587 B.C.) resulted in complete ruination for Judah. Only indirectly, and largely by inference, do we discern how sharply Jeremiah must have been opposed to the diplomatic moves and political tensions behind these disasters. The weight of blame is placed on the long-term religious faults and failings of Judah and Israel, rather than upon the more immediate, but short-lived, political misjudgments and defections that brought disaster to Judah.

No doubt this reflects in large measure the direction of Jeremiah's own emphasis and castigation, thereby contrasting with the much more consistently political utterances of Isaiah (cf. Clements, *Isaiah 1—39*, pp. 11ff.). We should not lose sight however of the importance of the work of the editors of Jeremiah's prophecies, and more broadly of the entire Old Testament prophetic corpus. They were concerned to draw from prophecy its more timeless and enduring significance by stressing its fundamental moral and spiritual elements (cf. Clements "Prophecy as Literature," 59ff.).

Bearing these considerations in mind, it is important for the modern reader to be aware of the positive contribution editorial shaping made to the fuller understanding of the Book of Jeremiah. For the prophet himself the thrust of his message, as it is preserved in 8:4—10:25, was to stress the certainty of doom and judgment; the editors' concern is undoubtedly that of showing that the catastrophic events that had befallen Judah did not undermine the credibility of God. On the contrary they demonstrated the awful and fearful reality of the divine power and wrath.

54

Jeremiah 8:4–12 constitutes the opening section of a series

of indictments of Israel and Judah and establishes a comprehensive uncovering of the nature and persistence of Israel's wrongdoing. The character of the punishment shortly to befall Judah is outlined in verses 10,12 in pictures of suffering and devastation closely paralleled in 6:12–15. The ties of family life will be destroyed because wives will be taken away and given to other men. Fields will be taken over by other conquering peoples and many will die violently in battle: "they shall fall among the fallen" (8:12). These are familiar and conventional pictures of military defeat and its inevitable consequences. We should probably place these prophecies during the early, or middle, years of Jehoiakim's reign (609—598), but there is nothing to show positively that the prophet knew at this stage that he was foretelling invasion by the armies of Nebuchadnezzar or when they would arrive. Events themselves would establish the true identity of the enemy as the prophecies were fulfilled. Instead the chief interest of Jeremiah lies in uncovering the nature of Israel's gross and sinful behavior.

This is achieved on two fronts, first by establishing that what had marked the popular behavior for centuries was psychologically foolish and unreasonable. All people make mistakes, but most afterwards regret them and turn away from such conduct (v. 4). This was precisely what Israel had failed to do. Such turning away from right conduct should customarily lead, by way of reaction, to a turning back to a better and more upright way of life. But Israel had never done this and was showing no inclination whatsoever to do so in the present. Her bad behavior had passed over unregretted and unmodified into still worse conduct (v. 6). In this fashion Jeremiah insists that Israel's conduct had not simply been sinful, a truth which could be said of all people, but it had been a consistent pursuit of evil without a tinge of regret. This people had become as uncontrollable in their determination to do wrong as a horse galloping into battle.

The second characterization adopted by the prophet is to assert that the people's way of life had become wholly contrary to the order that pervades the natural world. Even birds responded to the changing seasons and showed by their instinctive awareness of such changes a need to conform to the divinely-established pattern of the natural world (v. 7). The imagery and line of argument adopted here by the prophet provides a deeply perceptive illustration concerning the Old

55

Testament understanding of sin. Far from this being comprehended in the manner of an infringement of a taboo—a breaking of a purely formal set of rules concerning the nature of holiness—it is understood in a deeply moral sense. In this measure the prophetic interpretation of sin breaks with any merely external cultic notion of its essential nature. Furthermore Jeremiah's penetrating diagnosis of Israel's wrongdoing is deeply psychological and his perception is that it lies in the human will. To this extent the prophet anticipates in surprising manner the argument of M. Luther concerning the bondage of the will. The heart of sin lies in the perverseness and corruption of the human will, not in outward signs of certain types of action. Inadvertent errors do not bring outrage to God, but rather the extent to which human hearts and minds are bent on achieving evil ends.

A further explanation of the meaning and nature of sin is then brought out in verse 8. This brings to the fore a much-discussed and important feature of the relationship between sin and the written law. The verse makes reference to "the law of the Lord." Implicitly it is a written collection of laws, since the false pen of the scribes has "made it into a lie" (Skinner, pp. 103ff.). Some commentators have seen here a reference to the Deuteronomic "book of the law" discovered in the temple during the great reform in Josiah's reign (II Kings 22:8–13). The sharply critical reference to this law-book and to the misuse of it by other scribes could be an indication of Jeremiah's turning away in disillusionment from the effect of this reform upon the people (cf. further Rowley, pp. 157ff.).

This could be so, or the editors may have consciously sought to represent Jeremiah as issuing a sharp admonition against a merely formal and external understanding of divine law. Obedience to God must involve the entire personality and derive from a deep and heart-searching love of what is right, not a merely formal and outward adherence to a code of legal precepts. Certainly such a bold reproof would be appropriate after Jeremiah's deep psychological uncovering of the mysterious perversity and wrong-seeking of the human will. Few more subtle perversions of moral behavior are to be found than the rigid submission to a written code of conduct combined with an inward determination to avoid its more demanding requirements whenever possible.

However, such an interpretation of this important verse in

56

Jeremiah's denunciation of Israel's sins is not the only one possible. It is nowhere directly substantiated that the reference to "the law of the Lord" is to the scroll discovered in the temple during Josiah's reign or to any part of the Book of Deuteronomy. Israel had many oral and written formulations of the demands and requirements of the divine law (Heb. *torah*), and any one of a number could have been the intended reference here.

An important feature of Jeremiah's indictment of Israel was that mere possession of the law of God, a fact so highly prized in popular religious and national feeling, could never of itself guarantee that Israel's behavior was pleasing to God. More was needed than simply knowing what was right; it was necessary to do it! The people of Israel are then compared to vines that bear no grapes and fig trees that produce no fruit (v. 13). To exist as the Chosen People of God was meant to include among its privileges a knowledge of the law of God. Yet the ultimate goal and purpose of such a relationship to God must be that it should bear godly fruit in the form of right conduct.

The short section that follows in 8:13—9:1 is made up of a composite of brief announcements of the certainty and inevitability of military attack and defeat of Israel. It would be brought about through an enemy from the north (vv. 13–17). This pronouncement of coming ruin and disaster is followed by an outburst of uncontrollable grief from the prophet (8:18—9:1). The latter passage naturally draws most attention from the reader on account of its memorable disclosure of the prophet's inner feelings and his expression of deep emotional alienation from the task which he must, of necessity, perform as God's messenger. Yet it is important not to pass over the telling images and allusions by which Jeremiah presses home his message about the inevitability and horror of the coming disaster. Two verbal images stand out; in verse 13 the national situation is compared to a barren and fruitless vineyard—there are no grapes on the vines. This is followed in verse 17 by a warning. Snakes lurking in the fields would prove to be a mortal danger to those who walked through them. Between the two word pictures designed to drive home the sense of reality of coming danger the prophet interjects a soliloquy, which he places on the lips of the people (vv. 14–15). This soliloquy gives voice to a note of despair and hopelessness. The people are stunned by the inevitability of ruin and probable death facing them as they come to the

57

point of recognizing the hopelessness of their presumed lines of defense in the face of the overwhelming military power that would descend upon them.

The short reflection conveys a kind of double emotional outpouring: Israel had been complacent and secure in feeling that it faced no serious danger from enemies; instead it would come to realize that it did indeed stand in the way of a most alarming threat; all of its complacency would be turned into despair. On the other side there is an awareness that the greatest temptation thrusting itself upon Israel was that of self-pity and despair. For those who had survived the ruinous events of the reigns of Jehoiakim and Zedekiah, the temptation was to regard these happenings as the arbitrary and violent outburst of an outraged God. By blaming God instead of the wrongdoing of the people, the tragedy could be interpreted as the mark of an irascible deity. The prophet insists that the people must recognize that they were ultimately responsible for their own misfortunes. This insistence is given greater force by the way in which his prophecies have been edited and put together. With such emphasis, the interpretations of doom and judgment retain a very high and potentially noble view of human nature. Human beings are responsible before God for the lives they live, and their fate is not arbitrary or undeserved. They are called by him to be the planners and architects of their own world.

We hear the authentic note of prophetic pronouncement in the way Jeremiah describes the "snorting of their horses" (v. 16), which could be heard from the distant city of Dan. This was the northernmost of the cities of the land and is mentioned to elaborate the prophet's theme: the enemy will come from the north. As the war-horses enter Dan, so the invasion of Israel and the threatened ruin would have begun to materialize. It is still worthy of note that the prophet does not make explicit at this juncture that Babylon would constitute Judah's great enemy in spite of the firm characterization of the nature of, and the direction from which, ruin would come. All through Jeremiah's book and in much of Old Testament prophecy, we find that there is a reluctance to trace coming events with more than the sketchiest of detail. Far more important, it should be understood that God was the agent active behind the changing order of events. Nor does Jeremiah seek to castigate the bad political choices of succeeding kings and counselors in the manner typical of Isaiah.

Rather Jeremiah insists that the causes of the unfolding course of history through which his people were destined to suffer so much lay in their own ripeness for judgment, not their political miscalculations.

The outpouring of grief and anguish which follows in 8:18—9:1 contains some of the most poignant and memorable of the prophet's utterances. Certain phrases by which he expresses his own intense personal involvement in the foretold events reveal a measure of division within Jeremiah's own mind. On the one hand he felt his own helplessness to do more to strike home a sense of the inevitability of coming catastrophe. Alongside this he was deeply aware that he would be personally caught up himself in every aspect of the suffering inflicted upon his people. He might have been tempted even to hope that he would be shown to have been mistaken. The conflict taking place within Jeremiah was a part of the conflict and tension latent within the prophetic office. Despite the prophetic necessity to warn of coming doom and judgment, this was not because such prophets adopted a sharply judgmental and adverse view of society. On the contrary their very office was a gift for the welfare and wellbeing of the nation as a whole.

Two of the prophet's utterances expressing his own growing submission to a sense of the inevitability of judgment have become familiar texts relating to the prophet's message: "The harvest is past, the summer is ended,/and we are not saved" (v. 20). "Is there no balm in Gilead?/Is there no physician there" (v. 22)? Both are intended to give voice to a note of alarm at the erosion of hope as it gives way to despair. Israel, through its divine election, had a great potential, just as the harvest season of the year should be an occasion for renewed confidence and joy. Israel's land was rich and fertile, and none was more so than the fertile grazing lands of Gilead. Yet all this richness and joyous potential was to be lost because the people lacked the will to amend their ways in order to find God.

Because so much was at stake and the coming downfall of Judah was so awful to contemplate the prophet then launches into the first of several outpourings of grief (9:1). If we bear in mind the conscious concern for an appropriate "reader response" as Jeremiah's prophecies continued to be read long after the time of their original utterance, we can see how very important these outbursts of prophetic grief are. On the one hand they do uncover a genuine feeling for the inner perplexity

59

and sense of alienation that Jeremiah experienced. He obtained no satisfaction whatsoever from uttering the warnings and seeing them materialize! At the same time these outpourings provide a kind of dramatic realism as the reader finds precisely his or her own feelings reflected in relation to what the prophet has said. They do not merely encourage the reader to sympathize with the prophet, but to feel wholly at one with him. He is seen to be hero, philosopher, and victim all at once.

This is the first of a number of such disclosures by the prophet. Frequently they have been adduced in support of the contention that Jeremiah found himself in an isolated and unique situation. They have been thought to support the notion that Jeremiah was something of a pioneer of religious individualism. Yet this is certainly to mistake their purpose, since in large measure the primary character of the prophet's sufferings is that they were shared and were not purely private and individual. It is true that they were not shared with Jeremiah's original hearers, but they were most profoundly shared in full measure by his readers! He was at one with them, having by a kind of prophetic anticipation passed through the very sufferings that they were called upon to endure.

One further theme is brought to the forefront in this soliloquizing in grief. In verse 19 Jeremiah cites words that must have been on the lips of his contemporaries frequently. They are enshrined for us in a number of psalms: "Is the Lord not in Zion? Is her king not in her?" (cf. Ps. 48:3). But in the face of the threat from Babylon its assurance proved inadequate and is a central theme of Lamentations (cf. Lam. 2:7,15). Jeremiah had had to face the confused and complacent response from his contemporaries in Jerusalem, which had been induced by too great an emphasis upon the protective will of God and too little concern with the divine righteousness. Therefore the issue of God's presence in Zion and its meaning for the people was of utmost importance and needed to be fully raised in his prophecies. The concluding lines of verse 19 make clear his understanding: God was indeed in Zion but he had been provoked to righteous anger by the idolatry of his people! It would be false therefore to conclude that there was a major conflict of theologies. Jeremiah was not seeking to repudiate the assurance given in the psalms of Zion but only to insist that it was not the whole truth about God.

60

There follows in 9:2–9 a further affirmation of the divine

punishment that was to befall Israel. The interests of the editors show clearly in the way 9:2, which originally had no connection, is set to follow directly on 9:1. In 9:1 the prophet cries out in grief and anguish as he foresaw the unspeakable horrors coming upon his people. He is a soul screaming out in pain at the certainty of his people's downfall. Then in 9:2 the editors skillfully juxtaposed the prophet's agonized yearning to flee to a place of refuge from his people. In this case, however, it is not because of the danger facing them but, by striking contrast, on account of the awfulness of their sin. To live among them, cried Jeremiah, was to be infected and contaminated by their evil and contemptible behavior. So he longs to flee to a desert place free from the continual hurts and shame of a community of adulterers, liars, and perpetrators of violence. Who indeed, he proclaims, would not want to run away from a people such as this? They pollute themselves with their misdeeds and falsehoods and thereby contaminate all who listen to them. In this way Jeremiah insists that no individual could trust another and that all were compelled to live in a world of falsehood created by their fabricated lies. The literary technique is effectively accomplished by matching a pronouncement of doom, in which Jeremiah yearns to pour out his grief, with a longing to be free from the doomed people.

By his bold and gaudily painted picture of the inner corruption and treachery of Israel's social behavior, Jeremiah presents his own powerful indictment of them. They are a people who have passed sentence on themselves; they have no right to complain that God was leading them on to political catastrophe and military defeat. Rather they had judged themselves, finding themselves totally unable to rebut the charges the prophet lays against them. Jeremiah does not offer in this section any words of alleviation or qualification in his outright condemnation of the people. The charges are undisputed and unanswerable and the demanded verdict must take effect without any element of mitigation. Within the larger context of the book there does emerge an ultimate message of hope and of a restored Israel purged from all its former misdeeds. Nevertheless it must be insisted that the whole of the section from 8:4—10:25 represents a central core for an understanding of the Jeremianic prophecies.

61

In many respects what we find here is typical of Jeremiah and characteristic of prophecy as a whole. By backing up pronouncements of God's punitive action with broad indictments of the corruption and wrong prevalent among the people, Jeremiah establishes the fearful nature of his message and the near certainty of its fulfillment. We may insist that it represents "near certainty" rather than an absolute certainty because neither Jeremiah nor any of the prophets of the Old Testament subscribe to a fatalistic view of a fixed and unalterable destiny for Israel. Such a conception of "fate" is essentially Greek rather than Hebraic, although it has often appeared in many guises in conjunction with prophecy. So far as Jeremiah was concerned he certainly left a measure of "openness" to make room for the possibility of future repentance. The sharpness of his warnings and threats and the intensity with which he castigates his people's sins must then be seen as an essential part of goading the people towards repentance and a thorough amendment of their way of life.

This reflection upon the prophetic understanding of history and of the divine control evidenced within it is important for a general understanding of the book. There can be little doubt that the editors have elaborated the prophet's words by more explicit invitations to repentance (e.g., 18:11; 22:4–6—addressed to the royal house). In doing this, however, they have certainly correctly interpreted the prophet's intentions and, moreover, have sought to take into account the comprehensive impact of Jeremiah's message as a whole. Here too it is essential that we continue to bear in mind the changed situation of those intended to read Jeremiah's book from that of his original hearers. The past was past and the judgments Jeremiah foretold had taken place. To this extent any reflection on other possible outcomes had become purely theoretical. What mattered for the future was that the reasons and valuations of human society explicit within his prophecies should be taken into account fully. Only then could the hoped for future, which also belonged authentically to what Jeremiah had declared about God's plans for Israel, be realized.

Jeremiah's sharp and intense condemnations of Israel's sins, especially the scathing exposure of their lying and general deceitfulness, further raises the question of Jeremiah's time being one of major social instability and unrest. Certainly we should bear in mind that ever since the days, more than a century earlier, when Judah had come under the control of the imperial power of Assyria the country had suffered a good deal of external political and economic interference. The influence this may have had upon the traditions and ethos of the community as a whole is impossible to determine with any useful degree of detail. It may be highly likely that the continual drain upon the nation's wealth to pay tribute-gifts to outside powers, combined with the socially divisive consequences for those who became collaborators with these powers, contributed to a serious breakdown of social order and trust. Such would certainly be suggested by the Old Testament prophets who do point to a high degree of violence, corruption, and dishonesty particularly attached to the wealthier and more powerful elements in Judah and Israel.

Against this, however, we should certainly place the recognition that most of the misdeeds and wrong-dealing of which the prophets complain—adultery, greed, lying accusations—were of a kind that have shown themselves to be almost endemic to most human societies without strong social and political institutions. Israel and Judah were essentially parts of a very young national community that had not had long to establish deep traditions and firm commitments to effective social institutions of law and economic stability. It may reasonably be assumed therefore that the impact of Mesopotamian imperialism upon Israel and Judah worsened an already vulnerable situation rather than being directly the cause of it. Therefore, we need not suppose that the prophets were either exaggerating the moral faults of the communities they addressed or living in uniquely iniquitous times to appreciate the power and force of their message. Its strength and greatness undoubtedly lies in its almost timeless exposure of fundamental social ills.

Jeremiah 9:10–26
Lamentation and Soliloquy

The unit in 9:10–26 is a composite containing two clear and unequivocal declarations of the destruction that Jeremiah foresaw as about to come upon Jerusalem (vv. 10–11, 17–22) combined with two reflections upon the divine reasons and the necessity for this catastrophe (vv. 12–16, 23–26). These

63

reflections are set out in the form of a didactic soliloquy. Thus it is highly improbable that they derive directly from Jeremiah. Their goal is to question the comprehensibility and purpose of Jerusalem's defeat and downfall set against the background of divine righteousness and commitment to Israel. They are concerned with theodicy—justifying the actions of God as part of an intelligible and moral world order. Yet they nevertheless truly belong to prophecy and need to be read and interpreted in relation to the prophetic declarations of impending doom and judgment.

Jeremiah's initial pronouncement of Jerusalem's threatened situation is set out vividly in poetic imagery as a summons to perform a lamentation for the death and destruction soon to come upon the city and the surrounding territory of Judah: "I will make Jerusalem a heap of ruins" (v. 11). The second prophetic pronouncement, closely similar in character, calls for the professional mourning women to come and perform their sad and mournful duties (vv. 17–22). It is evident from the dramatic word-pictures that are painted—"death has come up to our windows"—"the dead bodies of men shall fall like dung upon the open field"—that military defeat and the inevitable subsequent slaughter of wounded and fugitives is envisaged. Once again, as consistently throughout the section of 8:4—10:25, no precise political and historical context is given. We should certainly think however of the period of Jehoiakim's reign leading up to the first act of rebellion against Babylon. Yet this is never made explicit, even by so much as a brief allusion, and in the overall context of the book the two campaigns of Nebuchadnezzar against Judah (601–598; 588–587 B.C.) have effectively merged. The causes and consequences of both these tragic experiences during a period of a little over a decade were effectively the same, even when viewed in a contemporary political perspective. This was even more truly the case when they were seen against the prophet's understanding of Judah's moral and spiritual history.

We may nonetheless remark upon the surprising lack of any explicit criticism or indictment of Judah's political leadership, which lay behind the decisions to withhold allegiance to Babylon. The contrast with the directness with which such criticisms had been expressed by Isaiah when Hezekiah rebelled against the Assyrian overlordship is particularly marked (esp. Isa. 28—31). The deep concern that the populace of Judah as a whole should not be allowed to hide behind the robes of their leaders and politicians may account in part for Jeremiah's silence. All are denounced as guilty since all had contributed in their own way to the sins and dishonesty which promoted the chain of events leading to their country's downfall. The record is not allowed to single out a few to be held guilty and thereby be made scapegoats. Rather the nation as a whole is accused of base and apostate behavior so that none should escape acceptance of blame and accordingly evade the summons to repentance! All had sinned; therefore all must repent!

A further consideration must also be raised, even though it requires to be dealt with more fully in relation to the pronouncements of the coming downfall of Babylon in chapters 50—51. The main part of the Book of Jeremiah is remarkably free of sharp and violent antagonism towards Babylon, and it does not appear until the closing chapters of the book. At certain points the Babylonian overlordship of Judah is presented as essentially fair, as in chapters 42—44. The rise of Babylonian imperial power is presented as an act of God, necessary to punish Judah and the surrounding nations for their sins. Only after seventy years will the time come to punish the king of Babylon (cf. esp. 25:8–14). There is therefore a marked concern to deal with the issue of Judah's sufferings and the destruction of Jerusalem in terms relating to Israel's moral and spiritual life rather than its political ineptness. Nor should we leave out of account that so far as the readers of the Book of Jeremiah were concerned, whether in Judah or among the Babylonian exiles, continued submissive acceptance of Babylonian rule remained imperative. The possibility no longer existed for these readers to make any immediate political protest against Babylonian rule. Such had to be left for the future time of renewal and restoration.

The act of mourning, with all its conventional rituals, belongs to the wider context in which the prophet actualizes in advance the threat he had perceived and had proclaimed as imminent. The certainty of the impending disaster, not the question of its nearer or more remote immediacy, remained of paramount importance for the prophet. The vivid use of metaphor in declaring that "death has come up into our windows" (v. 20) recaptures features of the widespread mythological conception of death in the ancient world. A destructive power, divine in its strength and ferocity and demonic in its intentions,

65

sought to seek out and strike down the unwary and unguarded (cf. L.R. Bailey, pp. 39ff.). Almost certainly Jeremiah's hearers were fully familiar with the notion of the god Mot, the great opponent of Baal and master of all the powers of death and destruction. Clearly disease or famine, even though these may popularly have been thought to find entry through unprotected doors and windows, were not what the prophet envisaged here, but the violence of battle.

The interjection of the two didactic soliloquies in verses 12–16 and 23–26 highlight the extent to which prophecy, once set down in written form, acquired a new dimension and meaning. It was one of the fundamental features of spoken prophecy that it was addressed to a specific historical situation. To preserve such prophetic warnings and threats was to a certain extent to modify their original significance by detaching them from their original setting. Nevertheless the editors have endeavored to adapt the prophet's sayings to their readers' needs by reflecting afresh upon the justice of the divine action in punishing Israel. We may reflect upon the issue as set out by S. Kierkegaard:

> Oh, my hearer, if thou hast known the darkest hour in human life, when all went black before thy soul, as if there were no love in heaven, or as if he who is in heaven after all were aught but love, and when it seemed to thee there was a choice that thou must make, the awful choice between: being in the wrong and gaining God, and being in the right and losing God (p.69).

It is noteworthy in this wisdom reflection in Jeremiah that the reason given why God had perforce to punish Israel is set out in surprisingly broad and comprehensive terms: "They have forsaken my law . . . ; . . . have gone after the Baals. . . ." In similar fashion the punishment spelled out is described in comparably general terms, but appears to hold out little by way of ultimate hope: "I will scatter them among the nations . . . until I have consumed them"(v. 16).

Couched in the language and form of a wisdom saying, the second didactic soliloquy falls into two parts: verses 23–24, 25–26. The celebration in praise of the knowledge of God—"let him who glories glory in this, that he understands and knows me, . . ." resembles very closely the thanksgiving for the hidden wisdom of God pronounced by Jesus after the sending out of the seventy disciples (Luke 10:21–22). The knowledge of God, which in the eyes of the world so often appears confusing and mysterious, becomes plain to the mind open to the possibilities of faith. Such faith then provides access to true wisdom in a manner comparable to faith that could recognize the revelation of God in Jesus. This provided a way to a deeper and more all-encompassing wisdom than that afforded by a surface reading of events (cf. further I Cor. 1:20–25). The purpose of the soliloquy in 10:23–24 appears to be to draw attention to the hidden, unfathomable dimension of the divine working (cf. M. Gilbert, pp. 105ff.; W. Brueggemann, *The Land,* pp. 85ff.). Even though, in human terms, it seemed practicable to offer reasons why God had had to punish Judah and Jerusalem, such human explanations could be no more than merely attempts and therefore could not hope to comprehend the whole range and majesty of divine providence. The knowledge of God and of his ways with humankind must ultimately be a knowledge that rests on faith.

The addition in verses 25–26 is evidently by a yet later hand and is concerned to point to the expectation of a future eschatological judgment upon Israel. It has undoubtedly been occasioned by reflection upon the mystery implicit in the idea of Israel's divine election and of the importance of circumcision as a sign of a covenant relationship to God (cf. Gen. 17:9–14). The primary point of reference in verse 25 was evidently to Israel alone as a people where circumcision was a mark of a divinely elect status. However this covenant-election required to be sealed and made evident by obedience to the requirements disclosed in the covenant law. Such demands of a moral and spiritual nature could be betrayed and rejected. The scribe has therefore proceeded to draw the conclusion that it was possible to bear the mark of circumcision and at the same time betray its deeper spiritual significance. As this was true of Israel so also could it be true of those other nations among Israel's neighbors who also practiced circumcision.

Jeremiah 10
The Condemnation of Idolatry

What would constitute the greatest of sins for a man or woman belonging to Israel? It would surely have to be the denial of God himself and replacing true knowledge of him with a spurious and make-believe knowledge that is nothing more than human invention. This then is precisely the sin of idolatry, for it is regarded in the Old Testament as not simply an unthinking act of homage to an object shaped from wood or metal. It is rather the fundamental denial and distortion of reality—the replacing of genuine openness to a transcendent, loving, and all powerful being, who alone is seen to be adequate as the ground and sustainer of human existence, by a spurious representation. It is in this light that the persistent, sharp, and repeated condemnation of idolatry set out in the pages of the Old Testament can be understood. Ultimately idolatry must be regarded as displacing and denying the central element of transcendence that belongs to the essential understanding of God (cf. G. von Rad, *Theology,* I, 212ff.). Deity without transcendence becomes a contradiction in itself and very dangerous because denying the ultimate transcendence of God leaves the way open for all kinds of false and destructive claims to transcendent authority on the part of human institutions and artefacts. By implication too those who manipulate and administer these institutions derive from them a spurious power. When God is no longer acknowledged as Lord, this does not put an end to the concept of lordship and authority but merely transfers it to unworthy and hostile claimants to the title.

It is in the light of these considerations that the fervor and tenacity with which the Old Testament condemns idolatry must be understood. Condemnation of idolatry is frequently combined with condemnation of gods other than the Lord, the God of Israel, since the two offenses—denying the transcendent nature of God and worshiping a distorted and alien representation of God—constitute for Israel a fundamental disorientation from reality. Both in its essential character and in its practical implications idolatry becomes inseparably linked with a departure from the grounds for Israel's existence as a people. It is no longer simply a practical turning aside to a different tradition of religion but a deeper spiritual and intellectual denial of the nature of reality.

The introduction in 10:1–16 of this long, mature, and deeply theological condemnation of the folly of idolatry is therefore to be understood as a further elaboration of the theme concerning the true knowledge of God set out in 9:24. It constitutes a primary illustration of the wisdom that understands the truth about God (cf. 9:24) and the contrast with the

68

false wisdom that rejects this and constructs instead a false and artificial representation of God the creator. The poetic unit here, largely praise of the true being of God, bears close comparison with the condemnation of idolatry in Isaiah 44:9–20. Almost certainly it is from the same late exilic period as the Isaianic diatribe and originates from prolonged reflection on Israel's past and not simply impatient frustration with the apostasy of some contemporary groups within Israel. It is couched in dignified poetic language into which a prose comment in Aramaic in verse 11, concerning the eventual time of abolition of all idolatries and misrepresentations of the one true God, has been inserted unexpectedly.

The temptation to idolatry had existed for Israel throughout the entire period leading up to the final collapse of the kingdom of Judah in 587 B.C. The prevalence of idolatry and the popularity of Baal and Anat images and other Canaanite deities had come to be regarded as a major cause of Israel's downfall. The prominent place accorded this carefully worded and forcefully presented piece of poetic polemic, which appears in Isaiah, Jeremiah, and Ezekiel, points us to recognize the persistent continuance of the use of images in worship throughout the exilic and early post-exilic periods. In fact it appears to have possessed an almost timeless attraction for Israel and continued to do so down to the very close of the Old Testament period.

It would be mistaken, however, to regard the sharp condemnation of idolatry in these prophetic books as no more than the opportunistic rejection of a feature of religion that had attracted official unpopularity but continued to enjoy a good deal of general support among the less religiously perceptive. The editors of the prophetic books have evidently recognized in idolatry a betrayal of Israel's own essential identity, a basic attitude of mind and heart expressing on the part of those who practiced it a fundamental rejection of the true knowledge of God.

This condemnation of a false representation of God is followed in verses 17–25 by a unit that is a composite of several short sayings, some self-evidently clear in their meaning whereas others have aroused intense discussion and leave a number of basic issues unclear. The command of God in verses 17–18 to the inhabitants of the land that they should prepare themselves for exile envisages that Jerusalem has already either fallen under siege, or at least has become seriously threatened by this

69

possibility. The circumstances must be those of the threat posed by the Babylonian campaigns involving attacks upon Jerusalem in 598 or 587, which have become effectively merged into each other (see commentary on 9:10–26). However, for the reader of this prophecy, a difficulty arises with the need to identify the "I" who speaks in verses 19–21. Either the prophet himself may be envisaged as expressing his own grief and agony at the picture of ruin and devastation shortly to burst forth upon his homeland or it is Jerusalem personified as a mother grieving over her ruined home and lost children, which is most probably how these moving verses were intended to be read. Jerusalem, by the action of rebellion against Babylon, seen at the same time to constitute rebellion against God, has sealed her fate. Now the inevitable consequences must be borne, although when the words were originally voiced these consequences were no doubt still to be faced in all their stark horror.

In such poignant lamentation the complex nature of the text, with its resort at times to deliberate and skillfully formulated multiple layers of meaning, becomes apparent. Jeremiah is presented as being one of the people so that even though he speaks against them and addresses them as over against himself, he nevertheless remains bound up with them and must share their fate. Their lamentation and grief is therefore his lament and grief—in a sense the misfortune is doubly his since he bears it with them, even though he had fought desperately and fervently to persuade them to act otherwise. Yet their fate is sealed, and with whatever seeming injustice, it has also become his fate. In crying out in grief and pain he voices the genuine pain of his own feelings and projects upon his hearers the sounds and sentiments they will themselves soon be experiencing in full measure.

Then clearly and firmly verse 22 spells out the nature of the events that will bring about this physical and spiritual devastation: An enemy will come from the north (undoubtedly Babylon is now understood as being referred to) who will ravage the cities of Judah. The penetrating and near despairing words of verses 23–24 cry out at the injustice of the prophet's fate. He has been destined to share the hurt and unyielding grief that he had sought to spare his people. These words voice a quiet commitment of submission to God that not all truth is comprehensible to the human mind and not all justice can be fathomed in one single event. The concluding comment in verse 25 attempts a further alleviation of the problem implicit in Judah's devastation and ruin at the hands of the Babylonian armies by looking to the longer term (eschatological) future. The sufferings of Israel are not a denial of its election; ultimately the full meaning and vindication of that election must be seen in God's judgment not only of Israel but of all nations.

PART TWO

God's Prophet in Conflict
JEREMIAH 11—20

The prophecies from Jeremiah in 8:4—10:25 appear to have been delivered originally in connection with Jehoiakim's revolt against Babylon in the period 605–598 B.C. They prepare for the devastation of Judah and Jerusalem and anticipate the heavy penalty imposed by the Babylonian imperial masters upon their recalcitrant subject people of Judah in the year 598 B.C. The disasters of this year resulted in Jehoiachin along with several of the leading priests (among whom was the prophet Ezekiel) being deported as prisoners to Babylon. Many other prominent citizens and landowners went with them. This action established the beginning of the Babylonian exile, which in turn was to mark the beginning of the period of many Jews being scattered among the nations, which has continued to the present. Without question, the year 598 B.C. marked one of the most significant turning points for Jewish faith and religious practice during the entire Old Testament period.

These events form the essential background to Jeremiah's prophecies and provide the unquestioned "fulfillment" of the threatening side of their message, so far as the editors of the Book of Jeremiah are concerned. At times Jeremiah's words about the coming military devastation of Judah and Jerusalem and the removal of citizens into exile are quite explicit (cf. 8:12, 16; 9:11,19,22). The unit that now commences in 11:1 and extends as far as 20:18 contains prophetic pronouncements that reflect in general the same message concerning the coming military defeat and the subsequent ruin and devastation of the land. These prophecies can therefore be assumed to belong most probably to the same period of Jehoiachin's reign (605–598 B.C.).

At the same time the surface layer of explicit prophetic pronouncements of coming national doom are greatly expanded in this section by the addition of an extensive range of outbursts and lamentations from the prophet that point to conflicts between the prophet and his audience. More deeply revealing than these, however, are outbursts that reflect conflicts within the mind of Jeremiah about his message and his role within the community of his Judahite compatriots. The overall theme of the section, therefore, is one of conflict both in a personal, individual sense applicable to Jeremiah and in a larger corporate sense reflecting divisions within the nation as a whole. Implicit in the tensions and turmoil of these spiritual and social conflicts is the most fundamental level of conflict between the nation of Israel and God. The theological background against which this dissension between God and people is to be understood is that of the covenant made on Mount Sinai (Horeb). Since Israel's beginning as a nation its fundamental goal of existence and the shaping of its destiny had been understood in terms of its election by Yahweh and its continued unique relationship to him.

This elect status and unique relationship between God and Israel had come to be given expression through the concept of a covenant (Heb. *berit*). Much has been written concerning the origins of such an idea, the extent to which an appropriate analogy is presented by treaties (or "covenants") between human parties, and the reasons why the term had come to enjoy great prominence in the last decades of Judah's national existence (cf. Hillers, pp. 120ff. Bright, *Covenant and Promise,* pp. 140ff.). The reason this idea enjoyed such prominence and appears so extensively in the edited collection of Jeremiah's prophecies (although it is doubtful whether Jeremiah himself used the term more than incidentally in his preaching) lies in the way it gives voice to an awareness of the mutually reciprocal demands of the relationship between God and Israel. As is widely assumed in the religious beliefs of humankind, the deity was expected to watch over and protect the interests and welfare of those men and women who worshiped him. Correspondingly, granting protection and blessing could honorably be expected only if those same men and women served God by living in accordance with the known directions of the divine will. Consistently Jeremiah's contention had been that Israel had failed to display precisely this mode of conduct pleasing to God.

74

The prophets as the representatives of God were to reveal God's anger and displeasure and thereby warn people away from the dangers implicit in their behavior. Such prophets would also act as intercessors to plead on behalf of the people and so to assist in averting the divine wrath. Either way the prophet acted as God's representative and the people's mediator so as to maintain the communion between the people and their God. A prophet who failed to warn the people of the dangers facing them or who failed through his prayers to avert the anger of God was accordingly seen as a failure. Should he not then be ignored as a failure and as a person of no account?

Jeremiah and those who have taken such care to preserve and interpret his prophecies contend that he was not a failure of this kind. Failure lay with Israel, by its refusal to listen to the prophet's message and to obey the known will of God. The ruin and disaster that befell Judah and Jerusalem could therefore be understood as the inevitable and necessary negative aspect of the relationship implicit in the covenant. The reverse side of God's pledge to protect and bless carried the necessity of punishment upon Israel's disobedience by bringing about military defeat and political ruination. Jeremiah's role as mediator and intercessor could achieve only so much in admonition and pleading; never of itself could it serve as a substitute obedience for Israel's rejection of God! Therefore, the entire section (11:1—20:18) presents the deepest and most heart-searching disclosure of the nature of Jeremiah's spiritual conflict and the role of one individual within a community. The prophet sensed that he was being torn apart by the conflicting demands of obedience to God and his commitment to be his people's representative.

Jeremiah 11:1–17
The Broken Covenant

Appropriately the opening section (11:1–17) of the larger unit of chapters 11—20 is concerned to reaffirm the existence, nature, and implications of the covenant established between God and Israel. The passage has certainly been formulated by Jeremiah's editors and not by the prophet himself, but necessarily it sets out what these editors saw as the implicit assumption behind all of Jeremiah's preaching. God and Israel were bound together in a covenant relationship that carried both privileges and obligations. A covenant with Israel by Yahweh to become their God, to protect and enrich them, had at the same time and by the same action brought upon the nation obligations and conditions which Israel had fully recognized. These conditions needed to be fulfilled if the covenant relationship was to continue. The references to "covenant" in this passage have frequently been linked by commentators with the great reform of Josiah (cf. II Kings 23:1–3): The king and elders of the people reaffirmed their loyalty and commitment to the covenant made between Israel and the Lord God on Mount Sinai (Horeb). The conditions of the covenant law were then set out in the scroll (or "book"); Israel was thereby bound "to perform the words of this covenant that were written in this book" (II Kings 23:3).

The relationship between the present "covenant" passage in the Book of Jeremiah and the central emphasis given to the finding of the law-book in the account of Josiah's reform is more complex than to suppose that Jeremiah was simply reflecting the course of events that took place in Josiah's reign (as Skinner, pp. 89ff.). Critical examination of the texts shows that on both sides, the manner in which Jeremiah's preaching has been recorded and edited and the way in which the events of Josiah's reign have been reported, there is revealed a conscious effort to bring the two into a clear relationship. Both reports are strongly aware of two major facts: Josiah's reform had raised expectations of a national revival and Jerusalem's defeat by the armies of Nebuchadnezzar had dashed these hopes. The concern of the editors in both cases has been to show the conditional nature of the covenant relationship between Israel and God. Israel's and Jerusalem's experiences of defeat did not imply that that relationship no longer existed but only that the nature of its obligations on Israel's part needed to be more fully appreciated.

It is strikingly evident from examination of the use of the relevant vocabulary that the term "covenant" as a way of defining the nature of Israel's relationship to God came to enjoy a period of sudden and extensive usage by Jerusalem (Deuteronomic) circles during the last days of the Judean monarchy. Nor is the reason for this rise in the popularity of a term that had had earlier and more perfunctory origins hard to find. It was a concept that expressed clearly and forcibly the two-sided nature of the relationship between Israel and God. Covenant not only assured Israel of God's protection but it also affirmed categorically the need for obedience on Israel's part. The scribes who have recorded for us the events of Josiah's reign, as well as the editors of Jeremiah's prophecies, have both been at pains to stress the theological implications of the relationship between the people and their God. This clearly is the case with 11:1–9, where it is heavily spelled out that the existence of the covenant carried major implications of obedience on Israel's part. The editors imply that such a point had readily and facilely been neglected by Israel with disastrous results. So in this section dealing with the subject of the covenant between Israel and God we find a major theological contribution by the editors towards understanding Jeremiah's prophecies in a broad historical perspective. The theme is unequivocally clear: Israel's relationship to God carried obligations to obedience which Israel had not in fact fulfilled (cf. esp. 11:4,7). Only if this obedience had been forthcoming did Israel have the right to expect that it would receive a special and privileged protection from God. Failure of obedience on Israel's part had been fully affirmed and Jeremiah's prophecies demonstrated that Israel had consistently and repeatedly failed to obey God (cf. v. 8).

The covenant had been broken many times and the evidence was to be seen all around—in every city and at every one of the abundant sanctuaries in the countryside dedicated to a false god. However, the disobedience by which Israel had broken the covenant and its primary obligations had now led to a deeper and more fundamental awareness of what "breaking" the covenant implied: The covenant could be broken so frequently and so radically that its very continuance could be set in doubt. The covenant then would be rescinded and rendered null and void! Such a situation is envisaged in 11:1–14, where God asserts his intention of bringing such great evil upon the people that there would be no way of escape. Then Israel might look in vain for help to the many spurious gods that they and their ancestors had worshiped. They would find them utterly empty and worthless, no more than a useless sham, which is how they had been warned all along they would find them to be.

The final affirmation regarding the irremedial breach of the covenant which had taken place comes in verse 14 where Jeremiah is warned personally by God to refrain from fulfilling his normally expected role as intercessor and mediator between Israel and their God. Prayers for leniency and mercy in such a context would only serve to paper over the cracks and leave Israel's condition more ambiguous and hopeless than ever. The theme of covenant therefore becomes a central key for understanding the entire section from 11:1—20:18. As the Lord's prophet, Jeremiah needed to be seen as a mediator of the covenant relationship. In a sense his very presence and activity implied the existence of the covenant. However the pain and agony he experienced through his prophesying, together with the apparent frustration and failure of his work as a prophet and mediator between God and people, could be understood to have only one possible explanation: the depth and willfulness of Israel's disobedience to God was so great that there had been no hope of averting the disasters that befell them.

This awareness of the final breaking off of the covenant relationship through Israel's disobedience is an essential part of the theological background to the doctrine of the new covenant that is set out as central to the prophetic message of hope in 31:31–34. The covenant had been broken in such a way that it had effectively been rendered void. Only a new covenant could repair the damage that Israel had inflicted upon itself. The full extent and radical nature of this breach of covenant on Israel's part is claimed by Jeremiah to have been everywhere evident: "as many as the streets of Jerusalem are the altars you have set up to shame, altars to burn incense to Baal" (11:13).

The divine injunction to Jeremiah to desist from making any intercessory prayer for "this people" (itself a deliberate designation implying the divine rejection of Israel who could no longer be addressed by God as "my people") must be understood as a necessary consequence of the fundamental breaking off of the covenant. The prophet's role had been that of mediator and intercessor of the covenant (cf. Deut. 18:15–22), as had been that of Moses himself in the nation's beginning. No longer, however, could Jeremiah honorably fulfill such a task of being a mediator, not through any failure on his part but on account of the radical failure on the part of the people to respond to the call for obedience. Radical sin had called forth radical punishment, and Jeremiah could do nothing further to avert this. He had done all that a prophet could be reasonably expected to do. The prophetic role of being a mediator and intercessor becomes a recurrent theme in the unit as far as 20:18, where

78

in fact the concluding section, beginning with the lament: "Cursed be the day on which I was born . . ." (20:14) marks a fitting conclusion to the whole. Overall the unit has as its theme the command of God to the prophet: "do not pray for this people." With such a command Jeremiah's whole ministry had become one of personal rejection, suffering, and tragedy.

The conclusion to the present section in verses 15–17 offers a brief summing-up of the indictment of Israel. The people had constantly provoked God to anger by their prevalent worship of his great rival Baal—the symbol of a man-made and falsely oriented religion devoted to the rituals of fertility and sexual power.

Jeremiah 11:18—12:6
A Prophet's Enemies—
Members of His Own House

Jeremiah's declaration that Israel had broken its covenant relationship with God in a fundamental and irremedial way set the prophet in a new role. From being mediator within the covenant Jeremiah had effectively stepped outside its range to declare that the covenant itself had suffered a mortal blow. To this extent Jeremiah now appeared to stand outside all the covenant possibilities and to be the spokesman of a new and previously unforeseen situation. In similar fashion his own personal position within the nation and within his own community had become seriously compromised. He belonged to the people and must share their fate and even their punishment, while at the same time he longed to flee from their shame (cf. 9:2–6) and to be freed from the burden of the message he was called upon to bring. His very position as that of a go-between, mediating between God and a godless nation, was tearing apart his own inner being. His message-bearing task imposed on him a tension between wanting to defend the people against God and wanting to defend God against the misunderstandings of the people. We now encounter, in two much-discussed sections, a glimpse into the prophet's inner doubts, fears, and agonies (11: 18–20 and 12:1–6). These outbursts are couched in the conventional language and imagery of Israel's psalms of individual

79

lamentation, but they have become intensely personal expressions of Jeremiah's private torment.

In the first section (11:18–20) Jeremiah records the hostile intent of enemies among his immediate town circle, including possibly even some from within his own family. They had resorted to planning attempts upon the prophet's life and understandably his sense of shock and bitterness leads to an outburst in which he calls upon God to exact vengeance on his behalf: "let me see thy vengeance upon them" (v. 20). The second complaint follows immediately upon this and asks a number of further questions: Why do the wicked prosper and why are they not swiftly stricken down with the punishment they deserve? (cf. 12:1–2). Once again the prophet feels tempted and goaded into appealing to God for vengeance to be inflicted on them: "Pull them out like sheep for slaughter, / and set them apart for the day of slaughter" (12:3). The total absence of any willingness to forgive, and more than a hint of impatient yearning on the prophet's part to see his enemies' downfall, has frequently been contrasted with the intercession made by Jesus on the cross for his tormentors (cf. Luke 23:34). It would be mistaken however to compare Jeremiah's action with that of Jesus almost six centuries later. Undoubtedly over the question of the forgiveness of enemies the Christian ethic has attained to a higher and more insightful standard. This does not, however, enable us to ignore the fact that Jeremiah's attitude was understandably human and was the outward expression of a deep and painful conflict that had taken place within his own mind and in relation to those of his own immediate circle. In recalling Jeremiah's experience the prophet's editors have not been concerned to highlight his personal ethical behavior so much as the nature of his message and the torment into which he was plunged on account of it. The word of God, which was intended to guide and heal, could not be truly the word of God if it did not also, where necessary, lead to alienation and division. In this case it could even lead to a mental division within the prophet himself.

The question of Jeremiah's vocation as a prophet was inevitably being called into doubt and uncertainty as a result of the reception his prophecies elicited from the people. Could he be truly faithful to his task if he were at the same time despised and physically rejected by those whom he was called upon to serve? The book of Jeremiah's prophecies begins with an account of his call but this should not imply that the issue for the prophet was settled once and for all. More probably his initial sense of uncertainty and inadequacy (cf. 1:6) remained a recurrent mood and occasion for doubt. We also learn (cf. chap. 36) that it was after an interval of twenty years that the need to record his early prophecies came to the prophet. There was a long and involved personal history affecting Jeremiah throughout the period of his prophetic activity which entailed the constant rethinking and reappropriation of the reality and implications of his divine call. What has been given to us in the final account in chapter 1 is the product of a lifetime of divine service, not a sweeping aside of any ground for doubt and uncertainty. For Jeremiah the sense of a divine mission acquired greater depth and meaning as it was tried and tested. Nor does it appear that the sense of divine call in any way exonerated Jeremiah from continued self-doubt and questioning. Vocation could be only an issue of faith.

In 12:5–6 we hear for the first time God's response to the prophet's inner struggle. Verse 5, in which God forewarns the prophet of even greater difficulties to come, suggests a kind of stiffening and reinforcement of the prophet's wavering convictions. He is assured that he is on the right track because the going is hard, and it will get harder! Verse 6, warning of the threat from within the prophet's own household and family, presents a rather ambiguous word of assurance. Jeremiah's brethren at one moment are in full cry after him and yet in the next moment may be speaking fair words to him. In neither case is the prophet to heed their words or threats. He is to be God's servant wholly and simply, undistracted by the trials or enticements of those who are nearest to him. Why the prophet's family turned against him is not spelled out and has inevitably occasioned a good deal of discussion.

We may venture to outline various possible avenues of understanding for the direct physical hostility displayed towards Jeremiah from within his own family circle as well as from the townspeople of Anathoth. We should bear in mind that Jeremiah was of the family in Anathoth descended from the priest Abiathar of David's time. On Solomon's accession Abiathar had been banished from Jerusalem for supporting Adonijah's claim to the throne (I Kings 2:26–27). Therefore it can be presumed that deep rivalry and bitterness existed between Abiathar's descendants and the Zadokite priesthood of Jerusalem. Josiah's effort to restrict Yahweh worship to the temple in

81

Jerusalem by suppression of the high places early in the time of Jeremiah's prophetic ministry certainly would have exacerbated this bitterness. Had Jeremiah shown even a moderate degree of support for Josiah's reforming measures this would have understandably provoked hostility from within his own family circle (cf. also II Kings 23:9; see commentary on Jer. 1, Superscription and Call).

Jeremiah's attitude to Josiah's reform is uncertain, so that we can presume to know very little about it. It is an event which lay at least twenty years in the past by the time the events reported in 11:21–23, 12:5–6 are most likely to have taken place. An issue of much wider national concern appears far more likely to have influenced the attitude of Jeremiah's family in Anathoth. This relates to the prophet's apparent lack of patriotism in maintaining a consistently threatening and admonitory tone in his prophecies throughout Jehoiakim's reign. Once the royal decision to withdraw allegiance to Nebuchadnezzar and his demands had been taken, we can confidently assume that many in the nation would have regarded Jeremiah's repeated warnings and threats as unpatriotic and contrary to what was expected of a major religious figure. Should not a prophet prophesy and pray for the protection and preservation of his people? Jeremiah's family may have felt that they too were being regarded with suspicion and distrust by the nation's leaders on account of Jeremiah's prophecies. Either by threats or enticing words, the efforts to silence him can be understood as intended to put an end to a dangerous member of the family. Jeremiah was seen as inviting a charge of treason against himself, which would certainly also have drawn suspicion upon other members of his family and even his whole community of townspeople.

There is a yet further consideration to be borne in mind. The narrative report of 11:21–23 regarding the threat to Jeremiah's life by "the men of Anathoth" is set out in prose; this may be taken as an indication that it has been composed in the light of the events of 599–598 and 588–587 B.C. During the Babylonian attacks upon Jerusalem the towns that lay a few miles outside of the major city undoubtedly suffered heavily as a result of the prolonged period of siege. It is likely that Anathoth was among these. We can then recognize a certain *post-eventum* eagerness to remember the events relating particularly to Anathoth, the town of Jeremiah. The threat in 11:22 had certainly been fulfilled by later events, and this may well have been seen to call for some special explanation. It was a point of deep interest to recall the hostility that had flared up between Jeremiah and his family and neighbors, since few of Jeremiah's fellow townspeople of Anathoth, unlike his scribe Baruch, survived the disaster of 587 (cf. 45:5). To this extent the fate of the townspeople of Anathoth mirrored directly the fate of the people of Judah more widely. They had had in their midst a true spokesman of God who had not flinched from proclaiming warnings of the dangers facing the people and its king. Instead of heeding these warnings, however, and trying to grasp their meaning and importance, these people ignored them and had instead turned against the one who might have been their savior and deliverer.

Jeremiah 12:7—13:27
The Inevitability of Jerusalem's Ruin

We now encounter a series of prophecies (seven in total; 12:7-13, 14-17; 13:1-11, 12-14, 15-17, 18-19, 20-27) which [with one exception] elaborate upon the theme of Jerusalem's coming downfall. They appear most probably to derive from the time of Jehoiakim's reign (609–598 B.C.) and from within the period after 601 when the king's intention of rebelling against Babylonian overlordship had become plain. The exception, 12:14-17, concerns the fate of Judah's neighbors, particularly in the longer-term future, once the time of the siege and destruction of Jerusalem had passed. This unit is in prose and, even more unexpectedly, is hopeful and reassuring in tone about the eventual conversion of these people to sincere worship of the Lord as God and about their ultimate welfare. A central theme of the foreign nation prophecies of chapters 46—51 is anticipated in this section and it will be considered separately after we have examined the remaining prophecies containing warnings and threats in 12:7—13:27.

It is convenient to take this group of sayings as a whole since they all convey essentially the same message: Jerusalem and Judah are shortly to be punished dramatically and extensively for their sins. This punishment will take the form of a

83

military invasion and defeat. The prophet foretells a massive ruination of the countryside accompanied by a fearful loss of life. In expressing this note of severe condemnation and inescapable doom facing the people, Jeremiah makes use of a number of fresh and vigorous word-images to convey his meaning.

The first of these threats in 12:7–13 is centered upon the theme of Israel as God's special "inheritance." Israel is and had for a long time been regarded as the unique "heritage" and "household" of the Lord God (cf. Deut. 32:9). Such affirmation bred a sense of wellbeing and security among the people of Israel since it was deemed to imply that God could be relied upon to look after those who shared such a special relationship with him. The way in which Jeremiah handles this deeply rooted assumption on the part of the people is simple and unequivocal. God has forsaken his household and abandoned his heritage. He has been compelled to do so by the people's behavior (12:7). There was, however, a further understanding of the concept of "heritage," or "inheritance," which had been given a quite unusual degree of prominence by the Deuteronomic literature (cf. Diepold, pp. 76ff.). This view regarded the land as Israel's inheritance; since the land was God's and had been given to Israel by him, the theme of inheritance had a dual significance. The land was the heritage of Israel and Israel was the heritage of God. The land, however, had been destroyed and ruined by those whom Jeremiah simply describes as "many shepherds." Who this metaphor referred to precisely is not further defined. It may indeed be the case that no specific individuals are in mind and that the image of irresponsible shepherds fits conveniently into the overall imagery of the metaphors of "vineyard" and "heritage." The metaphor of "shepherd" is used frequently of the kingship (cf. 23:1–4), and it may well be the case that Israel's bad and irresponsible kings are being referred to here. The theme of Jeremiah is clearly the defiling of God's "heritage" so that he has been compelled to abandon it. Israel's prided security and protection afforded by its special relationship to the Lord God was denied them by Jeremiah: Heritage of God they may be, but it was now an inheritance that God had been forced to abandon. Similarly the land was the people's "heritage," but they had defiled it so that it would now become nothing more than a place of dreadful slaughter "from one end of the land to the other" (v. 12).

84

Certainly this theme of the land as Israel's "inheritance" has called forth the editorial summary in verses 14–17 about the future of the land.

The second of Jeremiah's threats regarding the coming destruction of Judah and Jerusalem takes the form of an acted parable (13:1–11). What Jeremiah performs constitutes a "sign-action" in which he sets out to demonstrate that a necessary result follows from a particular action. This then provides the basis of an argument from analogy which is shown to apply to the situation, which the onlookers of the action will readily recognize. It is for them to draw the inevitable implications of this analogy for themselves. In this instance the sign-action consists of the purchase of a new loin-cloth, which Jeremiah proceeds to wear. He then took this off and buried it at a location described as "the Euphrates" (vv. 4, 6–7). Several commentators have suggested that this must have been the Wadi Farah, situated close to Anathoth, or it may simply have been a location designated by Jeremiah to be "the Euphrates" for the purposes of the symbolism of the action. The prose composition of the narrative suggests that it has been remembered and reflected upon after the events of Judah's collapse in 587 B.C.; it is quite possible that this naming of the location has been the work of Jeremiah's editors, who have introduced into the account a further level of symbolism. The fate of the loincloth is taken to represent the fate of the citizens of Judah deported to Babylon.

The original point of Jeremiah's action is clear. The loincloth is the most private and personal of the garments a person wears, which can be reliably expected to receive care and close attention. It may however become so soiled and dirtied by burying in the ground as to become useless. It will then have to be thrown away. The action then speaks for itself: "For as the waistcloth clings to the loins of a man, so I made the whole house of Israel and the whole house of Judah cling to me, says the LORD, that they might be for me a people, a name, a praise, and a glory, but they would not listen" (13:11). The hidden question behind the entire action hinges on this: Can God, who is "The God of Israel" be thought capable of disowning and rejecting his people? The answer shown by the analogy of the loincloth is "Yes, if they become so soiled as to be no longer usable." It would appear that a secondary level of interpretation, understanding the loincloth to represent Israel, has

85

interpreted the act of "soiling" to have been brought about by the deportation of the people to Babylon (the Euphrates).

There then follow four brief fragments all carrying very much the same general message that Judah and Jerusalem are ripe for judgment and this must inevitably come. The first of these fragments in 13:12–14 fastens upon what appears to have been a popular proverb that "Every jar shall be filled with wine" (v.12). The precise intent of this saying is rather elusive, but appears to devolve upon a paranomasia between the Hebrew words for "jar" *(nebel)* and "fool, thickhead" (Heb. *nabal*). The implication would then be that fools tend to drink too much, akin to the modern euphemism of being "fond of the bottle." The prophetic meaning of this saying is then made perfectly explicit in verses 13–14 that Jerusalem, including its leading inhabitants ("kings, priests, prophets"), will be made drunk with the "cup" of God's anger. The saying is probably not from Jeremiah himself and simply develops in a contrived fashion the message of the impending threat to Jerusalem.

The next fragment, 13:15–17, takes up the familiar theme of Israel's "pride" and appears to have been suggested by the idea that Israel's land constituted its "pride," being a feature of its existence as a nation of which it was justly proud. The message is now spelled out that this "pride" would soon cease to be a source of joy and satisfaction to the people. Instead it would provide an occasion for weeping and grief (v. 17) because of the ruin and death that would come upon it.

The short unit in 13:18–19 refers directly to the deportation of the young king Jehoiachin to Babylon, which took place in 598 B.C. (cf. II Kings 24:12). The reference to the fate of the king, along with that of the queen mother Nehushta (II Kings 24:8, 15), may have been occasioned by a further interpretation of the meaning of the nation's "pride." The fate of the royal house of David in 598 and 587 B.C. was a matter of particular concern to Jeremiah and apparently was even more so to his editors (cf. 22:24–27, 28–30). The saying must have originated shortly after the capture and imprisoning of Jehoiachin in 598 B.C. Verse 19 expresses with significant hyperbole the fate of Judah, since all Judah was certainly not taken to Babylon. The intention, however, may have been to stress that in the removal of Jehoiachin the hopes of the nation had suffered a major blow.

The concluding threat in 13:20–27 centers its theme upon the citation of a proverbial saying: "Can the Ethiopian change his skin, or the leopard his spots" (13:23)? The purpose of quoting such a popular dogma, affirming rhetorically that there are some things in life which cannot be changed, is to assert that Israel had sealed its fate, not solely as a consequence of its outward actions and contemporary decisions but as a consequence of its inner disposition. This short saying was designed to draw attention to the fact that God had not shut off his mercy nor precluded the possibility of repentance but that Israel had developed a disposition it was now unable to change.

From this the prophetic threat proceeds to spell out in personal terms the fate that awaits Jerusalem and its citizens. Pictured in the guise of a young woman who has abandoned all moral restraints (v. 27), Jerusalem is now to be faced with the inevitable fate of violence and rape that awaited a young woman captured as a prisoner of war (v. 26). The language is stark and the imagery has become rather conventional in the wake of the earlier prophecies of Hosea. There is therefore a certain lack of originality about it. The new feature introduced is that provided by the citation of the proverb of verse 23 concerning the inability of the dark-skinned Ethiopian to change the color of his skin. Israel, and Jerusalem in particular, had acquired a firmly delineated character as a result of all its past actions. Now it must bear the inevitable consequences of that acquired character. Judgment had become inevitable, not because God was merciless and unpitying but because Jerusalem could not change from being the disloyal and insensitive rebel against God that, over the centuries, it had shown itself to be.

It is not difficult to see that by using these powerful and dramatic images and by coupling them with imagined scenes of the violence and suffering that would ensue upon defeat in battle these short prophecies are attempting to deal with the realities of a human historical situation. Undoubtedly the popular understanding of what it meant for Israel to be the Chosen People of God, and for Jerusalem to be the site of his chosen "dwelling place" with its beautiful temple, had contained a deeply rooted expectation of divine protection. What Jeremiah had seen to be imminently threatened was the complete military collapse of Judah and the destruction of Jerusalem, brought on by a foolhardy belief that God would never let such a thing happen to his very own people. In the aftermath of what took place, first in 598 and then more seriously still in 587, reality

87

turned such complacent hopes into stultifying despair and disbelief. The purpose of recalling and preserving a knowledge of Jeremiah's prophecies, and even of reinforcing still more clearly what they declared, was to show that a true knowledge of the will of God neither justified the original complacency nor the subsequent despair. Either way the people were eagerly placing the blame for their tragic misfortunes upon God and regarding themselves self-pityingly as the unfortunate victims of a fate that they had not deserved. It was the concern of the prophet, as well as of his editors and followers, to show that the people could not evade the acceptance of responsibility for what they had suffered.

To a certain degree the affirmation of what was undoubtedly a more widely used popular saying "Can the Ethiopian change his skin, or the leopard his spots?" implies an element of divine necessity and inevitability. People are what they are, and this cannot be changed. Yet from the overall context of this prophecy within a range of other similar warnings of the inevitability of Jerusalem's fate, it is clear that it was not intended to imply such a complete loss of human freedom. The analogy must not be pressed too far. Human freedom and responsibility are strongly and consistently affirmed throughout the prophetic literature of the Old Testament. This is not allowed to be pressed, however, to the point of thinking of human choices and decisions as a series of totally separate and disconnected actions. Men and women acquire a character as a result of their past actions, and this character eventually takes on a set form. Jerusalem had indeed acquired such a character from which it could not now break free. It could no longer change its ways, however necessary and urgent it had become to do so. In this way the disasters of 598 and 587 B.C. had, in the prophetic theology, become inevitable. What such prophesying offered to those who had lived through such tragic events was a theodicy—a reason for holding on to faith in God—by reaffirming the two aspects of divine love and divine justice. The tensions implicit in these two divine attributes remain, and it is not the immediate concern of the prophet or his editors to resolve them. Indeed it may be claimed that even today it is very difficult to find a satisfactory intellectual resolution of them. From the biblical perspective of Jeremiah, however, which was set within a specific series of events, the resolution lay within the ambiguity of these events. The fall of Judah and Jerusalem needed to be seen

as manifestations of divine love and divine wrath which toler-
ated despair over the past but demanded hope for the future.

Jeremiah 14:1—15:9
Lamentation and Despair for Prophet and People

The section that now follows in 14:1—15:9 is composed of
a number of separate parts dealing directly with the prophet
and his role in the Judean community. "Nowhere in the book
of Jeremiah is the intercessory function of the prophet's office
better attested than here" (Polk, p. 75). The section as a whole
is built around the common understanding that it was an essential part of a prophet's duty to intecede on behalf of his people.
The extent to which it may have reflected Jeremiah's personal
conception of the prophet's task (cf. R.R. Wilson, pp. 238ff.) is
possibly more problematic, since the major concern is less to
demonstrate Jeremiah's attitude than to show that Judah's
wounds were such that intercession could not heal them. This
inevitably entails a richly rewarding and profound exploration
of the theme of intercession. Running through the entire section there is a felt but unexpressed question: If Jeremiah was so
great a prophet, why did he not intercede as Moses had on
behalf of the people (cf. Deut. 9:25–29)? The answer is presented that the divine command requisite to the nature of
Israel's sinfulness had forbidden it. In arriving at such a conclusion, however, the account of Jeremiah's inner struggle
points to a new understanding of the prophet's task and, with
this, a new understanding of the coming salvation (cf. Gerstenberger, p. 407). The prophet "becomes a paradigmatic figure of
salvation."

The character and significance of the individual units
(14:1–10, description of drought followed by a prayer of lamentation and oracular response; vv. 11–16, dialogue between God
and his prophet; vv. 17–22, prophetic lament followed by an act
of communal confession; 15:1–4, final oracular response; vv. 5–9
final lamentation over the people's downfall) is not in dispute,
in spite of a few uncertainties. Noteworthy is the very careful way in which the material has been structured to draw

89

attention to certain deeper implications concerning Israel's fate and Jeremiah's role as a true prophet of God. The message in fact is clear and straightforward. It simply repeats in varied words and with different images what has already been set out in chapter 13 about Judah's coming defeat and ruination. This much is taken for granted. It is the prophet's role in announcing this destruction and yet failing to turn the people away from their downfall which holds the center of attention.

This could undoubtedly have been construed to mean that Jeremiah had failed as a prophet, since it was his twofold duty to warn of coming danger and to plead and intercede with God so that the people might be spared destruction's horrors. Jeremiah clearly had not achieved this goal. However by skillfully expounding the nature of prophecy, and by exploring more fully than is to be found in any earlier prophecy the full implications of the nature of human freedom and responsibility, the editors find the answer in the nature of this human freedom and all that this entails about the nature of sin. It is important to bear in mind that they were working with the extant materials of Jeremiah's prophesying and with an immensely old tradition concerning the nature of prophecy. By the aid of these materials they were endeavoring to make sense of a history that had already happened and which had plunged its victims into despair. Once again the theme is that of theodicy: How could God be God and yet allow such things to happen?

The initial unit in 14:1–10 consists of a description of a time of serious drought threatening the crops as they grew, followed by a short prayer of lamentation in verses 7–9, and an oracular response from God through his prophet refusing to revoke the punishment implied by the drought. The presentation of the situation in this fashion can only have been introduced to set forth the typical pattern of prayer-lament in a time of national distress and the manner in which any prophet, not necessarily Jeremiah, would have behaved. The prophet serves as the intermediary between God and the people; so he offers the intercessory prayer of verses 7–9, confessing the people's sins and pleading for mercy, and then proceeds to offer the divine response to this.

We find a roughly similar dialogue between God and people reflected in the first two visions reported by the prophet Amos (Amos 7:1–6). In the case of the visions received by Amos the divine response to the prophetic intercession is favorable in that the developing threat is removed (Amos 7:3, 6). The instance adduced in Jeremiah 14:1–6 portrays very graphically the misery inflicted on people and animals by the intense heat and drought and is contrastingly followed by a message of reaffirmed threat: "Now he will remember their iniquity and punish their sins" (v. 10).

The purpose of introducing this incident concerning a drought and its effects, which stands somewhat apart from the historical and military concerns that otherwise dominate the Book of Jeremiah, is to recall the realities of divine-human interaction and the limits of what even a skilled prophet can achieve. Prophecy is not based on a body of abstract truths but is indissolubly linked to the realities of a given situation. It is, in its original form, addressed to a specific people in a specific context of experience and events. It cannot therefore be content with reproducing conventional palliatives concerning divine mercy and forgiveness when these basic truths are no longer the whole truth relative to a given situation. There will have to be times when God says "No"! In this way the seeming isolation and irrelevance of the concern with a time of drought is shown to be profoundly important and relevant to Jeremiah's message. The prophet must speak the truth about God, and there are times when this truth will be painful and hurtful for the people to hear! The people have always known this. They clearly would not venture to argue with the prophet when an experience of drought, which must even at its worst be only a temporary suffering, was at issue. What they cannot envisage is that God's answer might still be negative in the far more dangerous and appalling situation of the military threat from Babylon and all that this entailed about the survival of Judah as a kingdom and the safety and wellbeing of Jerusalem and its inhabitants. Having established the reality of the subordination of the prophetic word to the will of God, Jeremiah declares that the true prophet will sometimes be called upon to declare a painful and unwelcome response from God. Far from this rendering him a bad and undesirable prophet, as many had judged him to be, it rather established Jeremiah's claim to be the true and reliable spokesman of God. God had indeed determined to judge his people, and in passing this word to the people, Jeremiah was only fulfilling faithfully his God-given task.

It is on the basis of this liturgical sequence concerning drought that the larger and more alarming case is then introduced concerning the judgment of Judah and Jerusalem by military conquest and defeat (14:11—15:9). This introduces a

91

cry of lamentation from both prophet (vv. 17–18) and people (vv. 19–22) concerning the overwhelming nature of the threat of military catastrophe (undoubtedly to be inflicted by Babylon, although this is not actually said).

There is further reaffirmation of the by now familiar theme of the folly and sinfulness of Israel's ways. The unexpressed assumption that must have been in the minds of all the people who heard Jeremiah and that still remained a puzzling remonstrance for those who read his prophecies after tragedy had happened was this: "Surely God, who is gracious, merciful and long-suffering with his people, will forgive in the face of so dire a threat!" However the prophetic answer conveyed through Jeremiah is a terrifying and unrelenting "No" (15:1–4, 5–9)! The answer is based on the assertion that Israel's sins had become too deeply ingrained and too immense in their scale for God to forgive them, even on this occasion. The people could not now be delivered from their enemies without God's righteousness being so impugned by their sins that all sense of its reality would be destroyed. Once again, therefore, we see the primary intention of establishing a theodicy: justifying by the prophetic word the punitive action of God in allowing Judah to be defeated and Jerusalem to be destroyed by the Babylonians. In the minds of many who suffered the horrors of what took place in 598 and 587 B.C. (cf. Lam. 2:20), it may evoke the reply that the punishment far exceeded the demands of righteousness. However the prophetic insistence is that this cannot have been so, since God did not cease to be loving and gracious, even in the hour of his wrath. Israel's sins had been grievous and long-sustained, and the hour of punishment could be no longer delayed. In remembering its misfortune and misery, there lay the essential groundwork of hope for Israel's future (Lam. 3:21–24).

It is salutary to bear in mind that even so cherished a text as the affirmation "great is thy faithfulness" represents an insight into the nature of divine reality won, not against the backcloth of sustained comfort and happiness, but one secured painfully in a time of deepest horror and human misery. The instance of the experience of drought with which chapter 14 begins has been used to establish a fundamental principle that God remains loving, just, and merciful, even when he is compelled to refuse the bland cries and pleas of his people.

To those who read this account of Jeremiah's prophesying in the time of Judah's downfall it could appear that the covenant between God and Israel had been of no real benefit to them. Indeed it could have appeared that it had acted as a liability, since God appeared to have demanded of Israel a righteousness not expected from other nations. However, the aim of those who have structured the sequence of Jeremiah's prophecies in this fashion has been to convey the very opposite. The fact of the disasters that had overtaken Judah as a nation at the hands of the Babylonians was not in doubt, since these had occurred by the time the Book of Jeremiah was given its present form. Nor was there any doubt that Israel had believed in the central importance of its covenant relationship to the Lord as God. The concern that animated the scribes who have given the Jeremiah tradition its extant form was to demonstrate that both facts could be accepted with assurance, without one of them prejudicing the other. God was the God of Israel and he had indeed maintained a firm and loving relationship with it. In inflicting such grievous wounds upon his people God had acted in righteous wrath against their sins.

The divine action has in turn led on to a deep theological exploration of one of the most central themes of all theology: the relationship between divine justice and divine mercy. Nor is it possible for us, any more than it was possible for ancient Israel, to dismiss the problems inherent in such a tension by discounting the reality of God. The fact remains, human history and human experience amply testify to the ambiguities of the experience of human tragedy and suffering. The need for serious theological reflection upon these evident facts arises because the world and its history must be understood as a whole and not as a series of isolated and unrelated compartments. To the modern reader, enriched by the doctrine of atonement in the New Testament and by two millennia of Christian and Jewish reflection upon the theme, it is clear that any understanding of humanity's relationship with God must recognize that this cannot be easy or unconditional. In spite of the extensive attention to the warnings of coming judgment in Jeremiah's prophecies before Jerusalem's destruction in 587, it must be insisted that the fundamental aim of the entire Book of Jeremiah is to establish a theology of hope. If hope were to be simply on the basis of a few reassuring prophecies or by a return to the traditional and fundamental axioms implicit in Israel's belief in its divine election, it would be facile and unconvincing. The prophetic dilemma was to find a place for hope in the face of the deep despair experienced by many in Israel and by facing fully and unsentimentally the stark tragedy and grief that the

93

passage of two and a half thousand years has not been able to erase. The recollection of Jeremiah's warnings, threats, and his desisting from intercession speak more constructively and creatively about the theological foundations of hope in the midst of suffering than could possibly have been achieved by reaffirming conventional doctrines of divine love which ignore this.

In 15:1–4 a further issue is raised and permeates all the larger unit of 11:1—20:18. This concerns the function, and by implication also the personality, of the prophet. Traditionally the prophet had been seen in Israel as a mediator and intercessor between God and the community. How then could Jeremiah have failed so abysmally in his task of interceding for Judah when the nation had suffered so grievously? The answer is set forth unequivocally: God himself had forbidden his prophet Jeremiah to continue to pray and plead on behalf of Israel (11:14; 15:1). Israel's sins had exceeded the dimension for which prophetic intercession could provide relief, even by such giants of prayer as Moses and Samuel. The mention of Moses particularly highlights the intensity of reflection upon the unique status of this figure and the central idea of the covenant in the relationship between Israel and God. We may especially compare the portrait of Moses as intercessor in Numbers 14:13–25 and Deuteronomy 9:6–29 (for Samuel cf. I Sam. 7:5–11; 8:1–9, 19–22). It is highly probable from a literary perspective that the narrative accounts of the role of Moses as intercessor have been elaborated and developed in the light of the catastrophes of 598 and 587 with a deep concern for the role of prayer in human experience. Jeremiah was a "prophet like Moses" (cf. Deut. 18:15–22), but he had been forbidden to exercise his intercessory role. Where Moses had succeeded in averting disaster for Israel, their sins were now regarded as so severe that further intercession would represent an impossible affront to God.

This short prophecy concerning the impossibility of intercession for Judah offers nothing specifically new. It reaffirms the fourfold possibilities of death and disaster awaiting the citizens of Judah and Jerusalem: disease, death by the sword, famine, or a life in exile (v. 2). In verse 4 a further reflection has been added: the necessity for such a terrible fate on account of the sins of Manasseh (cf. II Kings 21:10–15), which adds a rather different dimension from the emphasis established earlier. The general sins of the people in their widespread apostasy from God narrow to the quite specific offenses attributed to Manas-

94

seh, for which he has been singled out as the worst of all the kings of Judah.

The mention of Manasseh in this fashion, which should probably be seen as the work of a scribe deliberately seeking to establish some cross-references to the historical narrative of First and Second Kings, raises some further points of interest concerning the prophetic interpretation of sin. In the Book of Jeremiah the prophet spread the blame for Israel's sinfulness widely. Although the kings and the ruling houses in Jerusalem are singled out as the subject of especially severe criticism, a matter of some importance for Jeremiah is that the people as a whole must share the blame for their fate. No scapegoats are singled out as guilty, and the widespread apostasy in which all shared is blamed for the nation's ruin. To all intents and purposes there are no innocent ones left in Judah (cf. 5:1). None could claim that their sufferings were personally undeserved; all had participated in the nation's shame and all were heirs of a nation that had offended God from its beginnings (cf. chap. 2).

This does not mean that we should lose sight of the fact that the social structure of the nation was such that some exercised leadership and control while others played only a minor role in national affairs. It is wholly striking therefore that the historian of First and Second Kings shares an attitude of deep ambivalence towards the kingship (cf. G. von Rad, *Theology,* I, p. 339). On the one hand the kings are heavily criticized and only David and Josiah escape censure. On the other hand portraying the entire people meekly following the individual kings vests in the institution of kingship an unrealistic level of authority and religious control. Singling Manasseh out both here and in II Kings 21:10–15 indicates a sentiment of deepest antipathy for this particular ruler. Why should this have been so? Two possibilities appear to have contributed to such an assessment. The first of these is of a political nature and must in part be conjectural. After Hezekiah's bold but unsuccessful attempt to throw off Assyrian suzerainty in 701 B.C., Manasseh may well have adopted a compliant attitude to Assyrian demands. What religious and economic subservience to Assyrian impositions meant is not explicit, but could have served to brand this king as a traitorous ruler, compliant to oppressive foreign demands and willingly sacrificing the interests of his subjects to maintain his own position.

95

Another consideration of a more directly historical nature must have certainly profoundly influenced the structuring of the historical accounts of Judah's eventual downfall. Josiah has been presented as a worthy reforming king, zealously seeking to display obedience to God and to make amends for the religious negligence of the past (I Kings 22:1—23:30). His violent and unanticipated death in battle (II Kings 23:29–30; II Chron. 35:20–24) came as a severe blow to those who had seen in his reign the signs of a great revival in Judah's and Israel's fortunes. Clearly the sympathies of Jeremiah's editors, and probably those of Jeremiah himself, were with Josiah and his death had been greatly mourned. In seeking to find some explanation for why all the good works of Josiah had not been enough to avert the final collapse of Judah, the excesses of Manasseh's reign were given a prominent place. This almost certainly explains the unexpected comment of 14:4, which otherwise stands apart from Jeremiah's concern to spread the blame for the nation's downfall as widely as possible.

The concluding pronouncement spells out the fearful and inevitable doom about to befall Jerusalem (15:5–9). The pronouncement, in words preserved from the prophet himself, probably should be dated to the time of Zedekiah's rebellion against Babylonian rule in 588–587 B.C. and seems to indicate that the military consequences of Zedekiah's withdrawal of allegiance had become plain for most of the population to see. As a forewarning of disaster and as a permanent record of the terrors and sufferings inflicted by warfare upon the human race, they deserve to be read and re-read. Human choices are real; those who make them must do so responsibly and with due regard for the consequences of what they determine. Decisions once made cannot be unmade, so neither Zedekiah nor the men and women for whom he was responsible could subsequently expect God to intervene by some miraculous thunderbolt and avert the ruin that Zedekiah had brought upon his kingdom.

Jeremiah 15:10—16:13
Jeremiah's Inner Conflict

The intense opposition Jeremiah experienced and the deep inner turmoil and conflict this brought to him has been highlighted in 12:1-6. The prophet's response from God in 12:5-6 indicates that no relief or lessening of the inner conflict and pain was to be expected. He was caught between two realms. On the one side his prophetic office drew him into the sphere of divine justice and holiness so that he could view the situation of Judah in light of this. On the other side his knowledge and experience of Israel's idolatry and blatant disregard of the divine law left him conscious of the danger his own people faced. In part he found himself on Israel's side. He belonged to this people, had been called to be their intercessor, and was committed to plead with God for them. That was an essential part of his task as a prophet. Yet he was necessarily also endeavoring to speak from God's side, castigating, rebuking, and pouring out bitter invective upon the prevalent wrongdoing of the people and yearning to be free from the very contagion that living among them involved (cf. 9:2-3). From God's side he had been forbidden to pray and intercede further on Israel's behalf; yet from Israel's side he had found himself shunned and disbelieved and made into an object of mockery and fun. It is no wonder then that Jeremiah sensed that he was being torn apart emotionally and that his innermost being was divided. We may also begin to sense the awakening of a deeper intellectual turmoil, a theological conflict between the prophetic understanding of divine justice and divine mercy. How could they be reconciled?

We may begin to see the consequences of this conflict forcing Jeremiah into a new awareness of the nature and ambivalences in the prophetic office. To be the people's spokesman before God and, responsively, God's spokesman to the people had been conceived as that of intermediary and message-bearer. He was the go-between for God and nation. Now his go-between status was rising into a position where his mind, heart, and will were caught up in the tension the relationship between God and people had brought. The people could no longer bear him, and he in turn found that he could no longer bear to fulfill the tasks and duties his ministry of the divine word entailed. He was becoming a prophet without an audience—an object of mockery and scorn which he experienced as a situation of despair. Verses 10-12 reflect this situation by giving vent to some of the most poignant words in the entire book. It is the Kierkegaardian situation of despair. By totally abandoning the desire and will to live, he discovers his deepest sense of personal identity (Kierkegaard, pp. 42ff.).

97

By reaching the point of rejecting his life and despairing of it, he became compelled to reconsider what his life and prophetic office truly meant. Verses 13–14 are a variant of what is set out in 17:3–4 and appear here as God's response to Jeremiah's daring and despairing plea on behalf of Israel. It is the complete and categorical divine negative: "No!" Israel's sins are such that the nation cannot now evade the punishment that they deserve. God's anger is such that, having been aroused, it will not be satisfied until the people are justly punished for what they have done. Doom has become inevitable!

It is quite evident that this cannot have been the original divine response to Jeremiah's outburst of personal despair but has been introduced editorially at a later stage. Its presence draws out a further side to the meaning and significance of the prophet's despair. This is no more a reflection of his personal sense of alienation from his people, but rather it is a total response to the awfulness of the message he has been called upon to bring. The prophet's agony and inner turmoil has become a foretaste of the agony and despair that will overtake the people. To this extent he has fully shared the misery of the condition experienced by those who read his prophecies in the light of what had happened in 587 B.C. "For because he himself has suffered and been tempted [to despair], he is able to help those who are tempted" (Heb. 2:18).

Verses 15–18 present a further cry of pain from the prophet. He has suffered the loss of everything for God's sake, save for the one possession which belongs to him by virtue of his prophetic office—the word of God! This alone can bring comfort and solace: "thy words became to me a joy and the delight of my heart" (v. 16). This is all that is left for Jeremiah; it is nothing and yet it is everything. It is nothing because he has been expelled from his home, rejected by his fellow townspeople from Anathoth, and can no longer find solace in the fun and laughter of his fellow human beings. Yet paradoxically it is everything, because it is the only key to understanding the realities of human experience and human history. The fun and laughter of an unthinking and complacent community proved to be a false guide to the peril facing Judah in the time of its defeat and collapse, while conversely the harsh seriousness of the prophetic word provided the firm platform of truth.

98

It is important to recognize the conscious many-sidedness of the preserved record of Jeremiah's utterances of despair.

Their origin is in Jeremiah's personal experience and must, presumably, have been recorded initially by the prophet himself. They emanated from wrestling with his own experiences. No matter how doom-laden and overwhelming his words of warning became, always one motive dominated all of them: It was the prophet's solemn responsibility before God to persuade his fellow citizens to amend their ways, especially those who exercised leadership and influence. Yet the more urgent and threatening his warnings became, the more he aroused hostility and caused offense. So it is not surprising that many of his sayings now appear to the modern reader to be frenetic, over-pessimistic, and unreasonably distressed by the common sins and failings of human nature. There is little evidence that Jeremiah's age was uncharacteristically distinct from others by the extent of its moral misdeeds. To the modern mind war came upon Judah and Jerusalem because of political miscalculation by its king and ruling oligarchy, rather than by the common failings of religious indifference and moral obtuseness. This would have been, in Jeremiah's mind, to generate the image of a scapegoat, which the circumstances did not warrant. Apparently this was fully endorsed by the editors, who have so carefully preserved his words for posterity. Consistently in the sharpness and range of the prophetic invective the sins of the people are set in the central position. So far as Jeremiah was concerned there could be no scapegoat, either in the persons of Jehoiakim, Zedekiah, nor even Nebuchadnezzar the king of Babylon. The people's own sins had plunged them into the abyss of misery and suffering.

The concluding outcry of Jeremiah is intense and memorable: "Why is my pain unceasing, / my wound incurable, / refusing to be healed" (15:18)? There is no hint of passive submission nor any suggestion that having done all he could do Jeremiah was prepared to leave the outcome to the will of God. His pain is real and persistent and does not leave him at a point of final surrender to the inevitable. In this we discover the extent to which Jeremiah has anticipated the sufferings of the people and participated fully in their despair. No agony of spirit the readers of these remarkable prophecies are experiencing has not been felt and faced in advance of them by Jeremiah, and in some measure on behalf of them. He would have spared them the grief which they now feel, but unable to deflect them from the reckless course of disaster on which they were set, he tasted beforehand the sufferings which now threatened to consume them! Surprisingly and paradoxically, the theme or purpose of these intensely personal outbursts is that of hope, but hope that cannot face the abyss of despair is not hope.

Only after this nadir in his inner despair had been reached could there be a turning-point in which some fixed platform of divine assurance was reestablished. This is to be found in verses 19–21:

> "If you return, I will restore you,
>   and you shall stand before me. . . .
> And I will make you . . .
>   a fortified wall of bronze; . . .
> for I am with you
>   to save you and deliver you, . . ."

Once again we encounter the skilled many-sidedness of the prophetic word. It is addressed to Jeremiah by God and affirms that Jeremiah must change his thinking and return to God so that the divine salvation might be realized. Yet God's word is also addressed to the despair of the people who were to read it in the light of their own sufferings. Their's is the ongoing mood of despair for which there appears to be no healing and from which there appears to be no avenue of escape. The ruin of their lives and the loss of the land has become complete. It is then to them also that the words are addressed: "If you return . . . then I am with you to save and deliver you, says the LORD". Jeremiah has become the paradigm of salvation, and it is vitally important that this should be seen in the depths of his own misery.

A further aspect of the way Jeremiah anticipated and shared in the misfortunes and sufferings of the people is set out in 16:1–13. His own life had been shaped and moulded to reflect the realities of the message of doom he had been called upon to proclaim. For those who mourned the loss of loved ones and grieved over the desolation wrought within their family life by the horrors of war, Jeremiah provided an example of courage and faith. He had been denied the normal human joy of marriage and family life, directly and precisely on account of his bearing the word of God. He had been compelled by the restraints set by the word of God to taste in advance the loneliness and isolation of one denied the solace of wife and children. It is important therefore to recognize that the command of God presented in 16:2 is in no way motivated by any form of cultic asceticism or taboo-ridden isolationism. Rather in living out the word of God Jeremiah is forced to experience before the hour of darkness strikes the terrors and tearing of the spirit that it will bring: "For thus says the LORD concerning the sons and daughters who are born in this place, and concerning their mothers. . . . They shall die . . . they shall perish by the sword . . ." (vv. 3–4).

Jeremiah was to experience what the men and women of his audience were soon to experience; theirs would be the grief of loss and lamentation for the deaths of mothers, husbands, fathers, and children. His had been the loss dictated by the divine word that he should have no normal family life. In this too he was a paradigm of salvation, sharing fully in the deprivation of those to whom his message was given and declaring that even in the despair engendered by such loss there still remained hope in the power and renewing of the word of God.

The entire section of 16:1–13 develops this theme. Verses 1–9 show how Jeremiah had been compelled to live his life as one in mourning, in prophetic anticipation of the national mourning that would soon shatter the people of Judah. Verses 10–13 then elaborate the familiar message of the prophet, showing why this day of national disaster must come: "Because your fathers have forsaken me, . . . and because you have done *worse than your fathers*" (vv. 11, 12, author's italics). We are startled once again by the breadth and comprehensiveness of the prophet's explanations, which are broad to the point of appearing bland. None are innocent! No leader, not even the figure of the king himself, is allowed to become a cover under which the sins of every man, woman, and child in Judah could be hidden. The blame is wholly and fully to be shared among all. Undoubtedly the reasons why the doctrine of human responsibility implicit in Jeremiah's affirmations about Israel's sins stresses this breadth and individuality lies in his awareness of the vengeful longing of human beings to seek out the guilty. Better to blame others than to shoulder the responsibility for disaster oneself! Jeremiah, however, allows no such excuses and affords no covering protection at all from the weight of blame he attaches to the people's misdeeds. In this he has clearly sensed the destructiveness of self-pity and of the human desire to lay blame upon others. Either would have meant a failure to attain fullness of inner repudiation of sin, from which alone a

101

new nation could be born. Only open acceptance of personal guilt could provide the antidote to despair. It was the deep necessity of choosing God by recognizing the extent of one's own personal waywardness from God.

Jeremiah 16:1–13 has occasioned a good deal of discussion concerning whether it is prose or poetry and whether part of it may not have been added at a late stage in the formation of the book. The section is symptomatic of a number of passages in the book where authentic words and reminiscences from Jeremiah have been shaped into a carefully structured unit. At times there is a resort to quite stereotyped phrases, which are more likely to be indicative of the work of editors rather than to represent Jeremiah's own words. Nevertheless the atmosphere of authenticity has been frequently sensed, Jeremiah's own words and life-style have been reflected upon in light of the events that transpired for Judah. Jeremiah has become the prophet of hope because there is no aspect of the sufferings of his people in which he has not in some deep and full measure personally shared. Finding hope through the word of God (cf. 15:19) had enabled him to become a representative and messenger of hope to men and women who had no other future than to recover hope or perish in their despair.

Jeremiah 16:14–21
Three Short Sayings

Reasons for the complex and sometimes confusing structure of the present Book of Jeremiah have frequently proved hard to discover. Difficulties occasioned by this for the present-day reader are apparent here, where we encounter three short sayings (16:14–15, 16–18, and 19–21). One of these affirms the absolute certainty and inevitability of judgment upon the guilty and is strongly threatening in tone (vv. 16–18), whereas the other two are markedly reassuring and hopeful (14–15, 19–21). Verses 16–18 begin with a declaration that God will send for fishermen and hunters who will hunt out their prey. In the general context of the political situation presupposed by Jeremiah, these metaphors clearly apply to Judah's enemies, the armies of Babylon. However, since the specific prey of the "hunters" are those who "have polluted my land with the carcasses of their detestable idols" (v. 18), it is possible that we are faced here with a later re-reading and reinterpretation of Jeremiah's threats of judgment. In this case later, post-exilic, idolators in the land of Judah are threatened with divine punishment. The situation presupposed by the addition would then be the complex social and religious tensions that arose later in the period of Babylonian rule over Judah. It is noteworthy that there is a return to the ancient concept of the pollution and defiling of the land (cf. Lev. 25:18–19). Since the land in theory belonged to God, it needed to be looked after and respected as a divine gift and was itself "holy" (cf. further W. Brueggemann, *The Land,* pp. 53ff.).

Set around this warning against further pollution of the land by idolatry are two promises of hope and of Israel's ultimate restoration to the land. We can plausibly suggest that the first of these, affirming an ultimate restoration of the exiles to their homeland: "For I will bring them back to their own land which I gave to their fathers" (v. 15), was first set down as the appropriate and necessary conclusion to the threat of verses 10–13. In turn this elicited the need to provide an admonition. Even those who had returned to the land after the Babylonian exile must not thereafter pollute it again with idolatry. In turn this has occasioned the final rounding off of the series of elaborative comments with an outpouring from a scribe in verses 19–20 concerning the absurd folly of idolatry: "Can man make for himself gods? Such are no gods" (v. 20)! Gone is the note of intense anger and bitterness which motivated the threat of verse 18. Those who worship idols are fools rather than evil-doers. They are attempting the impossible and succeeding in doing nothing other than creating an illusion. The comment is no doubt worthy of more prolonged reflection, since human history has suffered much from the violence and bitterness of iconoclasm. Those who oppose the use of idols have frequently displayed a vehemence and fanaticism that has proved worse than the idolatry they meant to eradicate! The author of the thanksgiving and reflection in verses 19–20 appears to have sensed as much and has rather blessed God for granting a knowledge of the truth. Those who turn to idols are more to be pitied than persecuted, since they are merely pursuing worthless things that can do them no good at all.

The entire short sequence of additional reflections concerning the importance of the land to Israel in its hope of a return is then brought to a fitting climax with the assuring

103

words of verse 21, which serve to sum up all that was intended by the prophetic message about the future: "they shall know that my name is the Lord."

Jeremiah 17:1–18
Short Sayings of Judgment and Lamentation

From a text-critical and literary point of view chapter 17 is significant and complex. It shows every sign of having been brought together by Jeremiah's editors from a short fragment of prophecy, supplemented by a measure of further reflection upon this. So we can trace no less than five short pieces here (vv. 1–4, 5–8, 9–11, 12–13, 14–18) that can best be considered as parts of one whole. These have been brought to a conclusion by a fairly long, and very perceptive, prose address in verses 19–27 regarding the importance of the observance of the sabbath. It represents a significant step in establishing the importance that observance of the sabbath came to enjoy as a sign of religious loyalty in the post-exilic Jewish community.

The opening section (vv. 1–4) is clearly the most basic as well as being the most straightforward of these. It is a typical prophetic saying consisting of a short and fervently expressed condemnation of Judah for the false worship by the people at the altars and Asherim. Asherim were wooden poles set up in the earth close to an altar. They were invested with a special symbolic meaning relating to the fertility rituals. Probably it is mistaken to abstract the notion of fertility too sharply from other aspects of the prevalent cultus of the land. Fertility and human sexuality were looked upon as aspects of the mysterious life force which pervaded all plant and animal existence. Such a life force was believed to derive from the union of the gods and goddesses and to be necessary not merely to ensure fertility in crops and herds but to combat the mysterious unseen forces of death. The fertility and sexual aspects were part of a constant life and death struggle taking place in the natural world. By participation in the rituals, men and women aligned themselves with the power of life given by God. The prevalence of this feature of ancient religion, which appeared in a variety of forms

104

over several thousand years, was the result of a deep anxiety for life to have victory over death.

At the same time, however, such ritual activity designed to promote "life" contained a prominent element of destructive sexual immorality, which was manifested and given justification in many forms. The repeated condemnation of the different forms of this cult in the literature of the Old Testament associate it particularly with Baal and Ashera, although the features of the cult tended to become associated with several deities. The notion of the cultic promotion of life gave rise to an immoral and destructive range of cult-practices that undermined the cohesion of family life. The presence of the prophetic condemnation of 17:1–4 is closely linked with the idea of the sanctity of the land. One of the primary goals of the cult of the Asherim "beside every green tree, and on the high hills" (v. 2) was to promote the fertility and food-producing usefulness of the land. The fundamental idea was that sexuality promoted life as a potent force affecting all things. In fact, the prophetic warning argues, all that the people had succeeded in doing was to defile the land, the heritage given to Israel by God. The appropriate punishment for so foolishly abusing the gift of the land would be to be cast out and taken to a land they did not know (v. 4). The saying is in prose in our text (RSV), but several scholars have endeavored to trace an underlying original poetic form. Whether it is directly from Jeremiah himself is not clear. It is, however, one of the most fundamental and widely adopted prophetic explanations for the punishment of exile inflicted upon Israel.

The next unit (vv. 5–8) can best be understood as a didactic reflection which does not originate from Jeremiah himself but marks a composition in the manner of the wisdom teachers and closely resembles the imagery of Psalm 1 (cf. further 9:12–16; 10:12–18 for similar wisdom reflections). It expresses a simple contrast between the folly of trusting in human wisdom and trusting in God. Humanity is to live under a curse of error and illusion, whereas trusting in God is the path of blessedness and security. The reason for interjecting the contrast here has evidently been to show that the tragic fate of Judah set out in verses 1–4 is to be traced essentially to these errors of human understanding. Those who went astray and pursued the worship of false gods and symbols of gods, such as the Asherim, were guilty of trusting merely human wisdom, which was worse than

105

ignorance. In contrast those who were wise enough to trust in God were enabled to avoid the path of error. At first glance the contrast appears to have been suggested by little more than the analogy between the wise man and the "tree planted by water." There may be a much deeper connection intended, based on the understanding that the way to life and fertility (cf. "for its leaves remain green") is not to be sought through misguided rituals but through obedient trusting in God.

A further wisdom-type reflection follows in verses 9–11, resembling very closely 10:23–24. It is concerned once again with true and false knowledge, which is viewed, as in 16:19–20, as closely allied to the contrast between idolatry and a true knowledge of God. In answer to the question "Why do human beings behave so badly and pursue such absurd illusions?" the answer is readily given: "Because they trust their own thinking rather than God's!" This is brought to a conclusion by a rather surprising analogy drawn from the supposed conduct of the partridge. The bird gathers a brood she did not hatch and they leave; so, it is argued, wealth dishonestly acquired does not last. Clearly at this stage the moralizing application of the great truths and teachings of the prophets is being undertaken in a down-to-earth and pragmatic fashion.

A third reflection in a more traditional vein on the meaning and significance of Jeremiah's prophecies is found in verses 12–13. These make the basic point that the temple of God in Jerusalem was a glorious throne, "set on high from the beginning," which reflects the beauty, grandeur, and greatness of the God whose sanctuary it is. It marks yet a different way of answering the question of how men and women can be sure of obtaining knowledge of the true God. The answer present in these lines is that the beauty and splendor of the visible sanctuary reflects the nobility, power, and greatness of the God who has deigned to use it as the means for revealing his presence to humankind.

By way of general comment upon this series of short didactic reflections about the meaning of Jeremiah's prophecies, we may note certain significant features. The original words of Jeremiah were clearly addressed to a particular community in a specific set of historical circumstances which were in fact the time of the greatest political and social crisis besetting Israel and Judah. From these great prophetic sayings grew the necessity to draw more timeless and ongoing lessons about the nature

106

of God's revelation of himself. They are certainly not the work of Jeremiah himself; but it is a false and mistaken conception of the nature of the prophetic writings to suppose that the intention has been to preserve only the prophet's words. Many important sections are reflections elaborating the meaning of what the prophet said; many are efforts to link various prophecies together to construct a more rounded picture of the plan and purpose of God. In this process the original sayings, with their close relationship to specific persons and situations, were broadened into a more widely applicable theology.

The message that these short elaborations present here is not difficult to follow: The people of Judah had sinned against the Lord their God and he had responded to their sin by sending the people into exile, since they had defiled his land (17:4). In turn God had brought in an enemy to take possession of their land. All of this was seen to result from the folly of trusting in merely human wisdom; in contrast, trusting in God would have brought security, prosperity, and happiness. Further, it is not simply the outward claim to trust in God that mattered but the genuine inner reality of doing so—"the heart is deceitful above all things" (v. 9). The comment introduces an almost Freudian awareness of the capacity of the human mind to indulge in self-deception. This in turn shades off into a rather more mundane reflection upon the dangers of wealth and the prevalent recognition that these too may be obtained by stealth and deception. A dogmatically confident assertion is made that wealth obtained in this fashion will not last (v. 11). A concluding comment adds that real hope and assurance belong to those who acknowledge the true God, who can be known from the beauty and dignity of the sanctuary that had been dedicated to his name in Jerusalem (vv. 12–13).

When we ask what motivated the addition to Jeremiah's prophecies of these general comments about truth and life (couched in the traditions of the wise), we can perceive several factors. The first must have been a deep sense of a failure to heed the lessons of the past. In the post-exilic Jewish community when the hope of restoration provided a vital goal and spiritual vision, there had appeared deep and violent divisions within the community motivated by greed and self-righteousness. Wounds had been inflicted by one section of the community upon others by greed, arrogant self-assertiveness, and an over-zealous tendency to condemn factions that were held to be in error. Pride had emerged among some within the Judean community; they alone were the authentic heirs of the prophets; they must assert their privileged knowledge. In doing so they merely repeated the sins of the past (cf. Matt. 23:29–36).

After this series of wisdom-style reflections we return in 17:14–18 to a passage widely recognized as constituting a further cry of anguish and lamentation from Jeremiah himself, forming part of the so-called "confessions" expressed by him. The appeal to God from the prophet is set out in the traditional language of lamentation familiar from the Psalter. It is a cry to God: "Heal me . . . ; save me!" Once again we are led to perceive Jeremiah struggling to find support and renewed confidence in God, pleading that he has never, in any spirit of vindictiveness, wanted to be proved right by seeing his threats and warnings of coming doom turned into fearful reality. This culminates in a final plea that the prophet's tormentors may be "put to shame" (v. 18).

The mention of shame in such a context implies far more than mere social embarrassment and conveys the idea of a completely overwhelming demonstration of being in the wrong. By such shaming of his enemies it becomes clear that when judgment falls on Israel Jeremiah will have been vindicated, and this will silence for all time the jibes and attacks of his enemies. More than this, however, it will have shown the obstinate folly of those who had set themselves against Jeremiah, demonstrating their unwillingness to listen responsively to the message of God's prophet and reaffirming the obduracy with which they had rejected the warnings of God. God had not willed judgment upon them as an inescapable fate, but had warned of its danger. They themselves had chosen to ignore the warning. Again the theme of theodicy, aroused in the minds of the readers by the consciousness that the disaster was past history, is uppermost. Even the most dire human tragedy is not the consequence of a predetermined fate, but the outcome of human obstinacy and unresponsiveness towards the word of God.

The prophet himself and the skillful way in which his words have been preserved serve to uncover the inner human dimension of choice and individual responsiveness that lies within every human historical situation. In a situation where every tendency was to "de-humanize" events by regarding them as beyond the control of human agencies, Jeremiah's anguish and pleas highlighted the essential dimension of individual responsibility and decision-making in the flow of events. In seeking to be like God "knowing good and evil" (cf. Gen. 3:1–7), human beings had sought to possess the power of moral decision-making. Yet in acquiring such greatness, they persistently endeavored to shrink from the pain of such choices and to evade all untoward consequences. The inner struggle Jeremiah experienced within himself, coupled with the outer conflict with forceful and vindictive enemies, served to show the pain that necessarily attended "choosing God and being in the wrong."

This short episodic outburst of Jeremiah's inner torment reveals the dilemma between the prophet's desire that his warnings be proved right, at a terrible cost in human life, and the fear of being proved wrong, with the total eclipse of his own credibility as a prophet.

Jeremiah 17:19–27
The Keeping of the Sabbath

This address on the keeping of the sabbath is set out in the elevated homiletical prose usually taken as a sign of the extensive editorial work of Jeremiah's Deuteronomistic editors (cf. Nicholson, pp. 13, 66). Several scholars have taken it to be undoubtedly Jeremianic in origin, but this can scarcely be the case for its extant literary form. Whether it does go back to an authentic incident in the prophet's career and reflects a public speech by him can be only a matter of conjecture. Much uncertainty surrounds the question of the degree of public religious concern attaching to the observance of the sabbath in Jerusalem before the catastrophes of 598 and 587 B.C. There are many features suggesting that a much increased conscientiousness about sabbath observance emerged during and after the Babylonian exile. This is not to deny that as a religious institution the sabbath had far older origins but merely to state that it was not a matter of such intense public concern as arose later.

If we accept that the address as now constructed was formulated during the exilic period, although based on authentic reminiscences of Jeremiah's preaching and of life in Jerusalem before the temple was destroyed, we can find in it an important witness to the rise of concern for sabbath observance in Judah

109

after the disasters of 587. With a widespread mood of religious despair and indifference, an increasingly disorganized population, and weak leadership by the remaining priestly officers the sabbath may quickly have appeared to be a religious irrelevance. The sermon can be seen then to directly address this situation and to seek reaffirmation of the sabbath and its careful observance. A number of features in the address stand out sharply and fully bear out the conviction that its concern was with the situation that befell those who remained in Judah after the temple had fallen.

Most marked of all is the conditional either/or manner in which the prophetic address is composed, warning of punishment for disobedience (v. 23) but concentrating more heavily on the rewards of conscientious observance of the sabbath as a holy day on which no work was done: "Then there shall enter by the gates of this city kings who sit on the throne of David, riding in chariots and on horses, . . ." (v. 25). Clearly with such unexpected words as these, the entire hope of national restoration, with the recovery of full political independence for Judah, was associated with sabbath observance. This indicates that it was felt that the carelessness about sabbath observance had been encouraged by the Babylonian administration during the exile. Undoubtedly, it must have displayed a marked coolness toward the distinctive religious traditions of cities such as Jerusalem.

A further consideration indicating that the normal pattern of sabbath observance in Jerusalem had been seriously, and very negatively, affected by the destruction of the temple is to be found in verse 26. Here the mention of people coming from all the cities of Judah, and even as far south as the towns of the Negeb, points us to a picture of what had been the usual practice in Jerusalem on a sabbath day; while the temple stood, it was set apart for worship. Such visitors brought with them their burnt offerings, sacrifices, and cereal offerings to present in the temple (cf. also 41:5). Once the temple had been destroyed, virtually all this religious traffic into Jerusalem for the sabbath had ceased. There remained little incentive to pay any attention at all to this ancient institution; so we can readily understand how easily the citizens of Jerusalem who had stayed in the city after 587 allowed interest in the sabbath to lapse. The purpose of the Jeremiah sermon, based on the preaching of the prophet but related to the later situation, was to inject a

110

new dimension of hope into the observance of the institution. It was a day of hope—of eager looking forward to a restored city of Jerusalem, with a recovery of its past glories and spiritual vitality.

In accepting the disappointments of the present and the impossibility of effective and impressive worship in the temple as it had once been, there was no reason why the sabbath should also be allowed to lapse. It was a symbol of hope concerning the future and the belief that God would fulfill his promise to make Jerusalem a splendid city and the center of pilgrimage again, as it had been in the past. On the other side a solemn warning was attached and set as the conclusion to the address (v. 27), pointing out that if the people remained indifferent to the demands of the sabbath which remained within their power to fulfill, then God would himself allow the city of Jerusalem to fall into complete and permanent ruin.

There can be little reason for seeking to relate this Jeremianic address to the period of Nehemiah, a century later than the period to which it more probably belongs in the middle of the sixth century B.C. (cf. Neh. 13:15–22). What is strikingly fresh here is the extent to which the institution of the sabbath has become filled with a rich range of expectations concerning Israel's restoration. The observance of the sabbath has become in itself a celebration of hope. Further interest in the question of sabbath observance during this period is displayed by the warnings concerning the punishments for failure to observe its holy character as set out in Ezekiel 20. Once again, as in the Jeremiah passage here, there is an awareness that the events of Jerusalem's defeat and destruction had set the regard for this institution under a cloud.

Jeremiah 18:1–12
The Visit to the Potter's House

We now encounter the first of several prophetic parables and sign-actions, narrated in prose, which provide further indications of the nature and extent of Israel's sin. Surprisingly for such prophetic material, there is only a broad identification of the conduct constituting rejection of the known law of God.

111

The disclosure of Israel's sinfulness is set out in relation to a visit made by Jeremiah to a potter's house. The action of the potter is interpreted by the prophet as a sign and an analogy for the actions of God to Israel. The incident must assuredly rest upon some authentic reminiscence of the prophet which has occasioned this interpretative elaboration. A further sign-action relating to pottery is to be found in 19:1–14, which centers upon the smashing of an earthenware pot.

The visit to the potter's house is reported in 18:1–6. To this has been appended verses 7–12, an extensive admonitory address in the first person prophetic style of divine speech, which many commentators regard as a later addition. As it stands, however, its message is inextricably bound up with the analogy provided by the work of the potter. It serves to make this demonstrably plain. The word of God connected with what Jeremiah was able to see in the potter's house is very simple: "Oh house of Israel, can I not do with you as this potter has done, says the LORD" (v. 6). The potter retains complete mastery over the material he uses, and the analogy between the potter working the clay and God fashioning human lives must have been an ancient and familiar one (cf. Gen. 2:7). However, this analogy is developed in a fresh direction to demonstrate that the destruction of the kingdom of Judah can properly be understood as the work of God. The perspective that this tragedy had already occurred breathes through the present form of the narrative, although it is appropriately referred to as no more than a future possibility. In working his material there are times when the potter is compelled to abandon the pot he is working on and to begin again. In this case he simply reworks the same piece of clay. This action provides the heart of the divine message: "Behold, like the clay in the potter's hand, so are you in my hand, O house of Israel" (v. 6). The elaboration in verses 7–12 then explains more fully what this means in terms of the divine action towards all peoples.

At first glance the primary point of the potter's action appears to be to counter the unspoken objection that it is inconceivable that God could bring about the destruction of Israel, since by their elect origin and status they are "the people of God." Can it be thought that God would permit, let alone ordain, the destruction of Israel when they are "his" people? The prophetic answer is that this can be so, as shown by the analogy of the potter beginning anew by reworking the original clay (v. 4). It becomes demonstrably clear that the destruction of Israel and Jerusalem is to be understood as fully within the range of the working of divine providence. There is a further hidden element in the analogy that may or may not have been intended: After the original pot had been spoiled, it was nonetheless "reworked into another vessel." We may discern in this feature of the analogy a positive message of hope indicating that God could begin to fashion his people Israel anew.

Elaboration of the message of the visit to the potter's house in verses 7–12 undertakes a more wide-ranging and philosophical reflection on how God deals with all peoples. In the wordy formal manner of a legal pronouncement it develops the principles by which divine providence operates for all nations and individuals. We may note especially the legal formulae: "If at any time I declare . . ., and if that nation, ... And if at any time . . . and if it does (vv. 7–10). This legal terminology has been employed to fulfill a didactic prophetic function, not without a certain reminiscence of wisdom. It points to a principle of conduct deduced from the cases specified: "Now, therefore, say to the men of Judah and the inhabitants of Jerusalem: 'Thus says the LORD, . . .'" (v. 11). This leads on to the conclusion: "But they say, 'That is in vain!'" (v. 12). In its conclusion this passage has a close relationship to the priestly legal formulation set out in Ezekiel 18, where the aim is to show the divine possibility of repentance effecting a total change in God's purposes towards Israel and towards individuals within the nation. The passage in Jeremiah serves a similar purpose in demonstrating that divine justice does not exclude the possibility of human repentance. Rather it demands and expects it! Thereby a full and effective human response to the divine will can open up a wholly changed prospect for the future. The form of address "to the men of Judah and the inhabitants of Jerusalem" (v. 11) should also be regarded as of special interest. What we may have expected as the national dimension of reference to "Israel" is instead narrowed down to Jerusalem and its immediate environs, almost certainly pointing to the community that survived in the land after 587 B.C.

The formulation of the argument establishes two central points. First it establishes that God's purpose allows the freedom of human response through repentance to determine the shape of the future—"Return every one from his evil way" (v. 11). The people of Judah had chosen wrongly against God and had necessarily suffered the consequences of their bad choice. They had thought: "We will follow our own plans . . ." (v. 12). Responsibility for the ruin and destruction of Judah and Jerusalem lay fully with their citizens. Blame could not be placed on an irascible and indifferent God, but destruction and ruin were the consequences of their own self-willed folly. By the same doctrine, however, repentance and a right choice towards God on a national and an individual basis could establish the ground for a wholly new beginning: "If at any time I declare concerning a nation, or a kingdom, that I will build and plant it . . ." (v. 9). The divine grace at work in providence was applicable to every nation and individual and was such that it both explained the past and held an open door towards a better future. By such a teaching, prophecy, which could so easily be regarded fatalistically, was shown to be opposed to all fatalistic reasonings.

Jeremiah 18:13–17
Further Condemnation of Israel's Conduct

This short poetic unit returns to the basic theme of Israel's repeated and excessive unfaithfulness to the Lord God. This pointed to judgment as a necessary and inevitable consequence. The primary point here lies in the specific way in which Israel's sinfulness is defined: "my people have forgotten me, they burn incense to false gods; . . ." (v. 15). The rest of the indictment is elaborate imagery enlarging upon the seriousness of such behavior and the awfulness of the consequences which must ensue as its punishment.

By now this theme of Israel "burning incense to false gods" (v. 15) has become a familiar accusation in the Book of Jeremiah. It represents a variant of the accusation that Israel has turned to idolatry. At first glance it appears simply as a distinctively religious explanation for Judah's social and political misfortunes, drawing attention to the mixed religious loyalties that had prevailed throughout the long history of the kingdom. In a modern secular context it is common enough to equate the "false gods" the people of Judah had revered with the goals and ideals of a modern secular society in which no formal religious commitment is required. The strongly sexual element in the ancient Baal-Anat rituals may serve to support such an analogy with aspects of modern popular culture. So the "false gods" are interpreted as false ideals of greed, sexual licentiousness, and a preoccupation with material objects. We may compare for such a basis of interpretation the Pauline interpretation of covetousness as idolatry (Col. 3:5). However, it is important to bear in mind a number of important, easily forgotten, historical considerations.

The very nature of the emphasis upon turning to false gods serves to strengthen the probability that this was a common feature of life, not only before Jerusalem and its temple had suffered destruction but also afterwards. The tradents of Jeremiah's prophecies had become deeply conscious of the despairing resort to a host of ill-considered and socially divisive religious practices, which took on a renewed popularity after the temple had been destroyed. In fact the very loss of the temple in Jerusalem had almost certainly encouraged a revival of alternative religious rites. To some, the Lord God of Israel appeared to have lost credibility as defender of those who had put their trust in him. It mattered greatly therefore to show through the words of prophecy that this was not the case. Israel's sins necessitated all that had taken place at the command of God. Following the political disasters of 598 and 587 with a conscious abandonment of worship of the Lord as God would add a dimension of inner spiritual disaster worse than the earlier political misfortunes. Prophecy had become a battle for the minds and hearts of the people of Judah. Only by giving full credence to the words of Jeremiah and by recognizing that he had correctly foreseen the likelihood of tragedy overtaking his people could this battle be won.

Strange as it may seem, this vital battlefield of religious ideas and ideals was also a struggle for retention of a worthy and responsible view of human nature. Fatalism, with its attendant submission to an irrational and unexplained destiny controlled by arbitrary and magical practices could be overcome only by faith. This entailed willingness to accept the reality of human responsibility, expressed through the action of repentance as a

115

truly human openness to God, and a recognition that this pointed to a divinely given trust in humanity, as those who had been called by the Creator to share the divine purpose for the world.

Jeremiah 18:18–23
A Plot Against the Life of Jeremiah

Again and again in this larger unit of prophecies (11:1—20: 18) the figure of the prophet comes to the foreground and his personal sufferings and violent response to them appear. Jeremiah is a persecuted prophet and this experience of hostility has bitten deeply and ineradicably into his inner spirit. So it is that in reporting plots against his life Jeremiah cries out in shock and indignation and pleads with God to bring terrible vengeance upon his personal enemies. An earlier account of a plot against the life of Jeremiah has been reported in 11:18–23; 12:1–6. Whether the plot here is the same one or, as seems more probable, a further instance in a series of repeated attacks against the person of Jeremiah is not made fully clear.

Commentators have frequently expressed surprise and dismay at the vehemence of Jeremiah's pleas to God to execute terrible vengeance upon his enemies (vv. 21–22). Jeremiah pleads that such attempts upon his life are unjust and unjustifiable (v. 20). It is true that Jeremiah's response contrasts negatively when compared with the later submission to suffering and prayers for forgiveness of enemies exemplified by Jesus Christ. However, this criticism cannot be fairly applied to Jeremiah more than five centuries earlier. His response is intelligible enough and human enough, nor are his words softened by recognizing that they echo the stereotypical language found in a number of lament psalms.

Jeremiah's enemies may be thought to have attacked him in part on the grounds of his seeming lack of patriotism and his willingness to acknowledge that Judah's national enemies were about to triumph. He was no doubt criticized because he appeared to be looking for confirmation of his pronouncements of coming doom. Yet more than this was at issue, in rejecting

116

God's message Jeremiah reasoned that his hearers were thereby rejecting God altogether. Nor was this viewpoint without foundation, and it must certainly have been a matter of great importance to the editors of Jeremiah's prophetic book. So it was that the conflict experienced by Jeremiah served to show the extent to which the prophet's contemporaries had rejected God. The inability of those who were faced with God's message of condemnation to take it seriously had been a potent factor in leading to the national ruin. Justifiable self-esteem on the part of Jeremiah's contemporaries had overflowed into a vicious campaign of hate and intended murder against the figure who had revealed the falsity of that personal pride.

What Jeremiah had been declaring to the citizens of Judah was to them unthinkable, and this had aroused a conviction that the only possible explanation for his message was that God himself must have deceived his prophet. Jeremiah's counter argument was that they had deceived themselves.

We can probe further, however, behind the heavy concentration in this part of the collection upon the theme of Jeremiah's personal sufferings. The God of Israel was not to be thought of as a "national" God, as the title "The God of Israel" appeared to imply. The creator God of all the world could not be envisaged as an exclusively national deity. Furthermore Jeremiah rightly recognized that there was a fundamental error in thinking of God primarily in terms of power—especially power available for the protection of his people—rather than in terms of love and righteousness. The very "Godness" of God would be impugned if it were thought to be a willingness to defend and uphold Israel regardless of their conduct. Jeremiah rightly recognized that a major issue of theology was at stake in the sharp hostility shown towards him. What may have naïvely appeared to his hearers as an acceptance that Marduk the god of Babylon was greater than the Lord God of Israel was in reality no such confrontation. All such nationalistic interpretations of deity were in their essence a form of atheism, since they failed to grasp the transcendent and other-worldly nature of the divine being. The long line of other prophets who, like Jeremiah, have suffered persecution and rejection (cf. II Kings 17: 13–14; Matt. 23:29–38) are witness to the fact that God cannot be confined within the framework of a purely human situation or institution.

117

Jeremiah 19:1—20:6
The Sign of the Broken Pot

The prophets of the Old Testament were messengers commissioned by God to deliver the divine word entrusted to them. Naturally enough this message was normally conveyed verbally on behalf of the deity who had sent the prophet. Yet it was conceivable that the word of God could also have been conveyed through a sign in which the forthcoming event, or divine action, was signified. We have encountered already in the activity of a potter, in working clay into a shapeless mass (18:4–6), a symbolic indication of God's intended action towards the people of Israel. The potter's action had become a sign of the action of God. Now we are presented with a report of an incident in which Jeremiah negotiates the purchase of an earthen pot to take along to "the Potsherd Gate" (19:2). There he would declare the word of God. Evidently the location was where shards of pottery were piled in heaps, and it must also have been close to the area where the potter worked. Jeremiah was commanded to smash the pot before the eyes of the people who had assembled to watch him. This action was then interpreted as a sign that God was about to break his people Israel (19:10–11). The action was a dramatic gesture providing an indication of the violence of the divine action coming to Israel. The people were to be broken into pieces "so that it can never be mended" (v. 11).

This action fits into a known and widely attested pattern of similar actions employed to convey the divine word. It is a form of street theatre, but with a far more serious purpose than merely to attract attention and entertain. The action both dramatized and served to give visual impact to the coming action of God. Much discussion has taken place concerning the extent to which this type of sign-action was thought to intensify, and even inaugurate, the action it signified. Yet this is to press the meaning of the action too far and to relate it too closely to forms of magical gesture and imitative action. There is no reason to suppose that it was thought to achieve more than an engagement of both eye and ear in encounter with the word of

118

God. We may compare Jeremiah's action with the linen girdle in 13:1–11. Signifying divine intention in this fashion gave it a note of suddenness. God would punish his people in an event that would be swift, terrible, and final!

In this fashion Jeremiah had no compunction about seeking an opportunity to startle his audience with his message. He needed to spread fear, alarm, and horror, since all other means of bringing home to his hearers the reality of the danger that faced them seemed to him to have been frustrated and nullified. Could this new and sudden gesture bring home to them the deadly seriousness of what he had to say? Words appeared to the prophet no longer enough to convey his meaning. His hearers saw only an isolated and mocked prophet, uttering assertions and threats they had heard many times before and which they dismissed as needlessly alarmist and defeatist. Tragedy, defeat, and terrible suffering did not fall within the range of providential activity that they cared to contemplate. God, they believed, could be only the author of good and beneficent actions towards them. As a result they had only a weakened and incomplete picture of how all of life, in all its many aspects, came under the range of the divine will and purpose. Even the horrors of war and the near certainty of national defeat could, as Jeremiah was earnestly insisting, come under the scheme of the divine plan for Israel.

The sign-action of smashing the pot Jeremiah had purchased concludes with a further attempt on the part of the people to silence him, this time led by Pashhur the priest (20:1–6). This is set out in a narrative which has evidently been placed at this juncture in the prophecies for a specific purpose. It brings further evidence to bear on the persons in high authority (Pashhur is described as a priest and as the chief officer of the temple, 20:1) to indicate the extent to which official approval was rallied behind the attempts to frustrate Jeremiah's prophetic activity. His sufferings were no hasty expression of popular mistrust and personal ill-will but a calculated expression on the part of officialdom to end Jeremiah's unwelcome prophesying. It is nonetheless noteworthy that punishing the prophet by submitting him to public humiliation in the stocks was less than might have been expected. What the prophet was declaring was treasonable, and yet he was spared the threat of capital punishment. We can discern in this a mark of the typical ambivalence towards the prophet of God—at one and the same time both feared and distrusted! He was not put to death as an enemy

119

of the people, since he was a prophet and was entitled to a certain respect as a messenger of God. At the same time his messages were not believed and the prophet needed to be ridiculed and set at nought. The reporting of the incident is intended less to focus upon the private sufferings of Jeremiah and more to show how, and why, his message had so little effect among the people. The fate Jeremiah had declared to be awaiting Jerusalem and Judah as a whole is then spelled out in a direct and forcible way as applicable to Jeremiah (20:4–6). This compares closely with the reaction from Amos towards Amaziah, the priest of Bethel, a century and a half earlier (cf. Amos 7:14–17). It is not private vindictiveness that has motivated Jeremiah's words but resolute conviction that the truth could not be altered, however much the religious authorities endeavored to do so!

The opposition of Pashhur to Jeremiah suggests a further reason why Jeremiah and those who have preserved and edited his prophecies saw that the destruction of the temple of Jerusalem was inevitable. The chief temple officers had been among those who most openly rejected God's word through the prophet. So the temple, and all that it stood for as a means of blessing and enlightenment for Israel's religious life, had become an obstacle to the true knowledge of God. Where a conflict between a great and historic religious institution and the word of God emerged, the word of God prevailed!

Jeremiah 20:7–18
Jeremiah Near to Breaking-point

The occasion of Jeremiah's public beating and humiliation in the stocks provides the background for the last of the prophet's so-called "confessions" (20:7–13). This is brought to a conclusion in verses 14–18 by a lament for his whole life. This takes the form of a curse upon the day of his birth. In verse 13 the short invocation to the praise of God, which marks a transition to the bitter personal cry of lamentation, reads strangely and appears to be out of place. It can best be understood perhaps as an addition by a later scribe introducing a note of thanksgiving for the courage and work of Jeremiah.

120

Central attention then must be focused on verses 7–12 in which Jeremiah accuses God in a shocking and almost blasphemous way of having deceived him (the Hebrew verb implies a meaning "to seduce, lead astray"). Jeremiah then turns from his accusations against God to the cruel mockery experienced at the hands of his friends, who had laughed at him for his endless threats of doom and disaster (v. 10). He calls out once more for God to execute vengeance against them for what they have done. His cry of frustration and inner rage receives no explicit answer from God. Possibly the addition of verse 13 has sought to give an answer by offering assurance that God does protect his faithful ones and does punish evildoers. However, there is no divine answer given and none properly can be expected, since the situation precludes any such personal vindication of Jeremiah. As every reader of the book would have known, the whole historical context provided the answer; tragedy had stricken Judah and Jerusalem and no subsequent cries or tears could undo the catastrophe that had overtaken Jeremiah's compatriots.

In what sense can we understand Jeremiah's claim that God had "deceived" or "seduced" him? The reference is undoubtedly intended to be understood in relation to the prophet's sense of call to his high task. How was it that God had deceived Jeremiah into believing and proclaiming that a disastrous future awaited Judah, wrought by a "foe from the north," when this had still, at the time of Jeremiah's complaint, not happened? Some have thought that Jeremiah's words refer to a sense of frustration and a feeling of public humiliation that had been heaped upon him because his warnings of coming doom had not so far proved to be reliable. We do not know, however, at what precise period in his ministry the outburst of distress and frustration mentioned here is to be located. It is true that we could think of Jeremiah, beginning in Josiah's reign, issuing a long series of repeated warnings concerning the threat of a "foe from the north." At this time all the available political evidence would have pointed to the increasing collapse of Assyrian influence in Judah. Not until twenty years after the moment of his call to prophesy was it that the reality of a further threat from Mesopotamia, this time led from Babylon, arose.

121

The incident involving Jeremiah's punishment through the agency of Pashhur the priest (20:4–6) had already referred to this threat from Babylon. We may conclude that much more likely Jeremiah's sense of having been deceived and misled by God was not because his prophecies appeared to lack fulfillment but because they lacked any adequate response in the hearts and minds of his hearers. What Jeremiah looked for was to be taken seriously as the mouthpiece of God, to be listened to, and to be able to evoke a deep and genuine repentance in the hearts of his people. This had not happened at all; instead his sombre warnings had been turned into the opportunity for mockery and ill-treatment. It had hurt him deeply and lastingly that men and women could joke about his seriousness and shrug off the intensity of his feelings of horror and alarm at the message he brought. He reasoned that if God had truly called him to be a prophet it was God's responsibility also to ensure that his calling as a prophet was respected and acknowledged by those to whom he testified. This too may be the implied sense behind the popular desire to see Jeremiah further deceived, as reported in verse 10. The people wanted to see whether he would be led into uttering from God such extreme and outrageous messages that their foolishness would be made plain and the opportunity would arise for his complete public disgrace. Such did not take place; Jeremiah found new strength and a new intensity of purpose in his knowledge that God was with him, compelling him to continue in the course he had begun.

Just as he had been unable to refrain from prophesying, even though he had made up his mind to do so (v. 9), so was he also unable to alter the content of his message in any way. What he declared was not of his choosing but the consequence of the truths God had given him.

As in the case of the other distraught outburst from Jeremiah, the purpose in recording and preserving this is twofold. These disclosures of Jeremiah's inner feelings highlight the reasons for Judah's downfall. God had been wholly faithful in revealing his hidden purpose through his prophet (cf. Amos 3:9), but the mystery of human freedom, even the freedom to reject the word of God, remained a reality. The entire sequence of Jeremiah's confessions and the collection of prophecies (11:1—20:18) in which the prophet's personal sufferings figure so prominently are then brought to a close with Jeremiah's cursing of the day of his birth (20:13-18).

Nowhere is the complexity of the prophet's language nor

the conscious ambivalence it expresses brought out more fully than here. Jeremiah speaks as one who has become isolated, frustrated, and utterly conscious of being alone and distraught in his sense of personal failure. Out of respect for a strongly felt social convention, he refrains from cursing either his parents or God outright. Instead he curses the day he was born and the messenger who brought the news of his birth. Nonetheless, the prophet's personal grief was to become the grief of a whole community; long after the terrifying events that had fulfilled his prophetic warnings had transpired, the reader too is enabled to pour out feelings of grief such as Jeremiah had felt. If the readers had heard the prophet speak in his time, would they not have listened and responded in an effective way? We may compare the words of Jesus in Matthew 23:29–39. Would it not have been easier to join in the mockery of the prophet and thereby hasten the day of Judah's ruination? Now in the aftermath of that disaster what words could more faithfully express the grief that men and women felt over their own obtuseness in not heeding this message while there was still time than those with which the prophet had declared his own misery?

It is reasonable to reflect how the sequence of Jeremiah's confessions recorded in chapters 11—20 serves to transform the understanding of his prophetic call and the entire understanding of the nature of the prophetic office. From being confident that he could serve as the mouthpiece of God, bearing messages stamped with all the authority of their divine source, Jeremiah had become frustrated, stricken with doubt, and even determined to resist the divine compulsion to prophesy.

We may question whether Jeremiah had not come to doubt, not once but many times, whether God had called him to be a prophet. At times his sense of a divine calling had become tarnished by doubts and misgivings, even though it was only through these doubts and misgivings that the genuine divine origin and strength of his call could be realized. So, in the light that it bears upon the nature of the prophetic office, we can discern a point of major theological significance in Jeremiah's self-curse with its implicit expression of despair. Truly this was one of the great turning-points that prophecy underwent during the biblical period. Jeremiah's success as a prophet was not to be measured by the extent to which he had been able to persuade his hearers to listen to the word of God and thereby avoid whatever dangers faced them, but rather in the firmness and consistency with which he bore testimony to the righteous purpose and grand design of God. A major theological issue was at stake; was the Lord, the God of Israel, to be regarded simply as "the national God of Israel" or as the Creator of the universe, the Source and Ground of righteousness, justice, and truth.

The exposure of the inner world of Jeremiah's turmoil, frustration, and temporary despair uncovers the way in which despair, so readily understood as the enemy of faith, may nonetheless fulfill a spiritual purpose. The fundamental nature of despair can ultimately be understood only in terms of humankind's spiritual self-awareness (cf. Kierkegaard, "The greater the degree of consciousness, the more intense the despair", p. 42). Discovery of the true nature of the self, the inner spiritual core of a person's identity, is promoted by despair that causes one to abandon desire to exist. In this sense it is the willingness and even longing to "lose" oneself that necessitates a rediscovery of one's true identity. In this way the individual's self is found anew. This is firmly pointed to in Jeremiah's understanding of what it meant for him to be a prophet of God. Despairing of the possibility of fulfilling the demands of such an office, Jeremiah discovered a wholly new understanding of the true nature of that office.

PART THREE

The Fate of the Nation and Its Institutions
JEREMIAH 21—29

A new section of prophecies which must derive from the period we have already been involved with now commences; that is from Josiah's death in 609 to the eve of Jerusalem's fall in 587 B.C. The latter event, implying as it did the end of the established political integrity of the kingdom of Judah and the removal of the Davidic monarchy from the throne in Jerusalem, provides a central point of focus for all the prophecies.

Jeremiah 21:1—23:8
The Faithless Leaders

Zedekiah (21)

The opening prophecy in 21:1–10 relates to an enquiry from Zedekiah king of Judah to Jeremiah at the time when Judah was imminently faced with the threat of siege by the armies of Babylon. This was either in 588 or early 587 B.C. Zedekiah, having already sealed his and his country's fate by his act of rebellion against Babylonian rule, appears to have been hopeful of receiving some word of assurance and support from Jeremiah. No doubt he had relied heavily upon promises of power- 125 ful Egyptian support and had made his plans in the expectation that he would thereby be free of the regular heavy payment of tribute money to Babylon. To what extent other irksome restraints and demands were involved in subjection to Mesopotamian imperial control are not wholly clear. Jeremiah firmly and decisively refused to offer any verbal support or message of hope to Zedekiah. He insisted that the king's action in withholding allegiance had been mistaken and would lead to ruinous consequences for him and his kingdom. Jeremiah further affirmed that the outcome of the Babylonian siege of Jerusalem would be terrifyingly destructive and would prove to be a political and social catastrophe for Judah. Instead of defending the city and nation that claimed to be "God's" people, God would be fighting against them with great wrath and fury (vv. 5–6).

The proper and expected role of a prophet would certainly be to serve the national interests and seek the welfare of his own people. He was in this sense expected to be their servant. The role of prophets in Israel's history in time of war had undoubtedly been that of committed members of the community which they felt bound to uphold. Their prayerful intercession was a way of working for the wellbeing of the people as a whole. Now Jeremiah was vociferously and starkly refusing to accept such a role and instead was declaring that the God of whom he was the servant also refused such a role. The Lord God would not defend his own people, but would instead fight against them. So there should be no doubt at all about the outcome of the imminent siege of Jerusalem (of which Jeremiah and the other citizens of the city were now fully aware), Jeremiah spells out its fearful consequences. The people would die in the city by one means or another or they would surrender in humiliating fashion to the Babylonian armies. The fate of the city, according to Jeremiah, could not be in doubt; and Zedekiah had nothing to look for from Jeremiah by way of assurance (v. 10).

The account presented here is stark and completely unequivocal. Set out in prose, it shows signs of having been written in retrospect in the wake of the events of 587 B.C. Nevertheless it must in all essentials represent closely the message of the prophet during the crucial days of Jerusalem's siege. In spite of their simplicity and clarity, it is difficult to penetrate the surface of the prophet's words to appreciate fully the thinking and motivation that characterized his message at this time. Why did Jeremiah appear to be so totally devoid of patriotic fervor and so wholly opposed to the rebellion of Zedekiah against Babylon? Jeremiah was convinced that the move the king had embarked

126

upon was hopeless. When we reflect upon the naturalness of ordinary patriotic feelings, which in other directions Jeremiah certainly did not lack, we do feel surprise at the sharpness of his message. Nor can we fail to feel some element of sympathy for Zedekiah, who had been anxious to rid his people of a burdensome economic drain upon their resources. In a multiplicity of administrative measures and religious activities, it must have been inevitable that Babylonian power could be dangerous and often cruel. A number of scholars have sought to picture Jeremiah as a firm and unremitting realist, aware of the extent of Babylonian military strength and of the hopelessness of the limited military resources of Judah. Yet clearly Zedekiah also knew this and must have relied heavily upon the promises of Egyptian military support.

If then we are to look for indications of why Jeremiah was so vehemently opposed to Zedekiah's policy, we can consider two possibilities. This is to leave aside the absurd notion that Jeremiah was completely unpatriotic and pro-Babylonian in his sympathies. First we must recognize the strong likelihood that Jeremiah felt deeply antagonistic to Zedekiah's misplaced trust in Egypt. For almost a century and a half, since the time of the prophet Isaiah, Judah had received a constant stream of promises from Egypt of military assistance against the imperialist expansion of Mesopotamia, first the Assyrian and then the Babylonian. Clearly the Egyptians had been fully aware of the danger to themselves of Mesopotamian interference and were more than willing to use Judah, Israel, and the other minor nations on their northern borders to fend off unwelcome intruders from afar. There had been many promises of Egyptian aid, but all of them had failed to provide the needed degree of resistance and protection. So a prophet such as Jeremiah would have been well aware that political alliances of this kind to support rebellion against Assyria and Babylon had shown themselves to be futile and unworkable. It is possible that we should recognize behind Jeremiah's uncompromising preaching against rebellion an element of serious political reflection and a determination not to be led astray by a false and emotional national optimism.

There is, however, a second and even more plausible understanding of the reasoning that underlay Jeremiah's preaching. The reader of the extant Book of Jeremiah cannot but be struck by the surprising absence of any form of clear-cut

127

political assessment or any firm indication of a partisan political stance. Instead we find with Jeremiah, and consistently throughout the book of his prophecies, an intense concentration on purely religious issues and a profound insight into the nature of religion. This strongly suggests that internal religious rather than external political factors in Judah's life more deeply affected Jeremiah. In particular he distrusted and openly opposed the strong national attachment displayed in Judah to the Davidic royal tradition. This is firmly borne out by two clear considerations. One of these is that the editors of the book have used this rebuff to Zedekiah to introduce a whole sequence of prophecies from Jeremiah concerning the Davidic kingship in 21:11—23:8. The implication is clearly that Jeremiah regarded the deeply rooted popular trust in the divine support for the Davidic kingship as dangerous and misplaced. Consistently we find that Jeremiah's prophecies concerning the office of the Davidic kingship are critical and hostile; the sole exceptions to this are the two prophecies set out in 23:5–8. Further pronouncements regarding the Davidic kingship are to be found in 33:14–26, but these quite certainly have been composed in light of what had happened in 587 and with a view to the long-term future of Israel's monarchy. The content of chapter 33 cannot be from Jeremiah himself.

Jeremiah's convictions about the nature and duties of the kingship are set out in 21:11–14. The address of this unit to the king has been obscured by the rendering in verse 13 "O inhabitant of the valley" (RSV). This should more correctly be understood as a reference to the king "You who are enthroned above the valley." Instead of acting as father and guardian of his people, each of Israel's (Judah's) kings had shown himself to be an exploiter and oppressor of the people. Few had been the exception to this! The traditional description of the royal duties as those of upholding justice and delivering those who are oppressed (cf. Ps. 101) had too often in practice been little more than a hollow fiction. At most this was a pretense, and sometimes scarcely even this. The kings had readily become agents of injustice and exploitation, as had been exemplified in the case of Jehoiakim (22:13–19; cf. also I. Sam. 8:11–17). Failure to implement a viable system for the administration of justice had remained one of the most frequently repeated and persistently felt criticisms of the kingship. In the case of Israel this had sometimes applied to non-Davidic kings, but the Davidic dy-

128

nasty too had been far from maintaining innocence on this front. It is readily understandable that Jeremiah felt no great affection for the royal house of David. Abiathar, a priestly ancestor of the prophet, had been banished by the Davidic royal house to the relatively minor sanctuary at Anathoth (cf. I Kings 2:26-27, 35).

Merely a fixed prejudice regarding the injustices perpetrated by the reigning royal house in Judah does not appear to have convinced Jeremiah that Zedekiah's policies would prove to be politically disastrous. Even more disturbing to the perceptive and critical mind of Jeremiah was the misplaced national confidence, at times almost an irrational euphoria, that rebellion against Babylon was bound to succeed. Ultimately this was encouraged by and in many ways derived from a wholly partisan and narrow view of God. While the Lord was regarded as the national God of Israel, there was a widespread belief that he could be relied upon to defend his people and to give them victory in all circumstances. Taken as proof of this was the way in which the previous century and a half of Assyrian rule over Israel and Judah was being interpreted, especially the singular fact that both Jerusalem and the Davidic dynasty had survived (cf. Clements, *Isaiah and the Deliverance of Jerusalem,* pp. 63ff.). The record of how Jerusalem had withstood the threatened siege by Sennacherib's forces in 701 B.C. saw the city's deliverance as having happened for the sake of God and the house of David (cf. II Kings 19:34). If there were two religious features of the contemporary outlook in Judah regarded by Jeremiah as dangerously and potentially fatally misleading they were these: trust that focused upon the temple of the Lord God in Jerusalem and trust in the royal house of David. These were both worthy institutions in themselves and were certainly not to be classed along with the high-places and idolatrous rites that marked the worst elements of the national life. Nevertheless, trust in such institutions was less than a genuine and wholehearted trust in God. Even such worthy institutions could come to stand between the people and a true knowledge of God and assume a destructive dimension.

What Jeremiah encountered in Judah, therefore, and what provoked within him a deep suspicion of and at times hostility towards the royal house of David was the way in which popular feeling abused it. It was made the object of a false faith and the basis for the pursuit of an illusion. So we can well understand

129

that common sense, military logistics, and a century and more of useless Egyptian promises of aid all failed to dislodge the popular belief that self-assertive nationalism and willful pride would succeed in throwing off the yoke of Babylon. What made Jeremiah so completely and resolutely certain that such hopes were false was precisely the unworthy and inadequate understanding of the character and universal power of God they implied. In choosing God he was compelled to recognize that so much of the popular religion he saw about him was in contradiction to the true nature of God.

A Threat to the Royal House (22:1–9)

The theme of the dangerous illusions that surrounded the Davidic kingship and its long history are spelled out with considerable firmness in 22:1–9. The section is partly in prose and partly in poetry, but its purpose is abundantly clear. The populace of Judah were convinced that the presence among them of a king of the royal house of David was an assured sign of God's favor and protection. More than three hundred years of history appeared to prove this belief, especially when contrasted with the fate of the short-lived dynasties of the Northern Kingdom, which had seceded from the Davidic kingship in Jerusalem after Solomon's death (cf. I Kings 12:16,20). The succumbing of this rebellious Northern Kingdom to Assyrian domination in a manner that destroyed any native monarchy and much of the national ethos had been popularly interpreted as a consequence of this abandonment of the divinely appointed Davidic royal house. So there was this widespread conviction that God had in the past blessed and protected Judah "for the sake of his servant David" and that he would continue to do so in the future.

Against such a popular conviction, we can see that it required a Jeremiah to recognize and expose this dangerous fallacy. Faith which had as its object a person or institution less than God himself was incomplete and inadequate. Only God could be the true author and ground of faith. This foreshortening of the true nature of faith was shown to be all the more dangerous when combined with a cruel indifference to the genuine moral and spiritual demands of divine rule. A king who indulged in oppression and abused the privileges of his position could not expect to receive the divine blessing and support (22:3). God had certainly not given Jehoiakim, or in fact any member of the royal house, the freedom to do only as he

130

pleased. If the kings became oppressors—even the kings of the Davidic line—they could indeed be removed from their high office (22:9; cf. I Sam. 12:25). It is this point that lies at the heart of Jeremiah's political theology: The Davidic kingship is not essential to the divine election of Israel. God had indeed in the past given Israel kings to lead them in the pursuit of a national life of peace and justice. The relationship of the kingship to God—even that of the kingship of David's line—did not guarantee Israel or Judah, which had remained loyal to the Davidic dynasty, an unlimited assurance of God's protection. In Jeremiah's understanding the kingship might even become an obstacle to a right relationship between the people and God. This, he argues, had been the case with Jehoiakim (609–598 B.C.). Jeremiah appears to have retained a more open verdict about his predecessor, Josiah, and his two successors, Jehoiachin and Zedekiah. The central feature, however, is what Jeremiah understood about the institution of kingship as a whole, not what he had to say in a purely personal way about the piety and justice of individual kings. Recognizing its divine origin and potential benefits, he nonetheless was impelled to assert that the kingship provided no unlimited guarantee of Judah's (and Israel's) welfare.

Lament for an Exiled King (22:10–12)

The short prophecy in 22:10–12 elaborates on the theme of the kingship with a prophecy from Jeremiah on the occasion of the deposition and removal of Shallum (Jehoahaz) into Egyptian exile (609 B.C.). This had been a momentous and tragic year for Judah, almost certainly more so in the reality of the time than the recorded biblical history of the events of that year now reveals. This is because the tragedy that brought an end to Josiah's long and illustrious reign (639–609 B.C.) was later overshadowed by even more alarming and painful events. The circumstances of Josiah's death had been wholly unexpected and it was probably unnecessary in the context of what was taking place in the struggle for power between Egypt and Mesopotamia (cf. II Chron. 35:20–25). After Josiah's death Shallum (Jehoahaz) reigned for a brief three-month period before he was removed by the Egyptian king Necho and replaced by his brother Eliakim (Jehoiakim). We find that for this king Jeremiah reserved his sharpest condemnations.

131

Jeremiah's short lament for Shallum's deportation and exile

is striking for what it reveals about the prophet's and the people's attitude to their kings: "Weep not for him who is dead [Josiah], ... but weep bitterly for him who goes away [Shallum] . . ." (22:10).

The injunction against an overwhelming sense of grief and loss for the death of Josiah, a king for whom Jeremiah had high regard (cf. 22:15), is balanced by the affirmation that the removal of Shallum is a national tragedy. He would never return to his homeland or regain his throne. It is surprising that more than a handful in Judah thought he might do so, and we can only conclude that many of the internal tensions and dissensions of Judah's political life lie hidden behind such expectations.

From what transpired, the brother of the deposed king of Judah was evidently perceived by the Egyptian king as likely to prove more compliant to Egyptian aims than the ruler first chosen. It is probable that Jeremiah also saw this to be the case. It may have been evident to the prophet that the loss of Shallum to the royal throne was a sad blow for policies of common sense and national wellbeing at a time when Judah could not afford to lose such a figure. In his place there came to the throne of Judah Jehoiakim, a man of a different stamp from his rejected brother; the bitter attack upon him in verses 13–19 forms the natural sequel to the brief lament for Shallum. Undoubtedly Jeremiah's editors have pieced together in 21:11—23:8 the sequence of prophecies concerning the kings of Judah's last years; in doing so they have provided us with an unrivaled window upon the prophetic view of the royal house at a most crucial period in its history. We can only marvel that a prophet could remain alive and free to say such things and to have them recorded!

Condemnation of Jehoiakim (22:13–19)

The sharpest indictment of a Davidic king by Jeremiah is reserved for Jehoiakim and follows in 22:13–19. We have a typically clear and reasoned prophetic saying that belongs to Jehoiakim's reign, possibly before the king had displayed his intention of withdrawing his allegiance to Babylon. He had come to the throne of Judah after Shallum's deportation and removal by Pharaoh Necho of Egypt in 609 B.C. (II Kings 23:24). He was himself another son of Josiah, and the report of the historian in II Kings 23:35 mentions heavy payment of silver and gold to the Egyptian king. This the king exacted from the people by imposing a form of tax assessment. The main thrust of Jeremiah's condemnation focuses upon the king's exaction from the people for funds to build himself a house. This points to some lavish extension of the royal palace complex (22:13–15), which the king paneled with cedar. There is possibly a certain play on the notion of the king "who builds his house by unrighteousness" (v. 13), since the record in II Kings 23:35 strongly hints that the payment of tribute to Pharaoh Necho was a calculated move on the king's part. Did he actively connive at Shallum's deportation by seeking to curry favor with the pharaoh of Egypt? If so, it seems possible that many in Judah would have viewed his occupancy of the throne as an act of usurpation, encouraging many to look for the eventual restoration of the legitimate king Shallum. The complexities of such internal political moves are not fully known to us, but such would undoubtedly serve to illuminate the intensity of Jeremiah's bitterness and condemnation of such a king.

The specific point of the prophetic invective concerns the fact that the king reduced many of his citizens to the level of slaves, compelling them to work on his palace but paying them no wages (22:13). This points to a system of compulsory labor in the royal service as a form of taxation, and it may well have been directly linked with the heavy exactions of silver and gold paid to the Egyptian king. Those who could not pay in kind had to pay in slave service! Memories of Solomon and the manner in which he had first built the royal palace and the temple in Jerusalem would have remained fresh in the popular mind (cf. I Kings 5:13–14; 12:3–4). Such compulsory slave service was understandably resented by the people as a whole, and it certainly would not have alleviated the feeling that it was primarily to minister to the king's vanity. Compare Jeremiah's words: "Do you think you are a king because you compete in cedar?" It is very probably the case that the king positively intended his action to demonstrate the firmness of his grip upon the people of the land and his control over their freedom.

A further point in regard to Jehoiakim is worth bearing in mind. After the defeat of the Egyptians at the battle of Carchemish in 605 B.C., it was clear that Jehoiakim's ally and supporter was now itself defeated and completely vulnerable to the westward ambitions of Nebuchadnezzar of Babylon. Once Judah was drawn into the area now falling under Babylonian control,

133

the fact that Jehoiakim retained his throne under this new master points to the almost cynical way in which Jehoiakim held onto power. The vehemence of Jeremiah's attack upon him remains one of the most precisely aimed condemnations of a ruler to be found in the Bible:

> "But you have eyes and heart
>   only for your dishonest gain,
> for shedding innocent blood,
>   and for practicing oppression and violence" (22:17).

The prophecy then proceeds in verses 18–19 to a sharp and vividly pictured description of the ignominious end awaiting Jehoiakim: "With the burial of an ass he shall be buried, dragged and cast forth beyond the gates of Jerusalem" (v. 19). The precise circumstances that eventually surrounded Jehoiakim's death are not clear, but his untimely and shameful end are again foretold in 36:30, after he had rejected the message of Jeremiah's prophetic scroll. Jehoiakim had rebelled against Nebuchadnezzar's imperial demands in 601 B.C.; it appears probable that both here and in 36:30 the prophecy regarding his end dates from the time after his withdrawal of allegiance had taken place. Undoubtedly, Jeremiah and probably many in the nation would see this act of rebellion as a disastrous step that would lead to a violent end for the king. This is clearly implied by the tone of what Jeremiah has declared. However the conventional phraseology used in II Kings 24:6 to describe the king's death, "he slept with his fathers," would seem to point to a death from natural causes even though he was only thirty-six years of age (II Kings 23:36). In this case, although such an early death could have been regarded as a divine punishment for his oppressive rule, it scarcely fits the precise terms of the prophetic prediction concerning it. It seems unlikely therefore that the prophecy has been composed as an interpretation of this death after it had actually occurred. However the truth is that we do not know all the circumstances surrounding his death while Jerusalem was under threat of siege by the Babylonians. He was succeeded briefly ("three months," II Kings 24:8) by his son Jehoiachin, who was then replaced by his uncle under the royal name of Zedekiah (II Kings 24:17). Some element of mystery surrounding the circumstances of Jehoiakim's end does remain, which cannot rule out altogether the possibility of popular action against him. He undoubtedly had many enemies

134

within the nation, which would have given strong cause for an assassination attempt. Besides this the king's hope of support from Egypt in his rebellion against Babylon had been shown to be misplaced (II Kings 24:7). There may possibly have been some internal action against Jehoiakim that the court historian was anxious not to disclose, or did not fully know about.

Refusing a formal state funeral and foretelling of the violence perpetrated against the dead body of the king (v. 19) would then have been related to this. However the fact that Jehoiakim's son succeeded him, if only briefly, would suggest that the king died from natural causes. If there was a literal fulfillment of the prophecy concerning the king's shameful final state, it would most likely have been desecration of the royal tomb once Jerusalem had surrendered to the Babylonians.

A Prophecy Against the City of Jerusalem (22:20–23)

The connected series of prophetic indictments of the Davidic kings of Judah by Jeremiah is interrupted in verses 20–23 with a strong warning of coming judgment upon the city of Jerusalem. It must originally have been proclaimed at a time close to that of the preceding prophecy, when Judah was threatened by the armies of Babylon in 599–598 B.C. The connection with the preceding prophecy lies especially in the condemnation of "the shepherds" (v. 22). Such a broad metaphor refers to the royal house of David together with other members of the ruling party in Jerusalem. We may consider the possibility that the editor intended to make clear that others besides the king himself shared in the blame for Jerusalem's downfall. The king was not to be the sole scapegoat for the nation's misfortunes when in fact he had been supported by counselors and others who shared his ambitions, who stood to gain from them, and who further encouraged him in his foolhardy political miscalculations in regard to the power of Babylon. At any rate Jeremiah declares that they are to suffer too for their share in the city's and the nation's excesses. This threat is given metaphorical expression through the description of Jerusalem as "Lebanon" (v. 23), hinting at the extensive use of cedarwood brought from Lebanon and used in the city's buildings. The indictment thereby shows how the king had certainly not been alone in the building ventures on which he had embarked.

135

Once Jeremiah's editors had established the primary focus on Zedekiah and the royal house of David he represented (21:4–7), a whole series of further prophecies from Jeremiah regarding the royal house were seen to be in order.

Two Prophecies Concerning Jehoiachin (22:24–30)

Jehoiakim died while Jerusalem was under threat of siege from the armies of Babylon in 598 B.C.; he was succeeded by his son Jehoiachin (Coniah). He reigned in the city for only three months (II Kings 24:8) before its surrender and he was deposed and taken as a prisoner to Babylon (II Kings 24:15). It appears that he was removed partly as punishment for his father's rebellious action and partly to keep him as a hostage. In any event he was destined to live out the rest of his days in Babylon, being released from close imprisonment after thirty-seven years (II Kings 25:27–30). We have from Jeremiah in 22:24–27 and 28–30 two separate prophecies concerning the fate of this king, the second of which certainly dates from a time after his deportation to Babylon. The first of these utterances addresses the king directly and, although it is in prose, it would appear to foretell the king's inevitable submission to Babylon and his being taken, along with the queen mother, into exile there. The threat is made under the image of a signet-ring set on God's right hand and torn off to be given to others. No doubt kings wore such rings as a mark of their divinely given office. The full implication of the imagery is not clear, but it would appear that not only Jehoiachin would forfeit his royal status but this would also mark the end of the Davidic dynasty he represented. The later reference to this prophecy by Haggai (2:23–24) made it clear that the prophet was well aware of the possibility of interpreting it in this way and was concerned to annul any such interpretation. Since the signet-ring was a badge of the kingly office, the use of the metaphor could be understood to imply even more; it could amount to a threat that Jehoiachin's deportation would mark the end of the royal office in Judah altogether. This in fact happened for a period of almost four centuries until the office of king was revived under the Hasmoneans.

A further prophetic threat concerning Jehoiachin, this time in poetic form and addressed to the people who bemoaned the loss of their king, is set in 22:28–30. The king is compared to a pot which when smashed is good for nothing and is thrown away. The meaning of this threat in terms of Jehoiachin's personal fate is then spelled out clearly: Neither he nor any of his children would succeed in ever again sitting on the throne of Judah. This undoubtedly must have marked much of the popular expectation concerning what had happened in 598 B.C. and this lingered on for some while afterwards. The hope was that Jehoiachin would return from his Babylonian exile, that he would regain his throne in Jerusalem, or at least his children would do so. The whole question of the future of the kingship over Judah and the significance of the Davidic dynasty was to remain a crucially important one during the years of the exile and for some time afterwards. It reappears again in a further dimension in the prophecies of Jeremiah 33, where further discussion is in order (see esp. on 33:14–26).

The attitude of the prophet, since we need not doubt the Jeremianic origin of 22:28–30, clearly rejected the possibility of any restoration of the Davidic monarchy through Jehoiachin or even of countenancing the possibility of the king's eventual return. Most likely we should take this as indicative of Jeremiah's attitude to the question of the kingship and its place in God's purpose for Israel. In his understanding its removal was not a catastrophe that seriously threatened the continuance of Israel as God's people. When Zedekiah was placed on the throne in place of Jehoiachin, Jeremiah appears to have gone along with this step quite willingly and co-operatively. Later, after the events of 587 B.C., he was equally willing to work with the non-Davidic Gedaliah in the office of governor. The Davidic kingship was, in his regard, entirely conditional upon the willingness of the individual kings to serve the genuine interests of the people and to guide them in the ways of God's law. If they failed to do this, then their place in the divine economy of Israel was forfeit and the nation could continue as God's people without a kingly office or a Davidic dynasty.

Three Prophecies of Hope (23:1–8)

We now encounter a series of three short prophecies, all prose, which are hopeful in their content and concerned with the future welfare and administration of Judah. It is unlikely that any one of them derives directly from Jeremiah. Rather they are in this position to amplify the picture of the future after the threatening prophecies of the preceding chapter and in particular to provide an affirmative theological stance with respect to the kingship. The first of these (23:1–4) takes up again the metaphor of "the shepherds" which has already been used in 22:22. In this fresh prophecy the point is made that God wholly condemns and repudiates the irresponsible and misguided shepherds of the past who had misled the people and brought them to destruction (vv. 1–2). The punishment they received (at the hands of the Babylonians) was therefore wholly deserved and necessary. Over against this condemnation there is a promise that God would provide in the future trustworthy and obedient shepherds who would care for the people and lead them with safety and care (vv. 3–4). It will be they who will bring the people back from the lands to which they had been driven.

The addition of this point at this juncture may appear at first to be needless and rather obvious. However it sets out a point of considerable importance. Since the preceding prophecies had presented a negative judgment upon the office of the king, it might have appeared that the role of the "shepherds," including that of the king at the head, would disappear altogether. Yet this was not to be so; it would be replaced by a new body of responsible and trustworthy leaders. No doubt the metaphor of "shepherd," as used of a king, is entirely self-explanatory and its use was undoubtedly very ancient. It was, however, sufficiently undefined to be applicable to leaders of many kinds, not necessarily those holding the office and title of "king." It is this possibility for the future that is now envisaged; it lends divine authority for the changing political structure and for the administration of the people of Israel and Judah that emerged after the debacle of 587 B.C. Not only would there be new forms of leadership and government in the land of Judah, such as that which emerged under Gedaliah, but leadership of other kinds would also emerge among Jews of the dispersion. In this way the prophecies of Jeremiah provided an important step in the transition from the hitherto prevailing concept of Israel as a nation to a new but not fully developed one in which Israel would emerge as a covenant people living in dispersion among the nations of many lands. There they would remain until the time when God would bring about the great "return" to the land of Israel (Judah).

138

A second prophetic comment, this time directly concerning the kingship, is set to follow in 23:5–6 and has aroused a good deal of discussion on account of the play it makes upon the name of Zedekiah. Many earlier commentators have taken it to be authentic to Jeremiah (cf. Skinner, pp. 311ff.). Others more recently have questioned this (cf. S. Herrmann, pp. 210ff.). The prophecy expresses a future hope that a king, who will bear the name "The LORD [Yahweh] is our righteousness" (v. 6), will be "raised up" (i.e., elevated to the throne) by God to fulfill the promise attached to the Davidic dynasty. This precisely is the meaning of the name Zedekiah; the Babylonian administration placed Zedekiah on the throne in place of the deported Jehoiachin. The interpretation favored by Skinner and others has seen this as an extremely subtle rejection of Zedekiah, implying that he was unworthy of his name (and royal office) and would be one day replaced by one who would bear it more appropriately.

We must consider, however, that Jeremiah's attitude towards Zedekiah appears to have been altogether more open and equivocal than is implicit in such an interpretation and that the saying itself fails to make clear the all-important point that Zedekiah is being rejected. Much more likely, Zedekiah was already dead at the time this prophecy was composed and it has been added here to find within the name of the last of Judah's kings a word of hope and assurance for the future. It is simply taking the last king's name as a prophecy, not about this king himself but about the royal dynasty he represented. In this way it is wholly in line with the prophecies set out in 33:14–26.

A final word of promise in 23:7–8 rounds off the assurances about the future leadership of Israel contained in the immediately preceding verses. This hope required the firm definition that it would lead on to a return of all who had been scattered among the nations, both from Israel and Judah, and their resettlement in their own land. So the final affirmation "Then they shall dwell in their own land" (v. 8) was to be and was to remain a central important feature of the message of hope for all Old Testament prophecy. Although there was a partial return after the fall of Babylon in 538 B.C., the unfolding process of history was to leave an ever expanding number of Jews scattered among the nations. They experienced, by their very survival, partial fulfillment of the promise of God for their future. Yet this was not to be the full and complete message of hope delivered through prophecy. There was to be a "great return," so alongside all other expressions of hope for the future and however

139

much its fulfillment was postponed, this needed to be kept constantly in view to remain a feature of Jewish hope throughout the later Old Testament period. The life of "dispersion" was to be understood as no more than an interim manifestation of God's providential purpose for the Chosen People of Israel.

Jeremiah 23:9–40
Five Prophecies Denouncing the False Prophets

The powerful series of denunciations in 21:1—23:8 clearly singled out Judah's monarchy as the institution most heavily to blame for the misfortunes of Judah; we now have a sequence of five short prophecies of the same general nature denouncing the false prophets: 23:9–12, 13–15, 16–22, 23–32 and 33–40. They lack specific circumstantial details which would show when they were proclaimed publicly and what particular messages Jeremiah so decisively brands as false. The folly and error of the messages of the prophets are condemned first on the grounds of the adulterous way of life some of them pursued (23:10, 14). They are further accused of stealing oracles one from another and of declaring things on the basis of their own invention (v. 16) or as an interpretation of their dreams (v. 25). A much fuller and more circumstantially detailed account of a major controversy between Jeremiah and a false prophet over an issue of substantial political importance is set out in 27:1—28:17. In this case the false prophet is named, and the occasion which provoked controversy was Hananiah's prophecy that Judah would shortly be free from the yoke of Babylonian imperial control.

The first of the denunciations by Jeremiah couples an accusation that the prophets were adulterers with a further accusation against the priests who were defiling God's house, the temple (v. 11). Almost certainly we should link this accusation of immorality with the cultic rituals derived from the worship of Baal where sexual fertility rites were regarded as a way of ensuring "life," productivity, and health. Jeremiah argues that instead such people achieve precisely the opposite effect and make their land barren and dry (v. 10). Instead of life they achieve death! The accusations are of a rather general nature

140

but must evidently have been readily open to confirmation on the part of any serious enquirer. Jeremiah confesses to having been deeply disturbed and broken by what he had witnessed (v. 9), suggesting that the flagrant way such prophets displayed their indifference to fundamental social obligations greatly shocked him.

The second of the denunciations of the false prophets in verses 13–15 reiterates the charge of adulterous conduct (v. 14) and identifies the prophets as directly and closely associated with Jerusalem (v. 15). All of this suggests that the false prophets were closely linked with the royal court and its policies. In this case they may also have been active in fomenting hostility towards Jeremiah and his message. Both the first and second of Jeremiah's denunciations conclude with firm pronouncements concerning the evil and untimely end God had reserved for such dangerous and misleading prophets (vv. 12, 15). Even so, the precise form their evil end will take is not specified.

The third of the short prophetic denunciations affirms in verses 16–17 that the false prophets were simply speaking words of delusion from their own hearts. What they had to say was characterized by words of assurance and consolation (v. 17) which bore no relationship to reality. They asserted that disaster would not befall the people, thereby encouraging headstrong and foolhardy policies. The imagery of the true prophet then used by Jeremiah is that of one who has effectively stood in the council of the Lord God (vv. 18, 22) and who as a consequence of this knew what God had prepared for his people. Jeremiah had consistently declared that this intention was punishment and judgment upon the wicked (vv. 19–20). Perhaps the most incisive point in Jeremiah's words had been his insistence that the people of Judah had become the enemies of God!

In all three of these short declarations from Jeremiah it is noteworthy that no circumstantial detail is given that would enable us to recognize at what period in his ministry such words were proclaimed publicly. The accusations against the prophets are linked with broad issues of misconduct such as could have occurred at any time. Possibly these sayings were uttered at various periods during Jeremiah's long career, so they can represent a persistent and distressing level of opposition and frustration encountered by him. However much he strove with full moral integrity and powerful speeches to proclaim the truth 141 concerning the purposes and intentions of God, he found his words contradicted by those of other prophets, especially those from Jerusalem. Very plausibly these prophets were themselves endeavoring to curry favor at the royal court by declaring words supportive of the king and his policies. Jeremiah had no way by which to establish the truth of his declarations against the falsity of what his prophetic opponents had to offer. It was a case of one prophet's words against those of another, who outwardly appeared as fully authorized and assured as the true prophet. Nor were there any inflexible and easily recognizable proofs by which Jeremiah could demonstrate that he was the true and faithful spokesman of God. In this regard he must have felt that the attention given to the charge of personal immorality of those who contradicted his message constituted proof and was a sign evident to all of their perversity and worthlessness as prophets. Nevertheless it appears to be clear to the reader that they still had listeners and followers who accepted the truth of what they had to say.

We find after these three denunciations of false prophets yet another sharp and forthright denunciation by Jeremiah of such figures (vv. 23–32). This unit is far from being uniform in structure, and it appears probable that two short poetic fragments from Jeremiah (vv. 23–24 and 28–29) have subsequently been expanded by Jeremiah's editors into a prose composition. It is possible to suggest a reconstruction of a poetic unit throughout, but this is neither necessary nor likely.

We have consistently noted that an important feature of the composition of the book has been that at several points the editors have placed the all too brief words of Jeremiah in a context which brought out their fuller implications. This appears to have been the case here. The starkness of the contrast between the true prophet who has nothing in his life to hide from God and the false prophet who has is stressed. The false prophets are shown as persons who make important and pretentious claims, but on the strength of wholly worthless and unreliable reasons. They have dreams, as all people do; then they proclaim a message from God on the basis of their interpretation of such dreams (vv. 28, 32). Their words have nothing more substantial behind them than this! They also steal prophetic sayings from one another (v. 30), thereby openly showing how empty they are of any true understanding of the will and purpose of God. Their preaching of the messages they dress up with their conventional phrases and stylized language purports to be the message of God, but is in reality nothing more than something they have themselves thought up (v. 31).

142

Throughout these four sections we have been brought face to face with a prominent theme in the Book of Jeremiah. False prophecy is a threat to the integrity of the true prophet and serves to undermine the force and clarity with which the word of God is heard. The charge by Jeremiah that the false prophets are guilty of flagrant moral misconduct in the form of adultery (23:10,14) is used to show the hollowness of their claims to be servants and messengers of God. Yet their persistent purveying of oracular revelations and their plausible claims of being recipients of divine messages show how difficult, almost to the point of impossibility, it was to make judgments between the competing claims of contradictory prophetic messages. The Book of Deuteronomy lays down certain tests for the discrimination of true from false prophecy (Deut. 13:1–5; 18:15–22). It becomes evident, however, that what is laid down here offered only partial and inadequate criteria for distinguishing between the true and the false. It could be argued that the true prophet proved himself by dire warnings of divinely ordained doom and judgment (28:8–9). This formula was too rigid and wooden to work with, since there was certainly a place for messages of assurance and hope within the divine purpose. Only a sensitive and morally alert understanding of the nature of God, awake also to the facts of the contemporary religious and political scene, could hope to recognize the true prophet from the false.

It must also be borne in mind that not only were there no clear-cut external criteria by which true prophecy could be distinguished from false but even the very idea of "true" prophecy is not in itself wholly clear. On one side truth in prophecy was linked to the foretelling of the true nature and future outcome of events. If prophets made threats and disasters followed them, then these disasters bore out the "truth" of the prophecy. However, as Deuteronomy 13:1–5 also points out, conformity to subsequent events could not be the sole criterion of truth; truth required also a genuine conformity to the demand for sole and effective allegiance to the Lord as the God of Israel. Even this however was not in itself enough, since there also needed to be a conformity to the authentic tradition of the Lord and his demands upon his people Israel (27:14; 29:8–9). The eventual resolution of this problem appears to have been achieved, insofar as it was at all resolved in a clear-cut fashion, only by the formation of a canonical corpus of prophecy (see further below on 27:1—28:17)

143

A concluding unit of the present section concerned with false prophets and false prophecy is set out in 23:33–40 under a series of word-plays on the theme of "burden." This Hebrew word *(massa')* means "what is lifted up (i.e., in speech [a declaration]) or in carrying (a burden). The section, which can scarcely derive from Jeremiah himself, represents a further reflection on the significance of prophecy and the reasons why Jeremiah's prophecies went unheeded at the time they were given. The prophet affirmed the divine origin of his message by using the traditional formula "the burden (oracle) of the LORD," thereby establishing a divine authority for it. Verse 33 affirms, however, that the hearer of such a bold claim should challenge the prophet or priest and his right to use such an authoritative mode of speech. The prophets and priests, far from proclaiming God's word and God's declaration (burden), were in fact offering a deadweight of useless and pretentious sayings. They merely dressed up their own ideas and their meaningless dreams with solemn affirmations that made them sound important but were in fact quite worthless.

It is on this basis that verses 36–40 aver that all such talk of the burden of the Lord must cease. It had become meaningless clap-trap that came between men and women and a true knowledge of God. Priests and prophets who had bolstered their own self-importance by use of such expressions would be hurled out of the land into exile (thereby bringing a yet further play on the idea of "lifting up"). The religious duties that they had customarily performed would become the subject of bitter reproach and shame. The whole section uses the various meanings of "burden" to explore the danger of religious hypocrisy. Priests and prophets were showing all the outward features of religious zeal and authoritative knowledge of God, when in fact what they had to say and teach was based on nothing more substantial than their own empty imaginings.

Jeremiah 24
The Good and Bad Figs

144

The vision of chapter 24 concerning the good and bad figs and the three summary reviews in chapter 25 that follow must be regarded as essentially editorial compilations of Jeremiah's book. This by no means rules out their being based on authentic reminiscences of sayings from the prophet himself, which is highly probable; nevertheless, they were put together in the light of what had happened with the fall of Jerusalem in 587 B.C. to the Babylonians and the new significance this brought for those who had already been exiled to Babylon in 598 B.C. Although when viewed superficially the vision of chapter 24 appears to be little more than a further warning of the judgment awaiting those who remained in Judah under Zedekiah's kingship in 598 B.C., it also contains within it more forward looking reflections concerning the hope of the nation's eventual restoration. It represents a divinely affirmed upholding of the position and status of the exiles who had been taken to Babylon in 598 and a decisive closing off of hope for the large segment of the population that had survived the initial impact of Babylonian intervention in Judah's affairs.

The vision itself is a simple one, undoubtedly suggesting an origin in an actual experience of Jeremiah in which he saw two baskets of figs set down in front of the temple. The time was shortly after the removal into Babylonian exile of the young king Jehoiachin (Coniah, 22:28, also called Jeconiah). Along with him had gone a large contingent of the wealthier and more able citizens of Judah (II Kings 24:10–17), where they became in effect Judean hostages of Babylon. Their deportation was to serve as a punishment for them, but it seems possible that they were also intended to be used as a political "lever" to ensure the good behavior of Zedekiah and those who had been left in Judah. Certainly the Babylonians were more concerned about the most effective way of retaining a grip upon Judah than they were about having prisoners closer to home, as had regularly been the fate of those defeated in war.

The interpretation of the vision of the two baskets of figs, one basket good and ready for eating and the other so bad that they could not be eaten at all (24:2–3), is transparent. The good figs represented the deportees who had been taken to Babylon and the bad figs those who had remained in Jerusalem under their new ruler Zedekiah. Corresponding to the evaluation of "good" and "bad" was the future destiny of the respective communities the prophet outlines. The good are those taken to Babylon and who will be cared for and treated favorably by God so that they will eventually be brought back to their land (vv.

145

6–7). Conversely the "bad" figs represent those who remained behind in Judah under Zedekiah. They were to suffer every kind of ruination and devastation—sword, famine, disease—until they were utterly wiped out (vv. 9–10).

Along with this group, whose destiny was to remain behind in Judah, was later to be added a third group, who fled to Egypt for political refuge after further setbacks and troubles had overtaken them in Judah (42—45). It is noteworthy that the negative assessment of the community that remained in Judah along with Zedekiah is further supported by Ezekiel 33:23–29, where a detailed list of the offenses committed by those in the land of Judah is given. It is not difficult to speculate that the original message delivered by Jeremiah to the community that remained in Jerusalem after 598, as Jeremiah himself had done, was to challenge the self-congratulation and mistaken self-esteem displayed by those who had been left as survivors in Judah. They counted themselves fortunate and singularly blessed by God, reasoning that they must have pleased God to have survived such dangers. In the present form of the account, however, which has clearly been composed after some interval from the original events (witnessed by its prose form and Deuteronomistic vocabulary), a much wider perspective is introduced. This undoubtedly has been influenced by what had happened for the community in Judah in the intervening years.

When we enquire as to the reason for such a categorical and inevitably onesided evaluation of the relative merits and expectations of the two communities, various possibilities present themselves. Certainly there has been a measure of hindsight imposed on a recollection of an earlier prophecy. Yet this cannot be the sole explanation. For this we need to bear in mind that much of the spiritual leadership had passed to Babylon, after Jeremiah and others along with him had felt forced to flee to Egypt. This Babylonian community of exiles, whose status must itself have been considerably affected by what had happened in 587, became the central focus for the hope of Israel's eventual restoration. Henceforth the idea of "return" (from exile, coupled with a "turning back" to God in repentance) was to become the central key to an understanding of the hope of Judaism.

146

This fact has become so fully established in the Old Testament, and most emphatically in the entire corpus of the pro-

phetic literature, that its surprising character is easily overlooked. The importance of the land itself, the temple site, as
well as the aspirations of those who had remained in Judah were
all set aside and the idea of the exiles' return, as the loyal bearers
of the Israelite tradition, to the homeland to restore the nation
was set in the forefront of hope. This is all the more startling
when we consider the limited chance of those deported to
Babylon and who survived there actually retaining a real sense
of purpose and identity living under such limited freedom. In
some respects the religious leadership in Judah after the murder of Gedaliah had become too compromised to retain confidence as the spiritual guardians of Israel's heritage and
probably the political administration imposed on the community failed to command widespread popular support. At all
events the torch of hope and expectation of Israel's eventual
restoration to greatness was handed on to the exiles in Babylon.
Jeremiah's account of his vision in chapter 24 is used as a platform for expressing this belief with absolute clarity. This undoubtedly entailed a deep spiritual reorientation as well as a
shift of political emphasis that brought about a long period of
tension and conflict before an acceptable religious community
could again thrive in Judah. This tension and conflict contained
the key to understanding many of the important changes that
emerged during the next two centuries.

However much we relate this vision of the good and bad
figs to the contemporary political situation Jeremiah and his
compatriots faced, in the end it pointed to the priority of the
moral and spiritual over the geographical and the political.
The community in exile came to be looked upon and certainly
to look upon themselves as the remnant chosen by God to
bring about a glorious future for Israel. The inherited and well
established commitments to the land as the most precious of
God's "gifts" to Israel (cf. Brueggemann, pp. 45ff.), the benefits deriving from the location of the temple on Mount Zion,
and to a certain degree the role of the Davidic kingship were
all set at a lower level of religious importance than a genuine
seeking after God with a whole heart (cf. 29:12–14). God is not
to be found through physical symbols of his presence but
through an inner spiritual movement of heart and will. These
features appear and reappear prominently in Jeremiah so that
this prophetic book has become a fundamental charter for the
spiritual development of Jewish life in diaspora. In line with

147

this the theme of "return" (Heb. *shub*) has been elevated to a central aim of Jewish piety, pointing to the return to God with a whole heart (cf. 24:7), which alone can be the foundation for an eventual return to the land and the recovery of full nationhood.

Jeremiah 25
God's Judgment

An Interpretative Summary (25:1–14)

The section we now encounter bears all the hallmarks of a major editorial piece designed and included to provide an overall assessment of the context and meaning of Jeremiah's prophecies. In the Greek (Septuagint) translation the main body of "foreign nation" prophecies (which occur in the Hebrew text in chapters 46—51) follow, in a different order, after 25:13 (see Introduction for the significance of this). The interpretative summary presents a perspective upon the whole initial period of Jeremiah's prophecies from the beginning in "the fourth year of Jehoiakim" (605/604 B.C.) until the first collapse of Jerusalem before Nebuchadnezzar's siege and capture of the city in 598 B.C. The section can hardly have been composed by Jeremiah himself and has clearly been intended to assist in the interpretation of a collected body of Jeremiah's prophecies. Such a collection must have existed in scroll form and presumably included the material from the scroll written for Jehoiakim and referred to in chapter 36. The summary contains a full survey of the basic themes of Jeremiah's message:

(1) Judah has sinned by worshiping false gods and must now turn from this evil way (vv. 5–6). Earlier prophets had also declared this message, but the people had remained unrepentant and had failed to change their conduct.

(2) The time had come for judgment to fall and this was now about to come in the person of the king of Babylon, Nebuchadnezzar. At his coming the land would be made desolate and ravaged (vv. 8–11).

148

(3) The period of Babylonian rule would extend for seventy years, thereby embracing the normal lifespan of Judah's citi-

zens (cf. further on 29:10). After this period had elapsed Babylon too would be punished.

(4) Other nations would also be caught up in the same web of violent international events brought on by Babylonian military conquest and ambitions. It would involve great human suffering (v. 14).

The fact that many other nations had been caught up in the same web of suffering raises the wide question: What divine purposes are served by this? This theme becomes central as a reason for the inclusion of the "foreign nation" prophecies of chapters 46—51.

The Divine Judgment
on the Nations (25:15-29)

The preceding section has clearly been intended as a concluding summary surveying the content and meaning of Jeremiah's prophecies in the face of the threat from, and attacks by, Babylon. The present section, which displays a number of affinities with its introductory summary, looks for the significance of God's acts of judgment upon Judah's bordering nations. Like Judah, they too had become involved with the extension of Mesopotamian power as far as Egypt and Arabia. At his call Jeremiah had been designated "a prophet to the nations" (1:5). Here, and in the prophecies set in chapters 46—51, we find the justification for this particular part of Jeremiah's prophetic office.

The prophecies addressed to non-Israelite cities and nations, represented in all the main collections of prophecies (Amos 1:3—2:6; Isa. 13—23; Ezek. 25—32), are in many of their features among the most impressive but most puzzling of all that has been preserved of prophecy in the Old Testament. Who was intended to hear them? How could the prophecies influence those to whom they were addressed if they could not be present to hear the prophet speak? How were the men and women of Judah expected to respond to the content of such prophecies? Were they simply matters of public interest, or were they recognized as possessing a direct link with the attitudes and policies being canvassed in Judah? Various perspectives are possible and several of them have been suggested as relevant. Such prophecies addressed to foreign powers represent in a number of ways one of the most fundamental forms

149

of prophecy. They provided an opportunity for the delivery of threats and warnings to foreign powers who might appear as a danger to Israel. We may compare Psalm 2, the royal coronation psalm which includes an element of warning to potential aggressors (cf. Ps 2:2–3, 10–11).

We should bear in mind that at times it would have been important for a prophet to declare God's verdict upon other nations with whom Israel or Judah had formed an alliance. Isaiah's prophecies against Egypt (cf. Isa. 30:1–17) readily fit this perspective in view of the importance of Hezekiah's treaty with Egypt as a part of his plan for rebellion against Assyria. Not all foreign nation prophecies, however, can be explained in this way, and we must certainly consider that a wider point of view was being sought by Jeremiah's editors.

It was evident that the impact of Babylonian power upon what remained of Israel had been immense, and Jeremiah's explanations for this in terms of Israel's apostasy were forthrightly presented. It was needful, however, to say something of those neighboring nations who had been victims of Babylon's imperial expansion but could not be accused of apostasy from the worship of the Lord God in the way Israel had been. The point can readily be seen to be of exceptional theological importance since it raised the question of whether the purpose of the Lord God included these other nations. Were they merely to be seen as the accidental victims of God's controversy with Israel? Even more controversially, Were the gods of each of these nations separately involved in similar plans of judgment against the peoples who worshiped them? It certainly could not have escaped popular attention that the Babylonian explanation being aggressively proclaimed was that Marduk, the great god of Babylon, was the dominant power behind all that had happened and that the gods of all the minor nations were showing themselves to be powerless and defeated. With immense boldness and great theological insight the editors and clearly the prophet Jeremiah himself saw the hand of the Lord, the God of the despised and defeated nation of Judah (Israel), as the real power behind all that had happened. This then clearly implied that the Lord God had a purpose and plan embracing the destinies of the nations who were at one and the same time neighbors to Judah and fellow victims of the Babylonian sweep into the west. This is more fully detailed in the prophecies now set in chapters 46—51. What we are offered in 25:15–29 is a summary outline of the prophetic conclusion concerning God's plans for the nations of the Levant. It was a plan tested in the light of events and was very far from being without hope for the future.

The Judgment of God Upon All Nations (25:30–38)

We are presented here with a further comprehensive summary of God's punitive actions towards the nations. What has preceded it shows that this primarily refers to the nations of the Levant who were overpowered by the might of Babylon in the years after 604 B.C. It represents a summary survey, this time couched in vivid poetic imagery, of the wrath of God against these nations such as is outlined in greater detail in the prophecies of chapters 46—51. God's violent anger against these nations is its single theme; this alone can explain the fearful punishment that had been inflicted upon them. Such a picture of an angry deity contrasts with the more familiar and congenial portrayal of God as loving, forebearing, and patient (cf. Exod. 34:6). It raises questions of considerable theological importance for an understanding of the biblical presentation of God as a revelatory whole. We are forced to note that such strong and persistent imagery in the biblical portrait of God is so deeply embedded in the biblical tradition as to require full attention. It cannot be claimed that this picture of an angry and violent God represents an "Old Testament perspective" contrasted with the loving and caring picture of God given in the New Testament, as popular apologetics has sometimes attempted. Both aspects—that God is loving and caring, but also sometimes angry and violent—are to be found in both Testaments.

It must furthermore be insisted that to dismiss the biblical language concerning the divine wrath as inappropriate, or even offensive, to the modern religious mind achieves nothing at all by way of resolving the tensions in the reality of human history and human experience. Once we accept that the prophetic literature arose directly and immediately as part of a human response to the realities of historical existence and in seeking to discover and interpret the divine meaning of this existence, then it is apparent that it had, of necessity, to relate to the painful, as well as the favorable, features of this. It is apparent that the great period of Old Testament prophecy derives from

151

Israel and Judah in the time when they encountered the imperial might of Mesopotamia, first with Assyria and then Babylon. The prophecies of Jeremiah derive from a pivotal point in this history. The belief that God could be angry and violent was directly related to the fact that events of great violence which incurred immense human suffering had taken place. To have dismissed such events as lying outside the range and purpose of God or as the consequence of the inability of the Lord God to cope with the rival power of other gods would have amounted to theological and spiritual defeat. Somehow these events had to be set within the divine scheme of things, so that the language and imagery of divine wrath provided an important step in the direction of asserting the unity, coherence, and ultimate purposefulness of human existence under the providential care of the one and only God. Whatever difficulties remain for us in reconciling the divine wrath with the divine love as theological concepts, they are each of them vitally important images for an interpretation of the nature of God.

In the Old Testament portrait of God there is undoubtedly an element of anthropomorphism which is never far away in all that the prophets have to say concerning God's plans and intentions. A purely wooden and arbitrary picture of God is never presented, but one which relates closely and directly to the realities of human experience. What makes the prophetic literature such a unique and important contribution to the religious understanding of life is its persistent concern to embrace the elements of catastrophe, defeat, and great human suffering in the overall understanding of God. In the face of the evident temptation at the time to resort to a fatalism which encouraged human despair and a sense of hopelessness, the prophets never lost sight of the ultimate beneficence of the divine purpose. Nor did they submit to the notion that human beings were of no account to God, who could therefore inflict whatever sufferings he wished upon them at a mere whim. The ultimate goodness, reasonableness, and intelligibility of the divine purpose are firmly insisted upon, even in the face of quite obvious difficulties in reconciling some of the tensions that such insistence brought into view. If the imagery of the divine "anger" retains a strong coloring from this anthropomorphic legacy in the Israelite understanding of God, it nevertheless made possible the keeping of theological ideas about God in line with the realities of human experience.

152

Jeremiah 26
Jeremiah and the Message About Jerusalem's Fall

The incident of Jeremiah's declaration of a threat to the very temple of God in Jerusalem begins a section of narrative biographical material which marks a new departure in the form of the book. The first of these sections, stretching from 26:1—29:32, deals with the general subject of the false prophets, which has already been initially raised in 23:9-40. The narrative section, which begins in 26:1 and stretches as far as 45:5, apart from the prophetic additions in 30—31; 33, has sometimes been described as "The Baruch Narrative," or even "The Baruch Biography" (see Introduction). It refers to Jeremiah in the third person and concludes with an address to Baruch personally (45:1-5), so that some measure of connection with Baruch must be postulated. Yet he cannot have been the author of it as a whole, however probable it is that he was an informant for some of its contents. The signs of connection with the Deuteronomistic ideas and language found elsewhere in other parts of the Book of Jeremiah are too marked for this to have been the case. Nor is it in the proper sense a biography, since it covers too short a period of Jeremiah's career for this to have been the author's intention. Further it is concerned with Jeremiah's message, rather than with the person of the prophet, and it selects only certain major illustrative themes as its subject matter.

We can best describe the material of this section of the book as a form of narrative prophecy, arising directly out of the actual utterances of the prophet, but clearly looked at with the benefit of hindsight and in an endeavor to use the prophet's message and experience to interpret a wider range of events. What these events are is left in no doubt: the destruction of Jerusalem by the Babylonians in 587 B.C.; the ruination of the temple, which is viewed as a major catastrophe; and the painful aftermath which followed these earlier tragedies. The overall theme concerns Israel and the divine purpose Jeremiah's prophecies had sought to declare.

153

That Jeremiah proclaimed a warning that even the presence of the temple of God in Jerusalem would not be sufficient to deliver Judah from judgment and that it could become a false symbol of hope and security has already been reported in 7:1–15. The report in 26:1–24 of a personal attack and threat to Jeremiah's life on account of threats he had proclaimed concerning the temple must undoubtedly point to essentially the same prophetic message. It is certainly possible that Jeremiah returned to the theme on more than one occasion. The rather vague date reference for the incident of chapter 26 ("In the beginning of the reign of Jehoiakim") may even point in this direction. It is possibly not meant too precisely but refers to Jehoiakim's early years, especially if we bear in mind that the written scroll of Jeremiah's prophecies is dated to the fourth year of this king's reign (36:1).

There can be no doubt whatsoever that the present report of Jeremiah's message about the temple has been composed sometime after this, and has clearly been affected by the knowledge of what actually took place in 587 B.C. Then, as part of a deliberate punitive act by the Babylonian commander, the temple was destroyed and burned (II Kings 25:9–10). Understandably this appeared to the popular mind of the time to be a massive demonstration of the powerlessness of the Lord God of Israel against the gods of Babylon. It was vitally important therefore to show that this was not the case, and the surest way of demonstrating this was to point out that the Lord God had himself, through his prophet, warned the people beforehand of what he was about to do. Yet was not such an action inconceivable—that God should order the destruction of his own most Holy Place?

It is in this light that we can understand how the recollection of Jeremiah's prophecy concerning the temple became thereby a matter of the greatest importance, and we should certainly not hesitate to conclude that it has been for this reason that the prophecy concerning the temple, and the events surrounding its public delivery, have been set first in the narrative section of the Book of Jeremiah. Whereas there is no very clear chronological order, the whole has been made to pivot around what took place in 587 B.C. Chapter 26 uses the prophet's temple address to provide a thematic introduction to the sequence of reports concerning the message of the prophet, its widespread popular rejection by those in authority, and its terrible fulfillment. A strikingly close parallel is to be found in the manner in which the report of the cleansing of the temple by Jesus has been made into a kind of preface to the ministry of Jesus in Saint John's Gospel (John 2:13–25). Here the conflict that surrounded Jeremiah's preaching opens with a report of the sharp antagonism between Jeremiah and Hananiah, occasioned by the reassuring prophecies of Hananiah and the threatening word of God through Jeremiah.

The message given by Jeremiah is reported briefly and clearly: "Thus says the Lord: If you will not listen to me, to walk in my law which I have set before you, . . . then I will make this house like Shiloh, and I will make this city a curse for all the nations of the earth" (26:4, 6). To be sure, this is only a summary outline of the prophet's words, composed after an interval of time. However, this in no way means that Jeremiah's foretelling of the destruction of the temple has simply been made up after the event with a view to justifying what had happened. On the contrary, the firm recollection that Jeremiah had preached in such terms and had suffered greatly as a consequence of doing so must have been readily accessible to the authors of the narrative. They have rightly and inevitably composed their report of Jeremiah's action in light of its immense bearing on what had subsequently happened. One thing particularly striking is the way in which both here and in 7:1–15 (cf. esp. 7:5–7) the whole issue of the threat to the temple is firmly conditional upon the repentance and good behavior of the people. This measured element of conditional appeal is markedly unlike the sharp categorical way in which Jeremiah usually voiced his threats and warnings. However much we may accept that such a conditional element was implicit in all prophecy, it is clearly the prophet's editors who have spelled it out so boldly.

The reason for making the conditional element in Jeremiah's preaching so explicit is at first not all that clear, even though it is in line with the general manner and theological perspective adopted by those who have shaped and edited the book. Obviously one prime reason for adopting such a position was to give full force to the reasons why it had become necessary for God to order the destruction of his own most sacred dwelling-place. A further reason also appears in the fact that those who have defined the situation in this manner certainly 155 did not wish to rule out the possibility that the temple would one day be rebuilt and refurbished by a restored and penitent community. The temple, of itself, was not offensive to God, only the shameful way in which unrighteous and disobedient people sought to hide within it from the wrath of the deity whom they were purporting to serve. Worship itself had become the ultimate lie; men and women were using worship to protect themselves from the wrath of their God whom they had so deeply offended by their daily manner of life!

A major feature of the theme and structure of chapter 26 concerns the fact that there had already been a most forthright declaration by the prophet Micah of Moresheth (26:16–19; cf. Micah 3:12) of the destruction of the temple in Jerusalem. The fact that Micah had earlier made this threat is drawn into the discussion about Jeremiah as a reason why he should not be punished for what he had declared. However it becomes clear on reflection that this is a rather puzzling and surprising feature to bring into the debate about Jeremiah. If Micah had truly proclaimed this warning, as he certainly had, but the temple had not in fact been destroyed in Micah's time, as it most certainly had not, then Micah was shown to be a misleading prophet. If his message were regarded in this fashion, then he might well have deserved to be punished for his false prophecy! However the whole point in adducing the parallel example of Micah and the fact that he had not been punished in Hezekiah's time (cf. 26:19) had a far deeper significance than this. So far as the compilers of this report were concerned Micah was indeed a true prophet and his message had been fulfilled. But this fulfillment had not come in Hezekiah's reign but in Zedekiah's!

We are here brought face to face with two of the most important developments that had occurred within Old Testament prophecy when this report was composed in Jeremiah's time. First of all it must be regarded as certain that there had come into being a written collection of prophecy establishing a basis of canonical prophetic understanding that now forms a fundamental element of our collection of "The Latter Prophets." Prophecy was being identified with an established body of collected writings in which its central themes and characteristics were established. We need hardly doubt that the precise record of Micah's words reported in 26:18 was drawn from such a preserved body of earlier prophecies.

To a certain degree such a collection of "old" prophecies such as this must be regarded as a surprising development, since they were, at a superficial level, "out of date"—the situations to which they had originally been addressed had passed into history. Yet clearly they were not regarded in this fashion, and this directs our attention to the second point: Micah's threat of the coming destruction of the temple of God in Jerusalem must certainly have been regarded as having been fulfilled in 587 B.C. Undoubtedly the catastrophic nature of this event for those who had experienced it had led to searching Micah's prophecy to find guidance for understanding it. Far from Micah's prophecy being out of date, it had shown itself to be very up to date, and more so than the words of most of the prophets who had been active in Zedekiah's reign. Micah stood as a further witness that the warning of the destruction of the temple, which Jeremiah had proclaimed as a divine possibility, was indeed a true word of God. Even more than this, the combination of Jeremiah's prophecy with that from the earlier Micah should have sufficed to warn citizens of Judah and Jerusalem of the danger facing them. Altogether a very distinctive view of prophecy is drawn upon, which took it for granted that fulfillment of prophecy could be very long delayed but would eventually take place. We find that precisely this distinctive viewpoint, that prophecy could be fulfilled after a long delay, strongly characterizes the theology of the entire history of Joshua—Second Kings (cf. G. von Rad, *Studies in Deuteronomy,* pp. 74ff., and Clements, *Prophecy and Tradition,* pp. 48ff.).

The distinctive handling of Jeremiah's prophecy concerning the threat to the temple of Jerusalem in 26:1–19 provides a central theme and motif for the narrative material that follows as far as chapter 45. It corroborates clearly the basic point (see Introduction) that the standpoint and the needs of the readers of the book were very different from those of the men and women who had first been the hearers of the prophet. The "hearers" had been faced with a prophet who challenged their foolish complacency; those who now read the edited and collected prophecies from Jeremiah were tempted to despair and a total loss of belief—in themselves, in their God, and in the entire notion of Israel's divine election. How, they reasoned, could such misfortunes have befallen them if they were indeed the chosen and beloved people of the Lord God? So it was of the greatest importance to show that Jeremiah had not been alone in declaring God's threat to destroy the temple in Jerusalem. For similar reasons the prophet Ezekiel had reached the most daring and provocative of ideas, that divine judgment

157

must of necessity begin at the very house of God (cf. Ezek. 9:6–10). Essentially we have described this fundamental motif in the structuring and presentation of Jeremiah's prophecies as a concern with theodicy. It was a deep theological development to show that God remained credible.

Micah's prophecy reinforced the contention that the message of Jeremiah concerning God's intended judgment upon Judah and Jerusalem was truly the word of God. Such a message already had a place within the prophetic tradition. This fact made it plain that the threat was not outlandish and impossible but very real. It demanded that the citizens of Judah willingly discern between the true and the false word of prophecy. This theme then occupies the center of attention in the following chapters as far as 29:32. The case of Uriah-ben-Shemaiah in 26:20–23 is then highlighted in anticipation of the question of the nature of true prophecy. The amount of circumstantial detail is surprising, amply attesting to the wealth of detailed information available to Jeremiah's editors. Uriah "prophesied against this city and against this land in words like those of Jeremiah" (v. 20). Unfortunately he suffered an even more severe fate than Jeremiah was to experience, and after having fled to Egypt he was brought back to Judah and executed. Such action serves to draw further attention to the marked ambivalence in the popular attitude towards Jeremiah. He might have been subjected to the same cruel treatment; there remained for him, however, sufficient respect and recognition that what he had to say had a truly authentic place within the prophetic tradition for him to be spared.

Through Micah's words, through those of Jeremiah, and even through such otherwise unknown figures as Uriah, the word of God was shown to be sharper than a two-edged sword, separating truth from falsehood and those of spiritual discernment from those who were blind. Inevitably it generated conflict, suffering, and sometimes martyrdom as the price of its reception. The important narrative of chapter 26 alerts the reader to recognize that to hear the word of God could in no way provide escape from the need to make clear and responsible choices. Rather it was a summons to do so. Far from the prophet guaranteeing the truth of his word, setting the people free from any need to discern whether he was speaking the truth, the very opposite was the case. Responsible preaching by the prophet needed to be matched by responsible hearing on the part of the people.

The concluding note in 26:24 regarding the fact that Jeremiah, unlike the hapless Uriah, was not put on trial for treason or forced to submit to any popular action against him as a traitor to his nation is interesting. Jeremiah's protection was a result of the intervention on his behalf by Ahikam-ben-Shaphan, and the family connections of this person arouse special interest. It appears his father Shaphan was "the Secretary" (cf. Mettinger, pp. 25ff.) in King Josiah's time (II Kings 22:8–14). This office was akin to that of a modern secretary of state, and Shaphan had been an active participant in Josiah's great reform. Furthermore, we learn later in Jeremiah's book that the son of Ahikam was no less than Gedaliah, the person chosen to be governor of Judah under Babylonian suzerainty [after Zedekiah had been deposed and taken to Babylon (39:14; 40:5–7; chap. 41)]. Evidently Ahikam was a powerful political figure from an influential family; his intervention on Jeremiah's behalf should be regarded not simply as an act of personal kindness but as related to a deep respect for Jeremiah's attitude and position. Ahikam clearly saw that Jeremiah was no mean-minded anti-patriot, but a deeply committed religious person who cared for the welfare of his nation and people. The incident, circumstantial as it appears to be at first note, highlights the fact that the whole period of Jeremiah's prophetic activity was fraught with political tension and that Jeremiah's message was one with strong political implications. His was no utopian vision of an unrealizable new social order but a serious contention for the paths of peace and safety.

When we come to analyze the most prominent elements of Jeremiah's message, we find that it rejected a number of the convictions and assumptions that were motivating the royal house and its most influential supporters. These concerned loyalty to the Babylonian suzerainty, with all the demands that this made in the form of heavy regular payments of tribute money. The nation was divided over the question whether the promises of Egyptian support for such a withdrawal of allegiance to a Mesopotamian master could be relied upon to prove effective. Behind such political decisions and popular support for such bold action there lay a number of religious and emotionally attractive beliefs that had taken firm hold in Judah. These focused primarily on the belief that Judah was the surviving part of the Chosen People of Israel and that the long years Judah maintained its sense of religious identity when the former Northern Kingdom had collapsed under Assyrian power was proof of special divine providence. The focal points and effective symbols of that providence were believed to rest in the kingship of the royal house of David and the presence of the temple of the Lord God in Jerusalem.

If we attempt to sum up the political implications of Jeremiah's message, we can see that it necessitated a continued submission on Judah's part to the painful and greedy demands of Nebuchadnezzar. For the time being Jeremiah saw no effective alternative to this continued submission, so that it was in no way misrepresenting his position to see in it a demand that "all nations" submit for a time to the king of Babylon. To do so was the will of God (cf. 27:6!). This was not a lapse into a form of cynical *realpolitik* nor even to despair of a better world order, since in God's time the end of Babylonian rule and the downfall of this great world power would come.

Jeremiah 27
Jeremiah's Warning Concerning the Conspiracy of Rebellion

The present chapter continues and develops the theme of false prophecy and does so by relating it to an event in which emissaries from Edom, Moab, Ammon, and the Phoenician cities of Tyre and Sidon came to Zedekiah in Jerusalem. The conspiracy to rebel is dated in verse 1 to "the beginning of the reign of Zedekiah" (the Hebrew says Jehoiakim, but this cannot be correct). The meeting, however, must have taken place a little later than this and should most probably be dated to the years 594–593 B.C., when Nebuchadnezzar led a military campaign into Syria (cf. Wiseman, pp. 37, 48). Verse 1 appears to have been added to the text at a late stage and is not in the Greek (LXX) (cf. J. A. Thompson, p. 529; R. P. Carroll, *Jeremiah*, pp. 526, 529). We must in any case conclude that chapter 27 represents a narrative compilation written down at some distance in time after the events it recounts had transpired. Certainly it shows an awareness of the devastating consequences of the conspiracy that took effect later and which led up to the siege of Jerusalem in 588–587 B.C. This year of catastrophe overshadows the entire Book of Jeremiah, dictating the selection of material and the emphases that are placed upon individual actions. We have argued consistently that this evidence of using the knowledge gained concerning the outcome of events should in no way be made into a reason for supposing that the report of individual prophecies and actions were simply fabricated later. Rather, the reporting of earlier events has been deeply, but also illuminatingly, colored by what they led to.

We may note that the conspiracy to withhold the payment of tribute money to Babylon and affirm rejection of political allegiance to it was negotiated in 594–593 B.C. It came to nothing; nonetheless, it appears to have established a broad basis of fundamental planning combined with a set of contingency proposals, which were eventually implemented four years later. The results then proved to be disastrous. We find a comparable situation in which the attitude of a prophet against one set of political proposals to rebel came to be revived and reactivated a few years later in Isaiah 20. In this case the rebellion of Philistia against Assyria in 714 has become linked with the later rebellion of Judah in 705–701 B.C.

It is impossible to determine how closely the report in 27:4–11 of what the prophet had to say to the assembled emissaries in Jerusalem corresponds to the actual words used at the time. They show the marks of later reflection and knowledge at many points and effectively regard the period of Babylonian intervention in Judah's affairs, which began in 604 B.C. right up to the time of the fall of Jerusalem in 587, as marking a single connected experience. They are nonetheless most informative and even striking for the way in which they attempt to offer a comprehensive religious explanation for Judah's experience of defeat under Babylonian aggression. From a detached modern standpoint we can define this experience as the understandable attempt of the surviving kingdom of Judah to resist Babylonian westward expansion. Babylon was simply taking over the role that Assyria had played for more than a century, drawn on by the prospect of taking plunder and wielding great international power. Egypt obviously had good reasons for encouraging all those minor nations on its northern borders, which might serve as a buffer against these incursions.

Then in 27:5–7, in words attributed to Jeremiah, there is the concise presentation of what had happened, what was happening, and what would eventually happen in the conflict between Judah and Babylon. It would be hard to overestimate its importance since it brings out clearly the overall understanding of the plan of God that had brought punishment upon Judah through the imperial might of Babylon. It provides a valuable key to understanding the aims which have served to give the Book of Jeremiah its present form and the theology underlying these:

> "It is I [God] who by my great power and my outstretched arm have made the earth, with the men and animals that are on the earth, and I give it to whomever it seems right to me. Now I have given all these lands into the hand of Nebuchadnezzar, the king of Babylon, my servant, and I have given him also the beasts of the field to serve him. All the nations shall serve him and his son and his grandson, until the time of his own land comes; then many nations and great kings shall make him their slave" (27:5–7).

The central message is clear: The Lord God is the creator of all the earth, and he has the power and the right to give it, with all its creatures, to whomever he wills. He has chosen, for reasons not explicitly defined, to give all nations and creatures into the power of Nebuchadnezzar of Babylon. For any nation or individual to resist this in the present time is to run counter to the plan of God. In God's (undefined) time, however, the end of Babylonian power would come and Nebuchadnezzar, who is presented as the central and representative figure of this power, would himself become a slave. The centrality of the theological assertion is complete: The Lord God is the creator of the earth and the controller of the destiny of all nations. The frequently asserted distinction between a God of creation and a God of history is totally rejected and swept aside, if it ever really existed in the minds of Israelites. However this assertion of divine sovereignty is tempered by a knowledge of the realities of history, even where this appears strange and unexpected. So it is that Nebuchadnezzar is regarded as God's servant (v. 6) who must be obeyed. The whole, which demands further reflection in the context of the foreign nation prophecies of chapters 46—51, is one of the most central theological assessments of the book and has wide political and theological implications for the development of Judaism.

162 When we ask how arrival at this advanced and realistic theological position came to be and how closely it corresponds to Jeremiah's own theological position, we may point to two important considerations. The first of these has a high degree

of moral significance, since it relates to the fact that Jeremiah and prophets who preceded him had come to know only too well the fearful consequences and political futility of rebellion against the major Mesopotamian powers, Assyria and Babylonia. Submission to Assyria had first become a political necessity for Judah and Israel from the middle of the eighth century, and resistance to this, with its economic, political, and religious demands, had proved disastrous. It had been the cause of the total collapse of the Northern Kingdom of Israel which thereby lost much of its political identity.

During the years since the middle of the eighth century B.C. both Israel and Judah had found themselves helpless in the face of a far superior military power bent on plunder and the exercise of firm suzerain control. Behind this power the great prophets of Israel had firmly believed that they could discern the righteous and punitive hand of God. Rebellion had been futile, bringing only an increase in bloodshed and further suffering and incurring more economic loss. The agriculture of the region, on which the peoples depended for their survival and which was never more than partially secure, was reduced to a ruinous level bringing famine and great poverty. In turn such violent pressures from outside the small kingdoms that were its victims encouraged internal dissension and fighting. We should not therefore dismiss as a sign of lack of patriotic fervor the Jeremian viewpoint: "If any nation will not serve this Nebuchadnezzar . . . I will punish that nation with the sword, with famine, and with pestilence . . ." (25:8). It is a sanguine and intelligible position, however much it leaves as a mystery the question why God should give such power into the hand of the king of Babylon. Rebellion simply provoked further needless slaughter and deeper suffering. There is therefore a note of political realism in the position presented in the Book of Jeremiah.

A second point is equally important, although it is clear that it could not have enjoyed more than an unclear and incomplete articulation at the time. Egypt and Mesopotamia had emerged as the great powers whose achievements and expansionist policies impressed themselves for good and ill across the whole of the ancient Near East. They established an early and strong pattern of regional control and military domination. Between them lay a large number of small communities, sometimes still existing as tribes and separate city-states but increasingly

163

forming themselves into emergent nations. The form, identity, and structure of a nation-state, such as Israel briefly became, was itself a relatively new socio-political unit. Even the concept of a nation was one only imperfectly formulated and even less perfectly realized. It is not wide of the mark to note that the clash of powers the prophetic message illuminates, from the time of its beginning with Amos until the very end of the Old Testament period, was a clash of ideologies. It marked a conflict between the greedy military imperialism of the Mesopotamian powers, Assyria and Babylon, and a small emergent nation, as exemplified in the case of Israel. The situation is yet further complicated because Israel had existed as a single national unit for only a very brief period under David and Solomon before breaking up into the divided kingdoms of Israel and Judah. Now, in the time of Jeremiah, only the smaller kingdom of Judah was left to face the considerable might of Babylon. Seen from the standpoint of the Old Testament prophets and historians, the division of Israel into two separate "houses" (cf. Isa. 8:14) had been a major stepping-stone to disaster.

In the light of this perspective of a conflict between the nation of Judah and the imperial power of Babylon, Jeremiah's prophecies have been formulated to express a deep conviction concerning the ultimate rightness and triumph of the individual nation-state over against the imperial power of Babylon. Such prophecies gave voice to an unshakable faith in the eventual triumph of justice and peace over policies of violence and plunder. In doing so they bore witness to the deep-rooted assurance that the ideal of a nation-state, vested with certain rights and responsibilities, more truly enabled the purpose of God for human society to be realized.

The section in 27:16–22 raises an interesting issue concerning the temple and its importance as a sign of God's protection and care for his people, even in the face of defeat. Almost certainly this issue is not from Jeremiah himself and points us to an area of speculation and religious apologetic that emerged during the years after 587 B.C. and came to enjoy a long and distinctive history (cf. Ackroyd, "The Temple Vessels," pp. 166ff.).

The facts are essentially simple, although their theological implications may easily escape adequate appreciation. When the military commander of the Babylonian forces in Jerusalem ordered the destruction of the temple, the valuable metal utensils, including also the massive bronze casting called "the sea,"

164

along with the metal from the large bronze pillars, were all taken to Babylon (II Kings 25:13–17). Such metal objects could have many uses and the metal itself could be reused easily. After this loss had occurred, prophets emerged in Judah foretelling the imminent return of these vessels (27:16), no doubt relying on the belief that God would look after his own holy objects. Their return was expected in the near future, and there was also an implicit expectation that many of the exiles, perhaps including the deported king Jehoiachin, would also return. We know from correspondence in chapter 29 that expectations were that the exile in Babylon would be short-lived, and Ezekiel seems to echo this hope (cf. Ezek. 11:14–21).

All these evidences simply highlight the fact that it was hard for the people of Judah, those remaining in the land as well as those taken into Babylon, to come to terms with a prolonged period of exile. The prophets who drew attention to the taking of the temple treasures and utensils to Babylon, and who saw this as a sign of hope, were simply exploiting an understandable human longing. Its falseness, however, was highly dangerous; in religious terms dangerous in relation to the superstitious and fetishistic attachment to the temple objects and in political terms in regard to the likelihood of a change in Babylonian policy. Ultimately such false and weakly based hope could only intensify the sense of despair and hopelessness. The sharp opposition ascribed to Jeremiah against these prophets and the misguided people who believed them was built on a sound awareness of the need for faith to be built on firm foundations. Rather surprisingly, the belief that these temple treasures were the subject of a special act of divine providence and the fact that they were eventually brought back to Judah came to be a prominent theme in showing how continuity in the spiritual role of the temple was maintained during the exile (cf. 27:22; 52:17–23; Ezra 1:7–11).

Jeremiah 28
Prophet Against Prophet

The issue now raised by an incident dated to the fourth year of Zedekiah (594–593 B.C.) serves to confirm and illustrate further the conflict of viewpoints presented to Zedekiah by

165

various prophets. Jeremiah had firmly and categorically coun-
seled the king not to join the proposed rebellion against Babylon (27:2–7), declaring this to be wholly contrary to the purpose
of God. Jeremiah's sign-action of wearing a wooden yoke-bar,
implying the inevitability of Judah's continued subservience to
Babylon, served to drive home this point. Now shortly afterwards another prophet, Hananiah from Gibeon [which was situated not far from Jeremiah's home town of Anathoth] appeared
with a conflicting message. He assured king Zedekiah that the
yoke of the king of Babylon would be broken, but also that this
would take place within an interval of two years. Furthermore
the theme of 27:16–22 is resumed with an assurance that the
temple vessels taken in plunder by Nebuchadnezzar in 598 (cf.
II Kings 24:13) would be returned to Jerusalem. Hananiah
elaborated and reinforced his message with a dramatic sign-
action by taking the yoke-bar from the neck of Jeremiah and
breaking it. Jeremiah appears to have been genuinely confused
and rendered uncertain by this action (28:12), but shortly he
received assurance from God that the prophet Hananiah's message was false and that God had in no way spoken through him
(v. 15). With this conviction Jeremiah roundly condemned
Hananiah's message as a lie and foretold that he (Hananiah)
would die within the year. His subsequent death is then reported as further proof of the falsity of his declarations (v. 17).

No doubt this account is based upon an authentic incident
relating to Jeremiah's activity and message, containing as it
does a number of circumstantial details. We should probably
assume that these details were reported through Baruch, or
some other figure equally close to Jeremiah. However it is clear
that the whole has been composed and shaped after an interval
of several years with a view to shedding fuller light on the major
event of Zedekiah's fateful rebellion against Babylon. The conflict of advice given to the king, the fact that the true word of
God had been given through Jeremiah but then refuted by false
prophecies, and the resultant confusion all served to explain
why disaster befell Jerusalem in 587. Consistently the deep and
searching questions of theodicy present themselves. Why had
God allowed such overwhelming tragedy to come upon Judah?
Why had both king and people not heeded the words of Jeremiah? Most especially the enigmatic question was Why had God
allowed his own temple—his very "dwelling-place" on earth—
to be destroyed? Perhaps less theological and more practical
was the question why the painful lessons of the unsuccessful

rebellion and consequent fall of Jerusalem in 598 B.C. had not been learned.

The response to these questions is strongly hinted at in this narrative. It is not so much a formal answer to the primary theological issues as drawing attention to the larger problem of false prophecy, with all its insidious dangers. By showing that Hananiah had categorically presented another perspective on the political situation in which Judah was placed and that his prophetic assertions accorded well with popular patriotic sentiment, the word of God itself had been contradicted. In fact the true word of God could only be grasped and acted upon through a process of responsive and critical discernment. The word of prophecy, when it is truly the word of God, is thereby shown to be wholly opposed to any notion of fatalism. Human destiny is not a fixed and unalterable future determined by God in advance of the reality of events. Nor is the prophetic word a means of escape from the pain and agony of serious decision-making. Rather it demands that such decisions be made in the most informed and responsible way; it is not part of the providential activity of God to override the plans and intentions of his creatures. Rather it is intrinsic to the nature of the divine glory that God shares this process of decision-making with his creatures. He enables them to fulfill their necessary role of participation in the fulfilling of creation and the shaping of human history.

Only when read as a single and compact whole does the story of Hananiah's false prophecy make it plain that this man's claim of having presented a true message from God is unsupportable. Quite obviously every reader of the story knew that Hananiah had been wrong, since events had subsequently proved this to be the case. What was needed was a better insight into the damage caused by Hananiah's words and the ever-present danger of false prophecy. No doubt many prophets like Hananiah, offering the same spurious appeal, were still known to the book's readers. Hananiah's grim fate was to be a warning to them! More deeply than this, however, we sense that the whole account has been designed to counter the nerveless and resigned fatalism that was the constant temptation for those who had survived the catastrophe of 587. They were tempted to "dehumanize" all historical and social action by regarding men and women as helpless victims of uncontrollable divine forces. Against this Jeremiah's prophecies called for courage, discernment, and genuine faith!

167

Clearly, prophecy in Israel had not been experienced as a single unequivocal message from God which obviated any need for careful evaluation and discrimination in acting upon its demands. All prophecy needed to be heard and responded to in the light of truths already known concerning the nature and will of God, the controller of history. The incident concerning Hananiah, dealt with at considerable length because of its direct bearing on what took place in 587 B.C., needs to be read and interpreted in light of warnings that had been given earlier about the danger of false prophecy (cf. 23:9–40). Not merely a complex historical event is illuminated by it but the whole nature of faith and the knowledge of God.

The word of God in prophecy called for a discriminating response if its truth was to become effective. The claim of a prophet to speak God's word could not be authenticated solely on the basis of the manner in which it had been given nor the formulas which accompanied it. Not even the confident performance of a dramatic sign-action could achieve this. Only hearing the word of God in light of the tradition regarding the entire prophetic revelation of God (cf. 28:8) could provide authentic and authoritative knowledge of the divine will. The confrontation between Hananiah and Jeremiah pointed to the essential spiritual inwardness and theological integrity of God's message: inner conformity to the nature of God that called for understanding the tradition of Israel's faith as a true guide to the power of God effective in history.

We have brought to light in this account certain basic features which contributed to the formation of a written collection of canonical prophecies (cf. Clements, "Patterns," pp. 42ff.; Blenkinsopp, pp. 96ff.). Prophecies required hearing and action, not in isolation from each other but in relation to a larger body of prophecy given to Israel. Each new prophecy required being related both to earlier prophecies (as in the case of Micah's prophecy concerning the temple) and to the reality of transpiring events. Through historical actuality alone was the ultimate revelation of truth to be found. However, knowledge of the nature and content of earlier prophecies, as preserved in writing, could assist in making this truth accessible. In the same way that Hananiah's death could be a demonstration of the falseness of his message and the presumptuousness of his claims, so similarly the event of Jerusalem's destruction in 587 B.C. served to validate Jeremiah's claim to have spoken the true word of God.

168

Lastly it cannot be too strongly emphasized that the idea of the Lord God of Israel disowning his own sanctuary and abandoning his people had appeared to be too terrible a situation to comprehend. Yet this had happened and Jeremiah had declared it could happen. Significantly and consistently what Hananiah had proclaimed as the divine purpose appeared to the popular mind to be more credible, it was so obviously a much more desirable future. He was reaffirming the traditional belief that God would intervene to protect the interests of Judah and Jerusalem, because the very understanding of the God-nation relationship took this for granted. This had not transpired, however; God had acted to defend his honor and righteousness and in doing so had inflicted a fearful judgment upon Jerusalem and Judah. In this action Jeremiah's interpretation of God's purpose made possible a more truly universal and absolute monotheism. Divine election did not mean that God protected a favorite people—Israel—but that Israel's destiny had to be seen as a specific instance of the universal providence of God. Patriotism required to be seen in the light of this larger universal truth of faith regarding the divine nature.

Prophets were naturally expected to pray for and to work for the ultimate welfare and "peace" (Heb. *shalom*) of their people (cf. 28:9). On the surface at least, Jeremiah's words appeared to contradict this expectation; consequently he had been forbidden to make intercessory prayers on their behalf (cf. 14: 11–12). In a more enduring and profound sense, however, there could be no true welfare and peace for Israel that did not conform to the reality and nature of God. By insisting that God would act to maintain a righteous and divine purpose, even when this meant punishing a rebellious people, Jeremiah ensured that the understanding of God remained superior to and apart from the understanding of Israel. God's existence was not to be thought of as being conditional upon the existence of Israel.

Jeremiah 29
Jeremiah's Correspondence with the Exiles in Babylon

The entire section from 26:1 to 28:17, in different ways, has been concerned with the question of true and false prophecy.

Now this section is brought to a conclusion in chapter 29 with extracts from letters between the Babylonian exiles from 598 and the community that had remained in Judah. These letters are probably four in number (Jeremiah to the exiles, vv. 1–15; Shemaiah in Babylon to Zephaniah in Jerusalem, vv. 21–23; Jeremiah to Shemaiah, v. 24, but broken off and no longer preserved in full; a further letter from Jeremiah to the exiles, vv. 31–32). The fullest report is undoubtedly Jeremiah's first letter to the exiles, dated in 29:2 to the time shortly after 597 B.C. when those who had experienced the first deportation to Babylon had been resident there only a short time. J.A. Thompson suggests plausibly that it belongs to the period 595–594 B.C. when there was a measure of political unrest in Babylon that may have encouraged premature expectations of a return on the part of the deportees. The correspondence is now reported comprehensively as an integral whole with extracts from other letters. These extracts elaborate further upon the contrast between Jeremiah's message and those of false prophets. Some of these were to be found among the exiles in Babylon, as were Ahab and Zedekiah (vv. 21–22). They were pronouncing the imminent fall of Babylon and a return of the exiles to their homeland. They paid for their falsely optimistic prophesying with their lives. Shemaiah was also in Babylon; others, like Hananiah, were to be found in Judah. Clearly false prophets did not belong to one group or one party.

The messages of all these men had been essentially similar in nature. Shemaiah's letter from Babylon to Judah had been concerned with matters of administration concerning the priesthood in Jerusalem (v. 26). The chapter as a whole is of considerable importance for the attention given to central issues relating to great changes in Israelite-Jewish life and faith that took place after the disaster of 598 B.C. It also raises a number of difficult questions for the interpreter.

We should note straightaway that the text is noticeably disturbed. Verses 16–20 are not in the Greek (Septuagint) and represent an interpretation couched in general terms of Jeremiah's message to those in exile. Altogether, from a textual point of view, the chapter displays many distinctive features with significant variations between the material in the Septuagint version and that of the Hebrew (details in Carroll, pp. 551ff.). The content of Jeremiah's letter appears to derive from a late stage in the book's composition and must be regarded as a summary outline of its main theme and not as a direct verbal transcript. How closely it stands to Jeremiah's actual words and why it has undergone expansion in this way can only be matters of conjecture. The text is evidently conscious of what had subsequently taken place with Jerusalem's destruction in 587 and the changed situation this entailed for those in Babylon and those in Judah. It therefore takes a longer perspective than Jeremiah's original letter appears to have done. It has become a focal point for understanding the nature and meaning of exile and the hope of return to Judah. Alongside this we must note the considerable amount of circumstantial detail regarding the activities of those in exile in Babylon and their continuing links with Judah; these make it certain that it does rest on an authentic text from Jeremiah. Nor should we ignore the fact that in antiquity letters were not simply written documents but were conveyed by messengers who would read out and interpret their contents. Precise verbal exactness was not demanded in the manner of modern correspondence.

The fact that a substantial exchange of correspondence took place at all between the community in Judah and the exiles in Babylon appears somewhat surprising. It would appear to have been carried out through the mediation of official envoys approved by the Babylonian authorities, since verse 3 refers by name to those who went from Judah. They were prominent officials; it is altogether likely that the correspondence concerning Jeremiah in Judah and Shemaiah of Nehelam in Babylon was also conveyed through these official channels. Why did the Babylonians encourage such continued links between the two communities? It is evident that those deported to Babylon were not dispersed and sold as slaves, as might have been expected. Instead they remained in tightly knit communities and were able to maintain regular communication with their homeland. The most likely explanation for this is that the Babylonian authorities firmly intended that those deported to Babylon should be kept informed of what was happening in Judah. Similarly they wished to ensure that Zedekiah, the appointed ruler in Judah, was not allowed to forget these exiles in Babylon who were in effect hostages. In varying ways their position was being used as a lever to help enforce the loyalty, subservience, and regular tribute payments from Zedekiah. It is interesting for us to learn from Ezekiel 17:11–21 something of the alarm felt

171

among the exiles in Babylon when news of Zedekiah's breach of loyalty to Babylon had become known.

It may also appear more than a little surprising that the two prophets executed in Babylon (v. 21) had been rash enough to proclaim the treasonable message of the imminent downfall of Babylon. How far this was encouraged by knowledge of internal problems for the royal house in Babylon and how far it represented ordinary human wishful thinking is not known. Yet it had become known and the officials acted promptly against the culprits, either acting upon information from informers among the Jews or more directly from their own observations. Clearly, active resistance among the exiles in Babylon to the will of the king was dangerous, even if only verbally expressed. It was obviously very important to ensure that all readers of the book fully recognized that for a given period of time (70 years) resistance to Babylon was tantamount to rebellion against God (cf. 27:14)! So this point remains a consistent theme of the Book of Jeremiah. Rather surprisingly, the book as well as the prophet himself counsels a rather quietistic acceptance of the sovereign demands of the king of Babylon for the present time. The bearing this had upon the outlook of the exiles of this period and in subsequent years for Jews of the dispersion on a large scale cannot be ignored.

The reference in Jeremiah's letter to a period of "seventy years" (29:10; cf. 25:12) was obviously intended to signify a full human lifetime (cf. Ps. 90:10). None of those who had been taken to Babylon could hope to return to their homeland. Only their children might hope to do so. Jeremiah's message, as it was originally given, was quite evidently meant to dampen and dispel premature expectations of a return to Judah. Understandably this remained a prime factor in the hope of those who had suffered the fate of exile. Only in retrospect, after an interval of some decades, did the words of Jeremiah begin to take on a more optimistic and reassuring note. To calculate how closely the precise number of seventy years corresponded to the period in which Babylonian control over Judah was enforced (604–538 B.C.) is of little consequence. More important is the fact that Jeremiah was initially anxious to counter the false optimism of anticipating an early recovery of homes and possessions (cf. Ezek. 11:15 for evidence of their anxiety on this point). For Jeremiah, hope and assurance were not to rest on naïve patriotic and unreasoned expectations that God would swiftly put an

172

end to the power of Babylon and so send the exiles back to their homes. Rather they were to be built upon the painful acceptance of the reality of Babylonian rule in the present. Consequently they had to adapt to this situation and learn to endure it.

The words in which Jeremiah's assurance of an ultimate return to Judah are couched point the reader to a remarkable and intense inwardness of religion: "You will seek me and find me; when you seek me with all your heart" (29:13). The period of waiting and surviving in a grim and threatening world of exile were to be years of spiritual discipline and an opportunity for repentance. When the time of discipline had been accomplished Israel could truly seek God "with a whole heart"; only then could a return to the homeland become a genuine possibility, because only then could it become spiritually meaningful. It is not out of place to note that by placing so much emphasis upon the inward and personal aspects of a true knowledge of God Jeremiah's letter established a spiritual foundation for a Jewish existence in the Diaspora (exile). Even though it was not possible in exile to give full expression to what it meant to "know the Lord," at the same time it would not be a way of life wholly devoid of such knowledge. Inevitably such an acceptance had important repercussions for the way in which the temple of the Lord God was understood and seen to be relevant for the knowledge and experience of God. Life in exile was to provide the essentials for an interim relationship to God; it would be less than full communion, a reality that would become possible only when Israel had once again been gathered "from all the nations" (v. 14). But life in exile was better than the extinction threatened upon those who had fled for safety to Egypt (cf. 42:16–17).

Shemaiah's concern for the appointment of Zephaniah as priest in Judah instead of Jehoiada suggests that Jehoiada was dead (in Babylon?). As the senior responsible figure for religious affairs in Judah, Zephaniah was now being commanded to take strong action against Jeremiah.

PART FOUR

The Promise of Restoration
JEREMIAH 30—33

Before examining in detail the first section of this unit, it is necessary to consider fully and carefully the many problems and questions that arise in chapters 30—33. These four chapters consistently and glowingly express a message of hope of an eventual restoration of Israel to its own land. This restoration was expected as the result of the return to the lands of Israel and Judah of the people from all the distant places of exile to which they had been scattered. Essentially the prerequisite of restoration is seen to lie in the message of "return," so that hope is wholly bound up with the idea of Israel as an independent nation with its own land and government in the form of the Davidic kingship being restored. Beyond the judgments which have taken place, therefore, the Book of Jeremiah asserts categorically that hope remained real: After all that had occurred in bringing ruin and devastation to Judah, there would be divine restoration. The twin themes of return and restoration to a full national existence provide the essential content of the prophetic message of hope, and this message is substantially the same in all four of the great prophetic collections. Eventually and certainly Israel would be saved (30:7); and this word of hope contains an implied assumption that salvation would consist of Israel's becoming a nation once again, free from all the restraints and impositions of foreign rule. Israel would become free, prosperous, and honored under the just government of a Davidic king (cf. 33:19–26).

In Jeremiah and Ezekiel we come closest to uncovering the circumstances and character of this prophetic message of hope (see below, esp. on chap. 32).

Various suggestions have been put forward to explain and

175

locate the time of origin of this message of hope in the ministry of Jeremiah, or alternatively and less probably to deny that it can properly and convincingly be ascribed to Jeremiah at all. The most credible interpretation of the situation is that in chapter 32 we are confronted with the moment when Jeremiah discovered the certainty and basis of this divinely given word of hope (cf. Clements, "Jeremiah, Prophet of Hope," pp. 345ff.). Jeremiah became convinced that Israel would be restored to a full and happy future on the very eve of Jerusalem's fall in 587. The light of hope shone brightest in Judah's darkest hour!

Attempts to find an earlier period in Jeremiah's ministry (? in Josiah's reign) for this word of hope show themselves to be wholly unlikely, since they entail major fluctuations in Jeremiah's outlook in different periods. Nor is it likely that the prophecies preserved in 30—33 are to be regarded as the precise words and formulations Jeremiah used. Rather, what we have here is the literary deposit outlining the message of hope that derived from Jeremiah's central conviction given in the hour of Judah's deepest crisis. It has been elaborated and filled out to offer a more complete picture of how renewal would come about, what it meant in theological and political terms, and also the range and nature of its authority. It would amount to a rebirth of the nation of Israel, drawing in not only the exiles from Babylon but also those far earlier exiles of Israel who had been thrown out from their homeland in the Northern Kingdom by Assyria (30:4–24).

Much of 30—33, it must be realized, is not Jeremiah's exact words, yet it can in no way be regarded as inauthentic on this account. Once the fundamental reality of the God-given message of Israel's renewal had been revealed through the prophet, it has necessarily called forth a fuller amplification of what this renewal meant in terms of the foreseeable political future of Israel. In many respects it is as important for what it leaves out, as for example any mention of the rebuilding of the temple, as for what it includes. The elaboration of Jeremiah's words has become an important feature in the process of giving clarity and direction to the prophet's message as the situation of Judah and the exiles continued to unfold.

It must also be borne in mind that so far as Old Testament prophecy is concerned the message of God was not regarded as a series of abstract theological propositions but rather the positive declarations of God's purpose for his people. It is this that has come so strongly into the structure of the book on account of the several confrontations between Jeremiah and the false prophets. Their message also was one of hope, but of a hope that Jeremiah insisted was not based on a clear knowledge of God. They either minimized or discounted altogether the idea of an effective work of divine judgment upon Judah. It was of the utmost importance, therefore, to Jeremiah and to those who have edited and elaborated the collection of his prophecies into book form to show the essential nature of this God-revealed hope. It was necessary to demonstrate that such a hope took full and serious account of the measure of Israel's sins.

In this context it is evident that such a hope could come to realization only through and beyond God's acts of judgment. Nor could such hope be satisfactorily represented by an abstract assurance that in the future all would be well for Israel. Rather it needed to take clear social and political form: assurance of a return from exile for those who had been carried away from their homeland and of a full restoration of Israel's national life. The situation of exile was to be viewed purely as an interim one. Peace and prosperity were thereby seen to be dependant on peaceable and prosperous structures within the order of the new Israel that was promised. The combination of authentic and original words from Jeremiah with subsequent elaborations and amplifications to give them fuller definition was a necessary and vital feature of the formation of the Book of Jeremiah. Like all the Old Testament prophetic collections, Jeremiah is essentially formulated as a message of hope throughout. This message of hope, however, needed to be seen in light of and in direct relation to the words of doom and judgment Jeremiah and his prophetic predecessors had proclaimed. To have ignored this would have been to ignore the reality of Israel's sinfulness and would ultimately have robbed the tragic experiences through which Israel and Judah had passed of their spiritual meaning.

Bearing in mind these larger considerations, we proceed to look in detail at the separate sections which make up this "Little Book of Consolation."

Jeremiah 30:1—31:1
Hope Through Judgment

Introduction to the Message of Hope (30:1–3)

This general introduction to the prophetic word of hope through Jeremiah comes without any indication of date or political context. It can be plausibly and reasonably argued that the actual historical setting of such a message is fully given in chapter 32. In this case it was during the fateful last days of Judah, when Jerusalem was under siege by the armies of Babylon in 587 B.C. It was a visionary glimpse of a renewal and rebirth of the life and national existence of Israel rooted in Jeremiah's knowledge of the character and purpose of God. Around this event the editors of Jeremiah's book have built up a more rounded and fully defined picture of the divine foundations of this hope and of the form and character of the New Israel in which it would be realized. The lack of a date reference in the short introductory note in 30:1–3 is of significance, since it lends to the promise of the divine renewal of Israel an ongoing and temporally extended importance. The assurance of this divinely empowered renewal was to rest wholly and securely on the word of God. It was not to be derived from the political possibilities of an external situation, such as a military threat to Babylon, nor upon earlier promises regarding the eternal nature of religious institutions, such as the temple or the Davidic kingship. It was to be separated from Israel's historical past and yet wholly justified in relation to it.

Strikingly, the promise of renewal is given birth at the moment when Judah's fortunes had reached their lowest point, with Jerusalem about to fall to the power of Babylon. Yet this too in its own distinctive way serves to strengthen the perception of the theological nature of Israel's hope. While the temple stood and while the Davidic kingship remained in Jerusalem these were seen as visible guarantees of divine protection for the nation. They were, however, both temporal and vulnerable, so that their removal enhanced the clarity with which the true basis of Israel's national hope in the word and purpose of God could be made plain. It was in a sense necessary for the outward physical symbols of hope to perish for the essentially inward and spiritual nature of hope to be revealed. It is also worthy of note that just as the extant symbols of hope were about to perish, it was a matter of relative unimportance through what agency or circumstances the realization of this hope was to be achieved. Although the Book of Jeremiah does include a number of declarations concerning the eventual downfall of Babylon (50—51; cf. 27:7), these can best be understood as part of the latest stratum to be added to it. In no sense do the political likelihood of the collapse of Babylonian rule or the experiences of unrest and turmoil within the imperial homeland occasion hope for Israel. This is too deeply spiritual and genuinely theological to need such circumstantial and temporal supports. The ultimate basis of hope lies in the nature of God and of his will for Israel as a people. Anything less than this would have been less than certain.

It is also significant that Jeremiah's assurance for the future does not build upon any expectations concerning the surviving vestiges of Israel's established existence and faith. Besides the kingship and the temple, even the land itself, so centrally valued in the Deuteronomic theology as the national "inheritance," now no longer appears as a central basis of assurance (cf. Brueggemann, *The Land,* pp. 107ff.).

In essence it is God's purpose for Israel that is shown to ensure a return to the land, not the nature of the land itself, which in some mythological fashion will call back her sons and daughters to dwell upon her once again. So the three great institutional and social realities—temple, kingship and land—that had previously provided the central evidence of the divine love and graciousness towards Israel are now set in a lesser position. The word of God, proclaimed and revealed to Israel by the mouths of prophets, provided the basis of hope and assurance for the future. Such a prophetic promise entailed stripping away the externals of religion for more fundamental theological realities to be made evident.

In this setting we should understand the necessity for an introduction of this broad and general kind and in which we can discern its deepest meaning: "For behold, days are coming, says the Lord, when I will restore the fortunes of my people, Israel

179

and Judah. . . ." All attention is concentrated on the "I" who speaks, for it is God himself and he alone who guarantees this promise. Similarly the impersonally formulated phrase "days are coming" carefully avoids drawing attention to any purely circumstantial detail of precisely when this would occur or through what agency it might be brought about. This would have been to lessen the certainty by drawing attention to purely minor issues. God remained free to fulfill his promise as and when and through what means he himself should choose. Such freedom was not simply the freedom of divine sovereignty but also the fullest guarantee of the reality and dignity of human freedom.

There is a singular significance to the open-endedness within the brief phrase "restore the fortunes" (Heb. *shub shebut*). The attendant concerns of to what political shape the new Israel must conform and what institutions must exist within it are left undefined and unspecified. They are rendered secondary to the fundamental issue that Israel would again exist within the envelope of the divine blessing and grace. As a people they would again enjoy the fruits of God's renewed blessing with all the wide range of meaning that this entailed.

A Threat and a Promise (30:4–11)

The unit of promise in 30:4–11 shows the literary form of being a composite structure in which a threat (vv. 4–7), addressed in the heading to both Israel and Judah, is countered and brought to completion by a word of promise (in prose, vv. 8–9). To this has been added a further confirmation of the assurance based upon the theme of the "full end" (Heb *kalah*) destined for the nations, but from which Israel will be saved (cf. also 46:28). The message of hope in verses 8–9 is formulated in broad and general terms and must be the work of the prophet's editors, who have taken up the words of a threat from the prophet and have shown that the people of Israel must pass through a period of judgment before salvation could come. Hope could be realized only through suffering, since in the prophetic understanding that suffering had become an essential part of the discipline of Israel.

Verse 9, with its description of the future age as one when Israel would serve the Lord their God and David their king," compares closely with Hosea 3:5. It sees in the restoration of the Davidic monarchy the divinely ordained means through which

180

the disunity of Israel and Judah would be overcome by a new central government and also the symbol and guarantee of Israel's freedom from foreign rule. The Davidic kingship embodied a revered tradition of a rich and successful past and Israel's claim to pre-eminence among the nations. So the new age promised to Israel by God was to be one in which it would be free from the yoke of servitude to foreign nations. As we find so consistently in the formulations of prophetic hope, the essential principles of freedom to live under a just government provided by a native kingship are thought to be assured by the divine will. Only by a monarchic government of this kind could true religion and genuine prosperity be achieved. So it comes about that the prophetic message of hope embodies an implicit ideology of Israel's return to nationhood.

Verses 10–11, which introduce the apocalyptic type theme of the "full end," must be regarded as a yet later addition. These verses betray a measure of anxiety concerning the delay in fulfillment of the divine promise of Israel's restoration and a measure of puzzlement over the theme that God had foreordained an "end" to Israel (cf. Amos 8:2). The message, built up on the basis of a desire to establish a coherent and comprehensive picture of what the prophetic message about Israel's future really foretold, presents a double assurance. This consists of a warning that the time would come when God would bring about a "full end" to the host nations among whom Israel lived in diaspora. Of Israel itself, however, he would not make a full end, even though there would have to be a continued and justly deserved chastening. Probably this passage, and the closely parallel one in 46:28, are among the latest units to have been added to the book, stretching the prophetic hope concerning the future into an apocalyptic picture of a cataclysmic warfare among the nations. It is also significant for the way it shows prophecy itself undergoing changes as the formation of a corpus of canonical prophecy led to attempts to establish a single harmonious picture concerning the future. So we find that the theme adumbrated here appears in close relationship to parts of other prophetic collections. The fundamental idea appears to have originated with Amos 8:2 and reappears in Ezekiel 7:2. Questions about what such an end may mean for Israel are to be found in II Kings 18:27; Isaiah 10:23; 28:22; Daniel 9:27.

The purpose of the addition here is to insist that the element of judgment prescribed for Israel is both necessary and inescapable but will not itself prove to be final ruination of the

181

people. Even when they have been scattered among many host nations and their weakness doubly exposed, yet the power of God will be with them and the word of promise contained in prophecy will be brought to fruition. We sense in this a drawing out of the Jeremianic message of hope into a more abstract and almost timeless frame of reference, seeking to hold together the ideas of the divine justice and the divine mercy in respect of God's purpose for Israel. The experience of exile in Babylon had begun to appear as an ambivalent experience, on one side affirming the just and punitive action of God to Israel and on the other side revealing a divinely ordained preservation of a faithful remnant of the nation.

Healing for Israel (30:12–17)

The unresolved and almost paradoxical note of ambivalence in verses 10–11 continues in verses 12–17, which provide a further promise of hope and restoration for Israel based upon the theme of Zion's incurable and grievous wound. These verses maintain a harsh and unrelenting message of threat and condemnation. Israel had suffered an incurable wound, inflicted on her justly for her sins and guilt (v. 14). Suddenly and paradoxically this announcement of Israel's fatal wound is altered in verses 16–17 to a declaration that the wound would be healed and that Zion would be restored to health and vitality once again. The astounding and unthinkable will happen: Zion will be restored to all her former health and vigor. There can be no doubt that this sharp contrast is a deliberate and carefully constructed pattern, putting into words the unconscious thoughts and fears of those who were smarting under the pains of their daily lives and the seeming futility and hopelessness of Zion's ruin and degradation. All this is indeed the case, declares the prophet; Zion is devastated and past healing, but with God the impossible becomes possible and the restoration of Zion, which in the present appears to be inconceivable, becomes a future certainty. There are a number of points of similarity and connection with the language and themes of Isaiah 40—55, but these need not lead us to conclude that there is a direct literary dependence. Rather it is the case that the fears, doubts, and constant temptation to despair that flourished in the wake of the disaster of 587 B.C. in Judah and Babylon have called forth several similar prophetic responses. The word of God alone is seen to be the antidote to despair.

182

The Ultimate Promise (30:18–22)

The picture is now filled out in verses 18–22 with an affirmation concerning the restoration of the city of Jerusalem ("the city" of v. 18). The city will be rebuilt, the royal palace will stand where it once was (v. 18), and the customary noise and bustle of city life will again echo through its streets. "The prince" of verse 21 is certainly a reference to a future ruler, or governor, and quite evidently the title "king" has been avoided deliberately for political or religious reasons. Particular emphasis is placed upon the identity of the ruler as "one of themselves," pointing to the increasing power and control over the land being exercised by persons of non-Judean origin. This may well have been what took place in Judah after the assassination of Gedaliah as a result of the conscious intention of the Babylonian authorities. It may alternatively have come about as a result of the weakness and instability of whatever basis of regional government had been set up in Judah by the Babylonians after Gedaliah's death (41:1–3). The strong insistence upon the piety of the future prince may also point to the indifference to religious observance which had come to characterize those who maintained temporary power in Judah during the years of exile. All too little is known by us of the conditions that prevailed in Judah during the years after 587 B.C. up until the time when the restoration of the temple took place in 520–516 B.C. (cf. Ackroyd, *Exile and Restoration,* pp. 20ff.).

The concluding formula of verse 22 expresses the full meaning of the covenant relationship between Israel and her God without actually using the word "covenant" (Heb. *berit*). It is noteworthy, however, that coming as it does at the close of a promise of Jacob's restoration, with Jerusalem as its central city, it was clearly intended to be much more than a theological abstraction and to point to the full reality of Israel's national and social life. For the Old Testament as a whole the idea of salvation retains a full political and physical embodiment.

A Threatening Word of Judgment (30:23—31:1)

This fragment is a brief and rather disconcerting piece repeated here from 23:19–20. It is possible that this repetition announcing the certainty of divine judgment upon Judah is

183

deliberate and is intended to present a warning; after the promises of the preceding verses, this hope was not to be taken for granted. God's promises and assurances did not cancel or circumvent a righteous anger against human sinfulness and wrongdoing. In this fashion there is an intention to alert the reader addressed in verse 24 to the need for taking seriously the warning implicit in all that Israel had suffered over the years. A further reaffirmation of divine wrath against human sin was felt to be necessary so that generations of the future would take note of Israel's sufferings and not repeat such sins. This short fragment is then rounded off in 31:1 with a return to the theme of 30:22, serving to make clear that the scope of the promised return would embrace "all the families of Israel." Quite evidently the loss of Israel's national identity as a consequence of the tragedies of 598 and 587 B.C., leading to the scattering of several small communities of Jews among the nations, now called for a broad, inclusive definition that would be decisive.

Jeremiah 31:2–40
Israel's Hope Is Based on God's Loving Faithfulness

The series of short positive affirmations of hope for Israel's eventual restoration in 31:2–40 are partly in prose and partly in poetic form. Altogether there are no less than eight short units (vv. 2–6, 7–14, 15–22, 23–26, 27–30, 31–34, 35–37, 38–40); several are easily identifiable by the formulaic introduction "Behold, the days are coming. . . ." While it would be mistaken to regard either the prose form or the stereotyped introductory formulae as infallible criteria for distinguishing what was authentically Jeremian, it is probable that only a little, and perhaps none at all, is a precise reporting of Jeremiah's own words.

As we have noted, the entire structure in this "Little Book of Consolation" is a careful compilation spelling out the certainty and character of Israel's future hope. This hope was firmly grounded in the message of salvation and renewal of normal social life given through Jeremiah in Judah's darkest hour (chap. 32). The collection of these brief assurances of the certainty of Israel's ultimate salvation contain some of the most poignant and memorable of all the words of hope the Old Testament has to offer. Furthermore, since the ultimate ground and certainty of this hope rested on the nature and purpose of God, these sayings bring to the surface some of the most vivid and theologically significant pictures of the divine nature. Precisely because Israel's assurance for the future rested on the word of God, and not the political will of human beings nor the favorable possibilities inherent in a specific set of historical circumstances, this hope remained valid and unprejudiced by any subsequent temporal delays or human weaknesses relating to its fulfillment. Jeremiah's hope made its appeal directly to the human heart and was inescapably theological in its nature, for it was neither a vague injunction "to look on the brighter side of things" nor an optimistic assessment of the potentiality of historical events. It made its appeal to the human heart by pointing to hope as the rediscovery of God as the creator. The nature of God is to create, and so the latent purpose of this creation will be surely carried forward to its God-given goal.

"Arise and Let Us Go Up to Zion" (31:2–6)

The first of these short promissory units is set out in 31:2–6 and expresses poetically a number of basic theological realities. It is addressed to all Israel, deliberately including Samaria and Zion in its scope (vv. 5–6) and recalling that Israel's existence as a people had its origin in an act of divine choice (vv. 2–3). How and why had Israel come to be, and how could its renewed existence as a national community become a reality once again? The answer set out in verse 3 is unequivocal. The Lord God had first appeared to Israel, loved it with an eternal love, and so could be relied upon to extend an enduring faithfulness of purpose. What seems at first glance to be familiar and conventional is nevertheless a truth that has been singled out to assert the most unshakable certainty. Israel does not and cannot exist in and of itself. It exists as a people only as the outward expression of a decision of divine love. Because that love does not and cannot cease, so will Israel's existence and restoration in the future remain assured. Neither the time nor circumstances of this restoration are specified, only the inner theological reality which made it a necessity of the divine love. All that needs to be said is that there will certainly be a day when watchmen will call out: "Arise, and let us go up to Zion . . ." (v. 6).

185

The Return to Zion (31:7–14)

The second unit of this series (vv. 7–14) requires little additional comment, since it simply spells out further, with some moving and memorable word-pictures, what this restoration of Israel will mean in human terms. It will provide a new beginning and renewed protection for the weak as well as the strong (v. 9). It will bring renewed prosperity and happiness to a suffering people (vv. 12–14). All of this will come about since God has never ceased to be the providential overseer of Israel's destiny, first having dispersed them among the nations in judgment, but now restoring them to their homeland. It is no doubt a point worthy of note that the devastation of Jerusalem and the destruction of the temple no longer constitute the primary basis of judgment upon Israel, nor the fall of the Davidic kingship, but rather the fact of exile and dispersion. Israel's existence in diaspora had become a long-term experience of judgment, which would soon be brought to an end.

The Everlasting Love (31:15–22)

These verses (15–22) further spell out the message of hope that restoration for Israel is certain and contain what are probably the most moving and poignant of all the prophetic expressions concerning the eternal nature of the divine love. It achieves its theological effectiveness with dramatic forcefulness by outlining poetically a sequence of deeply emotional human situations: Rachel, the maternal ancestress of the nation, appears bewailing her lost children (v. 15); her children then suddenly and unexpectedly appear, repentant and deeply ashamed of their foolish behavior (vv. 18–19). They return home after once having spurned and despised the love and protection offered there. In verse 20 the Lord appears as Israel's God, expressing his thoughts as a father over a rebellious and wayward son. Then Israel is addressed as a young woman who has abandoned the love and support of her home but now returns penitently to it (vv. 21–22). By blending together these domestic images of a home broken and disturbed by the loss and departure of children and the rejoicing at their return, the prophet portrays the intensity and nature of God's love for his people. If human beings behave in such a fashion when lost

186

children return to their home, how much more must this be true of God, who has created these human beings to be capable of loving in this way. If God so deeply wills the return of his wayward children, then how secure and certain must be the hope of that return, since its possibility is grounded in the very nature of God's love.

We are presented here with a singularly anthropomorphic portrayal of the nature of God and at the same time with a most perceptively theological exploration of the nature of hope. All significant theological reflection must relate to human existence in its method, since it must learn to understand God in terms of persons, not of things. Human relationships, which are of necessity only a partial and imperfect guide to the nature of God, may nevertheless be the most helpful and significant witnesses to the being of God that we possess. In consequence, the anthropomorphic view of God which so dominates the idea of the divine in the Old Testament may reveal itself to be an inescapable factor in any worthy understanding of the nature of deity.

The picture of Rachel, the matriarchal ancestress of Israel (cf. Gen. 35:16–20), weeping for her children vividly portrays the intensity of human emotions aroused by Israel's misfortunes (v. 15). We can discern here an unresolved element of tension between the love God is declared to feel for and show to the wayward and erring people of Israel and the parallel contention that these misfortunes are a divinely ordained and richly deserved punishment upon the people. While the scattering and departure from home are pictured here as an expression of willful human disobedience, elsewhere in the Book of Jeremiah they are affirmed to be the just and inevitable consequence of Israel's sinful behavior in the land (cf. 2:29–32).

The concluding affirmation of 31:22 "a woman protects (literally "encompasses") a man" has proven to be a quite enigmatic saying for interpreters to explain. It is scarcely resolvable by postulating an error of textual transmission; it appears to present a deliberately quizzical and provocative proverbial saying about the role of women towards men. Whether the image is a military one (as RSV's translation adopts) or whether it implies the taking of the sexual initiative by a woman, as some commentators suggest, is far from being clear. However the fuller implication in the remark appears to

187

be that the seemingly weak womanly virtues of loving and caring will achieve more than the physical strength of men.

The Return to Judah (31:23–26)

The short unit of 31:23–26 is perfectly straightforward and further elaborates upon the theme of restoration, this time spelling out in plain terms what this will mean for Judah and Jerusalem. It balances the previous section with its concern for Ephraim and the northern part of the kingdom of Israel. The hidden implication is a reaffirmation of the claim that Israel is one people. There is an unexpected and strange comment in verse 26: "Thereupon I awoke and looked, and my sleep (dream?) was pleasant to me." This bears no evident relationship to what has gone before. It possibly can be understood as an editor's note suggesting that all this hope is beautiful, but it is just a dream! If so, it serves to highlight the necessary element of vision and idealism which colors the portrayals of Israel's future set forth in chapters 30—33.

The Promise of New Life (31:27–30)

Two short sayings are introduced here to elicit from familiar and widely repeated sayings a spiritual message concerning the future of Israel. Israel will be sown with the new life of God to generate a new generation of people and animals. There is an allusion to the prophecy of Hosea 2:22 (Heb. v. 25), which is itself a play upon the name Jezreel. The close similarity of sound Jĕzrē'el-Israel may further have encouraged this verbal play. The sense is plain and it reaffirms what has already been said. Similarly the "building and planting" imagery of verse 28 takes up and counters the words given at the commissioning of Jeremiah in 1:10. The period of plucking up and destroying will have passed and the time for building and planting will have come. This careful balancing and interlocking of themes to make clear the passing of the period of judgment and the coming of the time for renewal and restoration is a significant feature in all the prophetic literature of the Old Testament (we can compare the "song of the vineyard" of Isa. 5:1–7 with the "new song of the vineyard," in Isa. 27:2–6).

188

The third of these three short sayings cites the popular proverbial saying "The fathers have eaten sour grapes and the

children's teeth are set on edge" (or more probably "blunted").
The point of this saying was clearly not to express a doctrine or
legal defense of the principle of shared family responsibility but
rather to give voice to despair. It is equivalent to "What is the
use of trying—our ancestors have done wrong and we are paying the price!" The importance of the prophecy that counters
this proverbial saying here (cf. also Ezek. 18:1–32) is to set God's
word of hope against the prevalent mood of despair that dominated the feelings of those who had remained in Judah after the
catastrophe of 587 B.C. Such a mood must also have been widely
felt among the exiles and further strengthens the contention
that the tendency of constantly recalling earlier prophecies
foretelling doom and judgment had been to encourage a widespread mood of fatalistic resignation to Israel's wretchedness in
the present. If what had taken place was a justly deserved
punishment for disobeying God, then it would appear to have
been useless trying to build again for the future. So we can see
that the citation of the principle "every one shall die for his own
sin . . . (v. 30) was not intended as a reformulation of a legal
principle but a demonstration of the total transformation made
possible for Israel through the gift of repentance. Israel's suffering in exile and Judah's devastation and ruin were not part of
an inexorable fate from which there could be no escape, but
they had been necessary punishments from God. Because renewal and restoration were possible, so repentance and renewal of commitment to God were wholly possible and meaningful
actions. It is questionable therefore whether the Old Testament
contains a concept of tragedy in anything like the Greek sense
in which the notion of "fate" carries a conception of an inescapable personal destiny. For the Old Testament understanding of
the nature of man there is an inalienable element of human
freedom, assured through the openness and reality of the
human relationship to God, which made repentance a genuine
possibility and the future an authentic part of God's creative
purpose.

The New Covenant (31:31–34)

The prophecy of the new covenant in 31:31–34 is unique
in the Old Testament and raises some of the most far-reaching
questions about the nature of the hope expressed in its literature. It may be stated at the outset of the exposition that it is

189

highly unlikely that the passage, in the precise words in which it is now formulated, is from Jeremiah's own lips (or pen!). The promise is couched in the elevated language and style of the homiletical prose which marks much of the editorial and developmental material in the book. It represents a concern to express the authoritative word of hope given through Jeremiah concerning the restoration of Israel (cf. 32:1–15) and to set this out in carefully defined theological terms. It endeavors to make clear and precise what restoration will mean for the future of Israel in regard to the nature and conditions of her relationship to God. The unspoken question that underlies what it has to declare is this: If Israel's sins in the past brought such fearful judgment upon the nation so that it came close to total annihilation, what assurance can there be that after a future restoration has taken place the same fate will not befall Israel again? The theologically conceived response to this is that God will, by the very creative power of his love, write the law of the covenant upon the hearts of the men and women who make up Israel. This is to be understood as a radically new type of covenant (cf. G. von Rad, *Theology*, Vol. 2, pp. 212–213). The old covenant of the law is dead; instead there will be an inner power and motivation towards obedience on the part of Israel written on the very hearts of the People of God, not on tablets of stone. Although the word "spirit" is not used, the implication is certainly that God's Spirit will move the hearts of Israel to be obedient to the divine law.

A number of major theological issues are raised by this understanding if the full reasoning or consequences that relate to them are not fully spelled out.

(1) Although the term "covenant" appears to have deep roots in Israel's religious history (cf. Hillers, pp. 46ff.), it was given fullest prominence in the Deuteronomistic literature of the late seventh and early sixth centuries B.C. (cf. Perlitt, pp. 54ff.). It is this Deuteronomistic language and theology that has so strongly colored the thinking of Jeremiah's editors. The term "covenant," drawn most directly from the sphere of international relations (perhaps more properly "treaty"), allowed for a flexible, two-sided portrayal of the mutual commitments involved in the relationship between God and Israel.

(2) A sense of the radical nature of Israel's "breaking" of the covenant implied not simply a transgressing of its demands but such a scale of transgression as to render the covenant effec-

190

tively annulled. It had been "broken" so that it was no longer in force. This radical breach is given force by the introduction of the analogy of a broken marriage (v. 32).

(3) In this promise of the new covenant the concepts of "law" and "covenant" are treated as virtually synonymous, which is also the case elsewhere in the Deuteronomistic usage.

(4) A measure of uncertainty is left over what exactly the new covenant will amount to. A new law is not properly envisaged at all, but only a new way of Israel's knowing and keeping the existing law of the covenant made on Sinai (Horeb). What is promised is not so much a radically different covenant but a renewed form of the earlier, broken covenant. Only later, in the thinking of the Jewish community at Qumran and among the early Christian community (cf. Luke 22: 20), did the idea begin to emerge that a wholly new covenant was intended by God. Certainly there came to exist in Jewish thought of the later Old Testament period very different understandings of what was foretold concerning the content of the "New Covenant" between God and his people. So too, among the early Christian communities, more than one understanding arose about the relationship of the new covenant to the law of Moses.

(5). The promise of verse 33, "I will put my law within them, and I will write it upon their hearts," closely recalls the words of Deuteronomy 6:6: "these words (of the law) which I command you this day shall be upon your heart." The concern in the Old Testament passages, in contrast to what emerged later in Christian thinking, was not for a law that could be summarized in certain succinct, fundamental principles. Rather it was for an obedient attitude towards the law. The central attention is upon the willingness to obey the known law, not for the clarification of obscure or conflicting elements within the law. The issue is focused on whether Israel is willing to obey the law that God has so graciously given.

(6) In noting the importance of the relationship between the new covenant and the Mosaic law, it should be noted that verse 33 defines the human partners to the covenant in a strikingly significant way as "the house of Israel." Use of the quite imprecisely defined term "house" instead of "nation" must be of set purpose. Israel was now no longer a nation but an emergent group of scattered communities in diaspora. Furthermore

191

the covenant itself, with its focus on the conscious moral bond between God and people based on a given law (torah), stands at some distance from the parallel notion that began to emerge of a relationship between a people and their God based on genetic descent and the sign of circumcision (cf. Gen. 17:9–14). From this we can see how later Judaism gradually became conscious of a tension in the understanding of divine election between the ideas of gift and obligation. This tension became very important in the conflicts within Judaism in the first century B.C. and is powerfully reflected in Paul (esp. Gal. 2:15–21).

The Certainty of God's Word (31:35–40)

Two short sections bring to a conclusion the ideas and themes of the promise of Israel's eventual restoration as God's people, the central point of chapter 31. Again it is important to bear in mind that hope as an abstract idea is not presented here. This prophetic affirmation of hope is built wholly upon the nature and will of God, not the possibilities inherent in human nature and human society. Such a hope, based upon the knowledge of God, is given direction through the firmly delineated promise of the historical restoration of Israel. Verses 35–37 draw an analogy between the natural order of the cosmos (v. 35) and the social and political order in which Israel's nationhood is assured (v. 36). As it is impossible for human beings to know the full range of the divine power and wisdom, so also is it impossible that God should fail to keep his word to make a great nation of Israel (cf. Gen. 12:1–3). The very strangeness of the contrast appears designed to counter unspoken fears or objections that God either has not the power or does not nurse the intention of restoring Israel to its former glory.

The second unit (vv. 38–40) concerns the rebuilding of Jerusalem as a central consequence of the hope of restoration. It spells out the major role this city is to play in the nation's future: It will never again be torn down or destroyed. There is clearly an understandable element of hyperbole, but it is nevertheless indicative of the exalted role the city was to enjoy in the restored life and faith of the people. Gradually we find that the rebuilding of Jerusalem and the exalting of the city as a symbol of hope and assurance for the future came to be one of the most popularly expressed themes of post-exilic Jewish faith (cf. Porteous, pp. 93ff.). As the expectation of Judah's obtaining the full restoration of its national existence receded in political terms, so the restoration and glorification of Jerusalem, and especially of its temple, took on a greater meaning.

Jeremiah 32
The Lessons of History Give Hope

The Sacramental Sign of Hope (32:1-15)

The whole of the remainder of "The Little Book of Consolation" (chaps. 30—33) is set out in prose and finds its central focus in the narrative report of 32:1-15. It is this narrative account of an event that took place while the city of Jerusalem was under siege from the Babylonians which has drawn to itself the more amplified collection of prophecies presenting Jeremiah's message of hope (30—33). We should probably assume that at one time this report was located where it properly belongs chronologically, with the several detailed accounts of actions and activities in which Jeremiah was personally involved during the later years of Zedekiah's reign. These led up to the account of Jerusalem's fall to the armies of Nebuchadnezzar in 587 B.C. (chaps. 37—39). Of the various prophetic sayings which follow the action of 32:1-15 (32:16-26), it is unlikely that any are now preserved precisely in words derived from Jeremiah. What we have here, as in other comparable sections of the book, is a series of elaborations showing how the word of hope declared by Jeremiah would take effect, what it would exclude, and what it certainly would include. The passages are couched in readily discernible Deuteronomistic language and fill out the picture of hope first proclaimed so dramatically at such a seemingly hopeless time. The message is all the more striking because it came when militarily and politically the situation had reached a point where no human resources of hope remained credible. In history, and yet grounded in a God who reigned above history, there was a reason for hope.

We can single out the salient points which are pivotal for an adequate understanding of the structure and meaning of 32:1-15. The historical setting is precisely recorded and shows

Jeremiah to have been placed under a form of house arrest in Jerusalem (v. 2), but certainly not debarred from receiving visitors. This restraint was almost certainly occasioned by the serious threat facing the city and the anxiety of the city authorities to prevent Jeremiah from acting in any way that might further undermine the people's morale. The city had been under siege by the forces of Babylon for some months, although it is possible the background to the incident was when the threat of an attack from Egypt forced the besiegers to briefly lift their blockade. This would explain the freedom of communication between Jerusalem and Anathoth, where the field Jeremiah was asked to purchase was, and could also provide a reason why the commercial deal had suddenly become important. It would also present a more significant feature of theological importance. The lifting of the siege, as we learn from what is reported in chapter 34, had provoked a great surge of hope and relief among the citizens of the city; they saw in it, however mistakenly and prematurely, a sign that their ordeal was over and the threat to their city and lives had been removed. Against such a false hope, based on unreasoned optimism and mistaken estimates of the value of Egyptian military support, Jeremiah was able to present the only true and worthy grounds for genuine hope. This could be established only by knowledge of the will and purpose of God.

It was most probably at the time of the temporary lifting of the siege of Jerusalem by the Babylonians that Jeremiah received a visit from his cousin Hanamel from Anathoth, who came to promote the sale of a field which was a part of Jeremiah's family heritage. In accordance with the laws regarding such sale of family property (cf. Lev. 25:25–31), the first claim to the right of purchase fell to the closest kin of the owner. Jeremiah must therefore have been the nearest of kin willing to consider this privileged right of purchase in such troubled times.

In deciding to purchase the field at Anathoth, Jeremiah took a step of faith in believing that there would be a return to normal commercial and social life in the land which would make such an acquisition of benefit to him. In doing so, he perceived that his action had taken on a sacramental significance as a sign more widely relevant concerning God's future intentions for his people (v. 15). The profundity of the sign is in fact almost masked by its simplicity as a straightforward com-

194

mercial transaction. It is therefore important to pay full attention to what is not declared in this simple divinely revealed message, since it serves to explain why a much fuller amplification of this word of hope is set out in 32:16—33:26 and why this was felt to be necessary.

It is first of all clear that although the sign of hope came to Jeremiah at a specific moment in his and Judah's fortunes and bore all the characteristics of being rooted in this historical situation, the hope was in no way derivative from the events themselves. Hope was based on God and his gracious plans for Israel, even though it was mediated to the prophet through a given set of historical circumstances. It was in this way God-given, timeless, and unconditional as an authentic prophetic word of hope. It is this that has made it so fundamental a feature of Old Testament faith. Hope is presented as a transcendent reality, not an inner-historical one, even though it must necessarily find expression in actual historical forms and situations.

Secondly it became of the greatest importance to make plain beyond question that this hope expressed through Jeremiah was not dependant on nor in any way occasioned by the temporary lifting of the siege by the armies of Babylon. It was not a hope that disaster would be averted, but rather that through judgment and disaster hope remained alive and meaningful. Israel's eventual restoration to normal life in which happiness and security would once again become possible was an inalienable part of the divine purpose for the people. Such hope existed in, through, and beyond the inevitable judgment that now loomed before the city of Jerusalem and its rulers. Almost certainly many of the citizens had become overjoyed at the temporary lifting of the siege (cf. chap. 34); this was to prove to be a quite illusory hope. The pain of disillusionment was to prove all the more destructive of courage and faith in the future. All the more significant therefore was Jeremiah's concern to ground hope on a deeper and more lasting foundation. Hope was no longer the short-lived possibility of averting or postponing disaster, but rather a discovery that there was no disaster that could take away a hope founded on God.

Thirdly it is noticeable that the message of hope is given expression in boldly human and social form: "Houses and fields and vineyards shall again be bought in this land" (v. 15). Genuinely God-given hope is neither an inner psychological

195

confidence that "all will be well," nor a transition to a wholly new and other-worldly basis of existence in another life. Its very reality, and therefore its power to convince and take hold of the imagination, lies in its this-worldly concreteness. All the essential interchange of commerce, trade, and investment in the land would serve to demonstrate that it would become once again a land blessed by God.

We may draw attention fourthly to the extent to which this message of hope provided a turning point for the entire corpus of written prophecy. It is no doubt true that at one time biblical scholarship was inclined to make too much of the fall of Jerusalem to the Babylonians in 587 B.C. as the turning point of prophecy, thereby tending to deny or ignore expressions of hope in earlier pre-exilic prophecies and paying too little heed to a sense of judgment still awaiting Israel in the post-exilic period. Not all warnings of judgment ended with the fall of Jerusalem, as is clear from any study of post-exilic prophecy. Nevertheless the focusing of attention on the events of the year 587, when Israel's fortunes stood at their lowest point and when afterwards the prophetic message of hope came to enjoy an increasingly large aspect of Jewish thinking, finds justification in the central position accorded to Jeremiah's experience here. Prophecy underwent a substantial change with the catastrophic events that took place in 587, and this is a year that casts its shadow across the entire Book of Jeremiah, and indeed the entire corpus of Old Testament prophecy.

The Prayer of Jeremiah (32:16–25)

Jeremiah's response to the message of hope is set out in the form of a prayer, placed in the mouth of the prophet but representative of the feelings of all Israel. The prophet has become the collective figure voicing the emotions and aspirations of an entire nation. The inclusion of a prayer at this juncture, rare in written prophecy and more typical of the narrative histories of the Old Testament, marks a strikingly significant new departure in the composition of the book. It is intended to draw attention yet more firmly to the word of hope given to Jeremiah and to serve as a special note of thanksgiving for it. For this reason it concentrates upon the theological quality of hope, showing that it is founded on God for whom all things are possible (v. 17). It comes in the face of and despite the awfulness and terrifying nature of inevitable judgment (v. 28). It must not be mistaken for an aspect of the political or military potential of any given situation. To all such it is irrelevant! It cannot be nullified or removed, because of the fact of Israel's sin (v. 23). Israel had persistently offended God by sinning against all the gracious gifts given to her. In spite of all this long-standing tradition of disobedience and ingratitude, this hope remained secure and certain, since the future of Israel and of all human-kind (cf. all mankind in v. 20) rested on the will and purpose of God. It was unconditional, since it rested on a transcendent divine will, and yet it was concretely embodied in the necessity to achieve realization in an actual form of human society. As a hope it remained solidly this-worldly and concrete, not other-worldly and abstract.

God Speaks Again to Jeremiah (32:26–44)

We are now presented with a reply from God addressed to Jeremiah closely and directly related to the prayer. It is effec-tively a continuation of the prayer in the form of a reflective meditation on how God responded to it. Its role in the literary structure is that of reaffirming the contrast between the two seemingly contradictory poles of the divine will for Israel. On the one hand God had surrendered his people to judgment, a threat from which they could not now escape since events had taken their course. Compare verse 28: "Behold, I am giving this city into the hands of the Chaldeans. . . ." On the other side, however, the divine grace and mercy would be in no way with-held from the people during this judgment; beyond its ravages there would be a subsequent act of divine renewal (vv. 37–44). It is a point of major importance in this for the authors to show that Jeremiah's hope encompassed those who had been scat-tered abroad into exile (v. 37). More than this, the hope espe-cially applied to these people. This feature takes increasing emphasis in the way in which the Book of Jeremiah has been edited. The hope of a renewed Israel, of a restored life of trade and agriculture in the land, and of all the normal routine of human life in a new Israel is declared to be assured for those who have been scattered in exile. For those who remained in the land after the disasters of 598 and 587 the way to hope and restoration became progressively narrower (cf. 24:8–10; 42:18–22; 44:11–14; also Ezek. 33:1–20).

197

Jeremiah 33
Temporal and Spiritual Rebuilding

The Restoration of Judah and Jerusalem (33:1–3)

This vivid poetic affirmation concerning the eventual restoration and rebuilding of the city of Jerusalem offers no new theological reflection on the reasons for this certainty, nor any further detail concerning the occasion of Jeremiah's receiving assurance of such a hope. Perhaps even more surprisingly there is no fuller indication concerning how soon or by what agency this rebuilding would come about. The contrast is simply and starkly drawn between the horror and despair occasioned by Jerusalem's destruction in 587 and the splendor and reassurance of its eventual rebuilding. Whether the words are directly from Jeremiah or are more convincingly regarded as a further application and development of his message reported in chapter 32 at the hands of later scribes makes no significant difference to its meaning.

There is, in any event, a striking aura surrounding the vigorous poetic images presented, clearly indicating that the devastation inflicted on Jerusalem by the Babylonian siege and destruction had brought a deep psychological shock. Pictures are presented of houses forcibly broken down to try to block the breaches occasioned by the building of a massive siege ramp by the Babylonians (v. 4); the victims of the battle lie unburied in the streets (v. 5). After the siege had ended and the fearful aftermath of willful plunder and destruction had taken place, an eerie desertedness had befallen the city (v. 10). All is portrayed as a near, terrifying, and overwhelming never-to-be-forgotten catastrophe. Could there ever be a new city built upon such a heap of ruins?

Set against this picture of devastation and suffering, the prophetic author pictures with remarkable sensitivity normal, healthy city life with all its sound and bustle. There will be marriage festivities, singing and worship, all expressive of hope and the joy of youth (v. 11). The contrast could hardly be more skillful and deliberate, and it marks a striking contribution of the poet's insight into the deepest human needs. In disaster the first casualty is often the will to survive! The word-imagery finds in human vitality and its many noisy outward forms of expression a sign of sacramental significance. Normal city life is presented as the most holy and sacred product of grace. God will ensure that such a renewal is brought about and the very antidote to shock and despair is to be found in the realization that ordinary involvement in busy human affairs will be the sign of grace and the true glory a rebuilt city, which to the reader's eye clearly presented so sad a spectacle.

Set against the grim and painful background of actual events, the inclusion of this portrayal of the rebuilding of Jerusalem as a central feature of Israel's hope for the future is itself a skillful achievement of poetic imagination. The possibility of a real and meaningful future needed to be presented in pictures that could sieze and hold the attention, rather than being left to abstract ideas and pallid assurances concerning the nature of humankind. The message given is altogether immediate, memorable, and compelling in its power to convince.

The Political and Religious Orders of the Future (33:14–26)

This whole section is missing in the Greek (Septuagint) translation of the Hebrew Bible and this should certainly be taken as an indication that the unit is a late addition to the book. This is a conclusion we should make from a consideration of its general content and character, besides its conscious effort to modify and develop themes that have been presented differently by Jeremiah himself. It possesses two distinct aspects, one dealing with the royal house of David and the other with the future of the Levitical priesthood. However both aspects are held together and were occasioned by the effects of the catastrophe of 587 B.C. In destroying the temple and removing Zedekiah from the royal throne in Jerusalem, the Babylonian powers had brought an end, at least for the foreseeable future, to the two institutions which served as visible and tangible expressions of God's presence with Israel. Through the temple God was seen to be "with" his people; through the kingship the divine will and justice were afforded them. Without these

199

institutional expressions how could Israel continue to be regarded as the People of God? On both counts it appears Jeremiah unequivocally believed that neither institution should be regarded as indispensable to Israel's welfare. Jeremiah warned of the possible destruction of the temple (7:1–15) and had roundly condemned those holding royal office (22:1—23:2).

When we look to the future hope for Jerusalem set forth in 3:15–17, although the actual words are certainly not originally from Jeremiah, it is clear that no replacement for the Ark was envisaged in the restored city. Since the Ark had been the most holy object set within the inner sanctuary of the royal Solomonic temple and was itself a direct symbol of God's presence and power, it might have appeared that a rebuilt temple without such an Ark could not possibly be regarded as truly the temple of God. Yet it soon becomes clear from both Jeremiah and Ezekiel that in spite of the severe misfortunes that had overtaken the temple of Jerusalem there existed a deeply felt and firmly established demand for its future restoration. Neither those who had survived in Judah nor those among the Babylonian exiles were ready for a purely spiritual religion devoid of a sacred shrine and all its symbolism (cf. Acts 7:48–50). Various prophetic voices in Babylon, as recorded in the books of Jeremiah and Ezekiel, regarded the rebuilding of the temple as the central and most necessary task for the restored people of Israel (Ezek. 40:5—44:4; Isa. 44:28). Along with such an attitude there went of necessity an implicit need for a continuing body of Levitical priests to serve within it (cf. 33:21–22).

If the question of the continuance of the Levitical priesthood in a restored temple in Jerusalem was to become a controversial issue for the future of Judaism (cf. Isa. 66:1–4; Ezek. 44:4–31), so also was this true of the desire to restore the Davidic family to the kingship. Jeremiah's prophecies appear not to have expressed a single and entirely clear commitment over this question, although this may well be the result of later editorial handling. Prophetically, Jeremiah had decisively ruled out any hope for the future of the royal house through the exiled king Jehoiachin ([Coniah] 22:24–27, 28–30). His attitude concerning the future of Zedekiah seems largely to have been negative. As a Judean citizen Jeremiah had been entirely willing to remain in Judah under the non-Davidic governor Gedaliah (39:14; 40:5–6). This suggests that Jeremiah did not regard the kingship as an essential office for the welfare of Israel (cf.

200

also Ezek. 19:14). Certainly there were many in later Judaism who came to embrace such a position positively and to regard the kingship as an institution of the past with no role to play in the renewed life of Judaism.

In spite of these affirmations, however, it is also evident that other factions not necessarily close to the royal court emerged. They saw the restoration of the heirs of David as central for hope, and they came to look upon such restoration as a vital feature of Israel's regaining a place of honor and prestige among the nations (so 33:14–16, 19–22; Ezek. 37:24–28). This hope for the kingship is found in this passage. It is not messianic in the same sense that such an adjective implied for later Judaism, although it proved to be an important step in the growth of the messianic hope. Rather, what is hoped for here is restoration of the surviving heirs of David's family to the royal throne in Jerusalem (through Jehoiachin, in spite of Jeremiah's prophecy in 22:24–27?). Such an expectation was certainly thought likely to take effect in the years immediately after the exile. The retention of a clearly preserved genealogy defining Jehoiachin's descendants in I Chronicles 3:16–24 points to one way in which this hope continued to affect Jewish expectations during the era of Persian domination of Judah.

PART FIVE

The Last Days of Judah

JEREMIAH 34—45

Almost the entire section from 34:1—45:5 consists of narrative reports referring to Jeremiah in the third person. For the most part these narratives concern events from the time when Jerusalem was under siege in the years 588–587 B.C., or from the period subsequent to this when Judah was seeking some kind of return to normal life. The events are not in chronological order and the earliest of them, chapter 36, come from a relatively early period in the sequence of covered events. It is dated to the fourth year of Jehoiakim's reign (605–604 B.C.). The conclusion to this series of narrative reports is to be found in chapter 45 and consists of a short prophecy from Jeremiah addressed to Baruch the scribe. He is named as Jeremiah's scribal assistant in 36:4–8 and was responsible for the preparation of a scroll recording Jeremiah's prophecies from the beginning. This would point us to conclude that Baruch was in a substantial measure personally involved in several of the incidents reported in chapters 34—45 and that he was directly responsible for recording them.

This was probably the case and has given rise to the belief that the narratives of these chapters, together with possibly material in chapters 26—28, constitute the "Baruch Narrative" or even the "Baruch Biography" of Jeremiah's career. However the title "biography" is certainly misleading, since the period covered is too selective and partial for this to have been the author's intention. Furthermore interest is focused upon conflicts and prophetic issues, not upon the figure of the prophet himself. There is emphasis upon the sufferings and rejection experienced by Jeremiah, but even this feature does not justify describing the narrative as a "passion narrative" of the prophet.

Throughout the chapters the primary focus is upon the events themselves, which involved the siege of Jerusalem by the Babylonians and the city's subsequent destruction. These events are followed by accounts of the painful period which followed for the surviving Jews in Judah, until they took the strongly condemned step of fleeing to Egypt to make a fresh start there. Against his will and in strong contradiction to his declared message from God, Jeremiah was taken forcibly to Egypt. The last we hear from him is a typical (and heavily stereotyped) condemnation of the religious apostasy of his fellow Jews in Egypt. Presumably the prophet died there. Whether his prophecies were compiled in Judah or among the Jewish exiles in Babylon or in some other location cannot be determined with any confidence. Probably a compilation in Judah best fits the general tenor of the work, although there are some factors which may weigh against this.

The basic message of the stories in chapters 34—45 finds its central focus in the sense of tragedy attached to the fall of Jerusalem to the Babylonians, the ensuing destruction of the temple, and the ending of the long period in which Davidic kings had ruled in the city. Thereafter Judah's whole political structure, and with this the religious inheritance of Israel, had to find new foundations and to learn to accommodate to wholly new conditions. A strongly marked and rather surprising feature of these narratives is that the Babylonian administration set up after Jerusalem fell is presented as fair and reasonable. The reader is made fully aware that life was tolerable and had to be accepted as a necessary part of the divine punishment for Israel. Attempts to violate this order or to flee from it are firmly condemned, for example Gedaliah's murder and the flight of some to Egypt. Life under Babylonian rule is presented as something that the readers and loyal Jews generally have to learn to live with. In spite of the fearful destruction brought upon Jerusalem by the Babylonians, there is no condemnation of them such as we find in full measure in Isaiah 13—14, 40—55.

It is regrettable that many details of the condition of Judah, and especially the administrative arrangements imposed on Jerusalem and its environs, are not spelled out. In fact after the vain and foolhardy flight to Egypt there is little concrete information about life in Judah for almost the next half-century. Undoubtedly some significant literary activity took place during this period, but in general it is apparent that the major

204

center of new religious developments and the major focus of interest was with the exiles in Babylon.

It is important to bear these broader considerations in mind to grasp the meaning and significance of the stories presented in these chapters of Jeremiah's book. Their primary role appears to be a concern to justify and explain why future developments of Jewish religion and social life took the form they did. Most especially there is evident concern to show why neither the community that had survived the disasters of 598 and 587 in the land of Judah nor those who sought political refuge in Egypt could play any effective role in preparing for the restoration of Israel. From this time on restoration means a prior act of return, and this return must first come from those who had been taken into Babylonian exile. They are henceforth looked upon as the spearhead of the new Israel that is to come into being. How much of this represents Jeremiah's attitude, promoted by disillusionment with his closest associates, and how much a more theoretical and considered approach by others is not clear.

Central to the theological purpose of the entire narrative section of chapters 34—45 is the concern for a theological understanding of the covenant relationship between God and Israel and the way in which the events of Judah's fall affected it. As the surviving part of Israel this people had suffered the collapse of their earlier religious and political foundations and were now faced with the need to confront a new situation, calling for a new order of life.

Jeremiah 34
The Dishonorable Behavior of Jerusalem's Citizens

The incident narrated at length in chapter 34 took place during the siege of Jerusalem in 588–587 B.C. Reports of a move by Egyptian forces to attack the Babylonians reached the commander of the besieging forces and he was forced temporarily to lift the attack on the city. This provided opportunity for action of a deeply perverse and dishonorable character on the part of the threatened citizens of Jerusalem. When the siege against the city set in, the slave-owners had released both male and female slaves (34:8–10). This was motivated partly by a form of genuine humane concern, recognizing that in such dangerous times each individual had to look to do the best for himself or herself. More cynically, it had been perpetrated out of a desire to abandon responsibility for feeding and protecting such enslaved persons. However, with the lifting of the siege the citizens hoped it would provide permanent relief from the threat, and the deep cynicism and treachery latent in the situation became plain. The slave-owners repossessed their former servants (v. 11)! Jeremiah saw in such an action a twofold significance. In the first place the possession of slaves in perpetuity was in contravention of the Deuteronomic law embedded in the covenant relationship between God and Israel made on Horeb (vv. 13–14). Such slavery of fellow Israelites on grounds of debt should have been limited to a maximum period of seven years (Exod. 21:2–6; Deut. 15:12–18, esp. v. 12). Secondly, as if this flagrant contravention of the divinely given covenant law were not enough, these callous citizens of Jerusalem profaned the very name of God in repossessing the slaves they had freed for so short a period (v. 16). They thereby broke the legal and solemn oath taken before God by which they had conferred freedom upon their slaves. Jeremiah carefully matched the words of his threat to the baseless disregard of human rights and feelings such actions displayed (v. 17). These citizens had disowned allegiance to God's covenant. How could they subsequently suppose that God would adhere to his side of the covenant commitment in protecting and upholding such people and their city?

The incident is transparent in the way in which it reveals the self-seeking and cruel mentality of the Judeans with whom Jeremiah had to deal. Almost certainly such behavior could be matched by instances of similar conduct in any nation where self-interest in time of war leads to fundamentally treacherous and selfish conduct. Such people fully deserved the fearful fate which awaited them once the Babylonian siege was reinstated. Furthermore their optimism proved to have been wholly misplaced; the respite from fear of starvation and violent death showed itself to be temporary. More deeply, the narrative account makes abundantly clear that Israel had not made any serious endeavor to keep its side of the covenant relationship to God. Their ancestors had failed to listen to God (v. 14); this

206

generation showed themselves also unprepared to do so. They openly flouted the covenant, despising its just and humane laws; thereby they ignored its claims upon them. How could they possibly expect God to protect them as a people deserving his special regard? They had reduced the covenant to an empty word; they no longer had any right whatsoever to expect God to hear their pleas and prayers for help. Their own behavior had sealed their fate.

It cannot be by mere chance that this narrative begins the longer section of detailed reports from Jerusalem during its period of crisis. It establishes the fundamental theme of all the scenes reported afterwards, even though some of them refer to earlier events. The covenant between God and Israel was at an end, not because God was no longer able or willing to maintain it but because the people themselves had effectively annulled it. Because they had altogether abandoned its demands upon them, they had reduced it to the level of a powerless institution. The narrative in a very real sense is prophecy interpreted through historical events, and this is essentially true of all that is reported in chapters 34—45. Reported human actions served to confirm and illustrate the charges of lawlessness and covenant-breaking the prophet had leveled against the citizens of Jerusalem. They are portrayed as fundamentally cynical and immoral in their disregard of the covenant law of God. So far as Jeremiah was concerned they had been caught "red-handed" in their godless misdemeanors. The sentence God passed was an entirely just and proper one, in accordance with the standards and laws the people themselves knew to be right: "Behold, I will command, says the LORD, and will bring them (i.e., the Babylonians) back to this city; and they will fight against it, and take it, and burn it with fire. I will make the cities of Judah a desolation without inhabitant" (34:22).

Jeremiah 35
Further Proof of Judah's Godlessness: Jeremiah and the Rechabites

207

The incident recorded here is interesting in a number of respects, some directly connected with the editors' primary purpose and some related to incidental information it brings to light. In the latter category we should first notice the remarkable way it brings to the surface the unexpected contrasts and tensions in the literary make-up of the Book of Jeremiah. The Rechabite presence seeking protection in Jerusalem at the time of the Babylonian invasion (v. 11) and the wealth of circumstantial detail concerning the names, identity, and chief characteristics of their way of life make it impossible to doubt the historical veracity of the incident. However this contrasts somewhat with the stereotyped phrases, familiar themes, and conventionalized homiletical structure of the speech Jeremiah delivers to the citizens of Judah and Jerusalem (vv. 13–17). This evidences all the essential features and themes of the heavily Deuteronomistic language which has consistently provoked scholars to ask whether Jeremiah himself could have spoken publicly in such rigidly defined terms. Although the action reported represents an accurate historical record, it is difficult not to accept that a substantial degree of editorial freedom has been shown in the composition and reporting of Jeremiah's formal speech. Most likely, although based upon records and memories of Jeremiah's encounter with the Rechabites, the editors have used this occasion to construct what they regarded as a typical prophetic admonition focused upon the basic themes supplied by the characters in the action and the demands of the situation. It is probable that the Pauline speeches in the Acts of the Apostles owe their origin to a similar editorial technique.

The essential message of the meeting with the Rechabites is remarkably simple and requires no elaborate religious or historical background to bring out its force. The Rechabites were a small community who had displayed great consistency, integrity, and loyalty to their inherited traditions and way of life. In contrast the heirs of the laws and traditions of Israel since the days of Moses had shown themselves to be deceitful, dishonorable, and disobedient since their very beginnings. The presence of the Rechabites in Jerusalem, therefore, was a testimony to the righteousness and justice of God and an irrefutable condemnation of the citizens of Judah, who were without excuse in their disobedience. They knew the right path, but they had deliberately chosen the wrong one in spite of repeated warnings concerning their folly.

The Rechabites were related to the Kenites of the southern

208

desert region of Judah (I Chron. 2:55; cf. Gen. 15:19; Num. 24:21–22; Judg. 1:16), and the incidental information provided regarding their way of life is of considerable interest. They lived only in tents, drank no wine (since viticulture was regarded by them as an alien "Canaanite' form of agriculture), and practiced no cereal-crop farming. They represented an extreme cultural conservatism, hostile to any features of life associated with urban and agrarian life and religion of the Canaanite city-states. At first their stance appears strongly negative; nonetheless, they served as a testimony to the close interweaving of economic, technological, and social factors in the religious life of the land settled by Israel. What may appear in retrospect to have been a simple choice between the near poverty of the older form of life closely attached to the desert and the more advanced civilization of the Canaanite city-states was no such thing when seen in the actuality of the contemporary setting. The promise of greater prosperity and security of the Canaanite way of life was inseparably linked with the religious ideas and rituals attached to the worship of Baal as lord and life-giver of the land. The agrarian economy and the worship of Baal were interwoven in such a way as to make it very difficult to embrace the benefits of the economy without also becoming enmeshed in the immoral rites and idolatrous practices of the worship of Baal and the goddess Anat.

Jeremiah's offer of wine to the Rechabites (v. 2) was a gesture the prophet knew must be refused, and it is striking that he made the invitation in the temple of the Lord. The solemn setting lent a sacramental significance to the inevitable refusal of the offer of wine by Jaazaniah and his brothers. They were saying "No" in the name of God, so that it was wholly fitting that it should have been spoken in the temple of God.

It should certainly be borne in mind that although the sharp reaction against involvement by the Rechabites in urban life and agriculture is presented as a praiseworthy action, this is not the overall perspective of the Old Testament prophets nor is it typical of the Bible as a whole. Ultimately the true realm of human society, lived in the sphere of divine grace, is portrayed as a city—the New Jerusalem—(cf. Rev. 21:2); this city organization is viewed as the gift of God. Human culture, as a necessary expression of human nature and human achievement, can be redeemed, sanctified, and enriched by a true knowledge of God. Without such knowledge human culture

209

readily succumbs to tensions and pressures that render it form-less and in conflict with itself.

Jeremiah 36
The Rejection of the Word of God

This narrative recounts in considerable detail the circum-stances surrounding the preparation, reading, destruction, and replacement of a scroll containing Jeremiah's prophecies. It is the most informative narrative in the entire Old Testament concerning the preservation of prophecies in writing. More clearly than anywhere else it provides insight into the reasons and concerns surrounding the transition from oral to written prophecy, a feature several scholars have noted (cf. Clements, "Prophecy as Literature," pp. 59ff.). We should also note the extent to which it reveals the ambivalence, already remarked upon, in respect to the structure and authenticity of the narra-tive traditions of the Book of Jeremiah. On the one hand it contains a wealth of circumstantial detail regarding events and personalities involved in the preparation and reading of the scroll of Jeremiah's prophecies, which cannot reasonably be thought to have been the invention of later scribes (as R.P.Car-roll, *From Chaos to Covenant,* pp. 14ff., *et al.*). On the other hand, however, it provides only very brief, heavily stereotyped summaries of the content and character of Jeremiah's actual prophetic message (cf. vv. 2–3, 7, 29). These summaries relate closely to the tenor and themes of the strongly Deuteronomistic passages in the Jeremiah tradition. Undoubtedly these factors support the view that the homiletic sermon discourses and the narrative reports of the Book of Jeremiah, with their markedly preaching intent, have passed through the minds of the Deuteronomistic editors. What we cannot do is use this fact to affirm any single monochrome solution to the historical and literary questions of how close we are in these sermons and narratives to the actual words and events of Jeremiah's life. Sometimes we appear to be very close, at other times we appear to see Jeremiah only at a distance and to hear his words in a heavily formalized way.

The purpose of recording and preserving a knowledge of

210

the circumstances surrounding the preparation of Jeremiah's scroll can scarcely have been simply to provide an aetiological basis for the existence of Jeremiah's book of prophecies. The account of the replacement of the scroll is altogether too minor and incidental an addendum (v. 32) for this to have been the case. Rather it must be concluded that the central purpose of the narrative is to demonstrate the rejection of the word of God by the responsible authorities in Jerusalem, especially King Jehoiakim. Replacement of the scroll, then, has become indispensable to show that Jeremiah's prophetic book was authentic to the prophet, even though the contemporary rejection of this message by the king in Jerusalem had led initially to complete official repudiation of the prophecies and of their implied demands upon the nation.

This issue is central in the detailed coverage given to the various persons, policies, and events dealt with. It leads on naturally to a powerful and stark pronouncement outlining the grim fate that awaits Jeremiah (vv. 30–31). We may well conclude, as have some commentators, that the precise circumstances surrounding the king's subsequent death in 598 have been allowed to reflect the prophecy concerning it. Once the city of Jerusalem had surrendered to the Babylonians in 598 B.C., it is very probable that, with Jehoiakim already dead, his corpse was ignominiously dug up and exposed as an act of Babylonian reprisal for his rebellion. However this feature of the narrative in no way lessens the significance of the account of Jeremiah's prophecy; the purpose has been to establish a connection between the failure of the rebellion and Jehoiakim's unseemly end, together with his refusal to respond positively to Jeremiah's word from God.

There is another prominent feature in the account. This concerns the fact that the summary accounts of Jeremiah's prophetic message strongly emphasize a theme: Repentance by the house of Judah (v. 3), had it been made seriously manifest in time, could have averted the destruction of Judah and the ruination of the land—". . . so that every one may turn from his evil way, and that I [God] may forgive their iniquity and their sin" (v. 3). Nowhere does Jeremiah directly speak out in such explicitly conditional terms about his warnings and threats. It is a summary of their import, not a citation of the prophet's exact words. We may, however, fully recognize that such an appeal for repentance was in varying degrees implicit in all

211

prophecy. The intention in recording Jeremiah's message in this fashion has been to focus attention on the special guilt of the king and his court advisors for all the destruction that befell Judah and Jerusalem. By doing so the possibility of genuine hope for the future, once the guilty persons had been punished, was firmly established. Far from God wanting to destroy Jerusalem, he had sought through his prophets to warn the people extensively and repeatedly of the threat facing them; they had failed to heed the warnings in time (cf. II Kings 17:13–14).

It is not difficult to see that the overwhelming concern of the chapter, as in fact of most of the narrative accounts in chapters 34—45, is one of theodicy. It is set on establishing the true understanding of the holy and just will of God towards Israel and Judah, which sought the welfare and ultimate good of the people. This had to be maintained and reflected upon in light of the tragic and ruinous events which had taken place since the kingdom of Judah had fallen under Babylonian control after the battle of Carchemish in 605 B.C. The precisely given date for the compilation of the scroll of Jeremiah's prophecies "in the fourth year of Jehoiakim" (36:1) and the mention that it was read out to the people in the ninth month of the fifth year (v. 9; this would have been December 604 B.C.) is therefore inseparably related to the nature of Jeremiah's message. Whether or not (as seems most likely) Jeremiah began from this time onward to identify explicitly "the foe from the north" of his earlier prophecies with the Mesopotamian power of Babylon, this was clearly the understanding assumed by the compilers of the narrative. It should also be borne in mind that we possess independent biblical corroboration, in the short book of the prophet Habakkuk (which probably dates from 605–604 B.C.), that the imposition of Babylonian power over Judah at this time was recognized as a major political turning-point. All that had been anticipated by way of national revival since the collapse of Assyrian rule over Judah in Josiah's time was now clearly set in jeopardy.

It also becomes evident from the complexity of the literary structure of the Book of Isaiah (with its combining together of Assyrian and Babylonian powers as the [Mesopotamian] opponents of Judah (cf. esp. Isa. 13—14, 40—55) that the theological meaning of the onset of Babylonian power in Judah was a subject reflected upon deeply in prophetic circles. After the enthusiasm that attended the ending of Assyrian control over Judah

212

since the middle years of Josiah's reign, the threat that emerged from Babylon appeared as a cruel sequel (cf. Hab. 1:13). Jeremiah's scroll was undoubtedly the major and probably most significant spiritual and religious response to the new political fact of Jehoiakim's reign. Judah had now fallen under the control of the king of Babylon; the age of Mesopotamian domination of the Fertile Crescent as far as the border of Egypt was by no means over. Where the grip of Assyria had slackened, that of Babylon was now tight and firm.

The detailed references to so many individuals in the narrative, Micaiah ben Gemariah, Elishama the Secretary of State, Delaiah and others (vv. 11–14) is significant. This is also the case with regard to the attempt to arrest Baruch and Jeremiah (v. 26) through Jerahmeel, Seraiah, and Shelemiah. Evidently the attempt failed because popular support for Jeremiah enabled him, together with Baruch, to remain in hiding. This suggests that Jerusalem had become divided in its political loyalties and the king's will was by no means sure of being enacted. In reporting these facts the narrator has evidently been at some pains to draw attention to those individuals upon whom a major portion of blame rested for the misfortunes that befell Jerusalem.

Without explaining in detail the fact of Jehoiakim's opposition to and total disregard for Jeremiah's role as the messenger of God (with the implication that this amounted to an overt rejection of God) this serves to show the extent of hostility the king displayed to Jeremiah. It is possible that there was a measure of strong personal antipathy between king and prophet (cf. 22:15–19), but it should not be ruled out that Jehoiakim and probably other of Judah's kings held prophets in general in low esteem. However, Jehoiakim may have already shown himself headstrong and willful in his disregard for the welfare of his kingdom; so Jeremiah sensed that the king was prepared to gamble with his kingdom in a vain attempt to oppose the king of Babylon. So far as we can identify any single policy issue that lay behind all of Jeremiah's prophecies, it was to be found here. The lessons of a century of Assyrian rule over Judah, as Jeremiah saw them, were that the power of Mesopotamian interference in Judah could not be resisted without incalculable hurt being inflicted upon so small a kingdom.

A further point regarding the event narrated at length in chapter 36 is deserving of extensive reflection. The transition from oral to written prophecy was to prove to be far reaching

213

in its consequences. It gave birth to a wholly new understanding of prophecy; its original and immediate historical setting and application gave way to a much longer-term and wider-ranging interpretation of prophecy as disclosure of the mind, character, and intention of God to Israel. From being a series of more or less separate and disconnected pronouncements concerning God's coming actions, prophecy became a collected and preserved sequence of utterances reflecting on the very nature and being of God. In this way it acquired a more theological form and frame of reference and as such it has been handed down in Judaism and the Christian church. It became a groundwork for a theology of far wider relevance than its original historical and temporal significance could have allowed. Not only did the written form establish its long-term preservation, but it also entailed a degree of development in its meaning. From providing a message of divine warning and admonition to a relatively small circle of people who heard it, it came to offer a word of God in relation to some of the most poignant and tragic events in the history of Old Testament times.

Initially the circumstances of this shift were not directly intended to achieve this but were simply to ensure a hearing for this divine message, to which the king and his court refused to listen. This refusal necessitated resorting to the medium of writing to obtain a relevant hearing. By refusing to hear this prophetic word, the king eventually brought about a situation in which a far greater number, both of his and of succeeding generations, became hearers of this word. Prophecy took on a new power and a new vitality in written form. It came to be read and re-read in many new situations. Far from destroying the word of God, Jehoiakim's attempt to burn the scroll of Jeremiah's prophecies led only to its acquiring new force and range.

The specific prophecy addressed to and threatening Jehoiakim with an untimely end (vv. 30–31) is itself deserving of careful attention. In one sense it may have appeared to be a false prophecy since (after his act of rebellion against Babylon in 601 B.C.) it appears Jehoiakim died peacefully and was buried before the frightful consequences of his action could be brought home to him. Exposing his corpse (v. 30) most probably took place after the city had surrendered to Nebuchadnezzar and was clearly regarded as a mark of divine and not merely Babylonian reprobation. It has probably been introduced proleptically into the narrative to provide a fitting conclusion and to focus

214

blame on the king specifically instead of on the citizens of Jerusalem more generally. The end of rule for the royal house of David (v. 30) did not become a reality until removal of Zedekiah from his throne in 587, eleven years after Jehoiakim's death. However it is noteworthy that Jehoiakim's action in refusing to listen to Jeremiah rather than the later action of Zedekiah in rebelling against Babylon appears to have been regarded as constituting the major offense against God that called for special punishment. We may usefully compare Ezekiel's concern to lay the greatest measure of blame upon Zedekiah for his culpable breach of loyalty to the king of Babylon (Ezek. 17:15).

Overall, the question of the longer term continuance of the line of Davidic kings upon the throne in Jerusalem receives a rather confused and changing picture in the final edited form of the Book of Jeremiah (see above esp. on chap. 33). This varied picture in the book concerning the future of the kingship as a divinely ordained office and of only the Davidic family as the authorized dynasty from which the kings could be drawn must undoubtedly reflect the way the political situation in Judah changed more than once during the sixth century B.C. The great importance of the kingship as the major administrative office of government and the deep sense of historical commitment to the family of David found themselves in evident conflict with the fact that the kings of Judah had merited a large share of blame for the final collapse of the kingdom as an effective political entity. Many of the same tensions are to be seen in the edited form of the books of First and Second Kings, at once blaming the kings for their apostasy while at the same time recognizing the exalted position occupied by such rulers.

Many themes chapter 36 touches upon provide in broad summary most of the central issues and features of the Book of Jeremiah. The word of God had been faithfully delivered to the people in spite of strong hostility to it. Jeremiah had suffered forcible restraint and had experienced much difficulty in fulfilling his role as God's messenger. He had made uncompromisingly plain the threatening nature of God's message to both king and people. However, the word of God through Jeremiah had been firmly, repeatedly, and aggressively rejected. There was nothing the prophet had failed to do. Responsibility for heeding its content lay elsewhere, since such a word could not impose its own acceptance. The prophet's concern to leave testimony to the fact that the word of God had been faithfully delivered had secured for later generations the privilege of

215

reading this message in a written scroll. Thereby these later generations of Jews would be enabled to see how heavily blame was to be laid at the door of the last kings of Judah and how determinedly the prophet Jeremiah had fulfilled the terms of his divinely given commission.

Jeremiah 37—38
Jeremiah and Zedekiah

The story that unfolds in chapters 37—38 has a sequel in the events of chapters 39—45; it concerns the events that took place after Zedekiah, chosen to replace his nephew Jehoiachin on the throne in Jerusalem, rebelled against Nebuchadnezzar. These years witnessed the collapse of the kingdom of Judah, the ending of the kingship, and the painful years that followed. What took place between 588 and 586 B.C. formed the climactic focus for all of Jeremiah's prophesying. In many of their central features these events form a historical pivot-point for the entire Old Testament. Before this time, Israel and its surviving part in the kingdom of Judah still formed a nation. After these years the nation had become so dispersed among other nations that a whole new perspective of Judaism had begun to emerge in diaspora. The major events in the minds of those who had survived these calamities were those which related to the ending of the Davidic kingship and the destruction of the Jerusalem temple built by Solomon. Through what took place in 587 the most deeply venerated visible expressions of God's presence with and divine election of Israel as a people had been removed.

No doubt to a considerable extent a modern sociological perspective would recognize the fact that these institutional changes were simply the outer shell of an inner change that took place within Israelite life and religion, enabling it to pass from an older, national frame of reference to a later, more amorphous one in which Jews existed as scattered communities among other nations. Religion was the bond that held them together and gave them their special identity. The nation came gradually to be replaced by a large number of small close-knit communities, living under the rule of larger powers (Persia, Greece, Rome). In the process of this transition from a national

216

entity to a number of smaller religious communities, the role of the temple slowly declined while the importance of written Torah—the record of the law given through Moses—increased. It eventually came to occupy the central place in the liturgy of worship itself. With these changes the outward form of a richly elaborate order of cultus became less significant than the inward ordering of the human spirit in repentance towards God, contrition for sin both private and communal, and an earnest striving after obedience toward the law of God.

We can see that all of these changes begin to show themselves in the edited book of the prophecies of Jeremiah. In many respects this prophetic book provides a charter for the new Israel beginning to emerge. It is wholly fitting that the prophecies of this outstanding figure who appeared during the period of Israel's deepest disaster contain a sequence of narratives related to the events of this disaster. During a span of almost twenty years the kingdom of Judah collapsed under Babylonian domination; in a prophetic ministry of more than thirty years Jeremiah foresaw and interpreted these events. Jeremiah's activities assumed a significant role, but the narratives recounting them are not a "biography" in the modern sense. The stories are detailed, but to the end, this detail concerns the continuing conflict between Jeremiah and those to whom he prophesied. By and large his words fell on deaf and unresponsive ears, although clearly the authors of the narratives recognize that their readers will not now find themselves so unresponsive. What had happened had been a terrifying uncovering of the folly of Judah's leaders; those who now read of this folly and of Jeremiah's attempts to unmask it would feel very different sympathies.

The men and women and the handful of powerful political leaders Jeremiah addressed had shown themselves eager to leap at every vain movement or eventuality offering some prospect of saving Jerusalem and the lives of its citizens. Yet they had remained obstinately unwilling to heed the prophet's message and to accept that they were under the judgment of God.

We may discern in this conflict between the prophet and the political leaders of Judah a number of contributory elements. Not the least important of these was the weak and vacillating attitude of king Zedekiah, revealed in these reports as a relatively indecisive figure who was half convinced of the 217 rightness of Jeremiah's diagnosis of the situation. His response to Jeremiah was affected by a band of headstrong courtiers and advisors determined to withdraw all submissive allegiance to Babylon. Furthermore, Judah's experienced and seductive southern neighbor Egypt was deeply concerned to promote rebellion against Babylon for reasons of its own. It looked for northern neighbors who would act as a buffer between Mesopotamian advances and the interests of Egypt. It is not surprising therefore that Egypt promised military support to Judah, which it honorably tried to substantiate. Even though such promises were serious they proved hopelessly inadequate to the task. Egypt's defeat at the battle of Carchemish was a demonstration of the worthlessness of reliance upon Egypt. This would certainly have been apparent to Jeremiah and to many others in Judah.

Alongside these purely political factors, however, we must reckon that a falsely assured and complacent religious attitude led many to believe that God would surely deliver Judah, if need be by a miracle, as he had once before delivered Jerusalem from the clutches of Sennacherib in Hezekiah's time (II Kings 18—19). Political miscalculation linked hands with an excessive and complacent belief that God could be called upon to act to protect Jerusalem whenever his people turned to him in prayer. Such complacency led Judah into the abyss.

The first account of this intricate series of confrontations between Jeremiah and royal authority (37:1–10) relates an interview between Zedekiah and Jeremiah during the time when the Babylonian siege of Jerusalem had been temporarily lifted in 587 B.C. (cf. 34:8–22). It centers upon an appeal to Jeremiah to pray on behalf of the people (v. 3). The Egyptian forces moved to strike against the Babylonian armies, they proved to be no match for them, and had swiftly been driven back to their homeland (v. 7). However, before reinstatement of the siege there had been an almost euphoric optimism in the beleaguered city of Jerusalem that its troubles had passed. This has already been made clear by those citizens who supposed that the Babylonian army had gone for good and repossessed their freed slaves (34:11). It is likely that Zedekiah was among those who thought this to be the case. Supposing that the most serious threat of which Jeremiah had spoken had now passed, his sending to Jeremiah (v. 3) would have been intended as a move towards reconciliation. Jeremiah's clear and unequivocal answer affirms that the threat of destruction of the city still remained operative (v. 9) and that there was to be no escape. If

218

Zedekiah had supposed that Jeremiah was at some disadvantage, he was seriously mistaken. The situation and his sending to Jeremiah serve to highlight very clearly the weakness, indecision, and facile clutching at every straw of political advantage which marked Zedekiah's years on the throne of Judah. He was a weak leader who led his people to disaster, even though both Jeremiah and the editors of the book have gone to considerable trouble to show that he had many qualities better than those of Jehoiakim.

In 37:11–20 the scene is switched to one in which Jeremiah is portrayed as suffering imprisonment during the period when the siege of Jerusalem had been temporarily lifted. The amount of circumstantial detail reported in this short narrative is remarkable. The prophet had set out to go to his home territory in the Benjaminite region of Anathoth and had been recognized and arrested by a guard at the Benjamin gate of Jerusalem. The event must have taken place before the incident reported in chapter 32 and serves to explain the circumstances which led to Jeremiah's being kept under arrest in the house of the guard (32:2; cf. 37:1). This was obviously a much healthier and safer place for the prophet to be than the prison location in the house of Jonathan the secretary (37:15, 20). It kept the prophet under the supervision of the king, enabled food to be given to him until the city's supply became exhausted, and protected him against any privately expressed ill-will of the people. Jeremiah had become a marked man, and yet the king continued to show the same ambivalent attitude of seeking his support and approval while at the same time continuing to reject his words.

So far as the theological purport of the account is concerned, we can see further the extent to which it highlights the degree of hostility and rejection the prophet experienced. The reporter, however, has clearly been anxious to recall the better features revealed in the king's attitude, including his willingness to listen to what the prophet had to say. All of this suggests both a strong historical knowledge derived from an individual who was very close to the prophet (Baruch?) and a concern to remember the king in his different moods. Since the concern of the book is to show the importance of the hope of an ultimate restoration of the Davidic dynasty (cf. 33:14–26), this feature too **219** must have played a significant part in the composition. However the fundamental impression remains the same: The people had among their number Jeremiah, the prophet of God, who understood the full spiritual meaning of what was taking place in the nation and the city, yet his words went unheeded. The people, like the king himself, wanted the assurance provided by having a prophet to consult; yet they lacked the courage and the will to heed the warnings he gave!

An account of a further consultation of Jeremiah by Zedekiah during the time of Jerusalem's siege follows in 38:1–28. It is widely thought to be a duplicate account of events already recounted in chapter 37, although there are some divergent details. Where chapter 37 tells of Jeremiah's arrest in attempting to journey to Benjaminite territory, chapter 38 makes it clear that the prophet was charged with treason for having encouraged the population of Jerusalem to flee to the Babylonian lines. Furthermore, 38:7–13 tells of the intervention of Ebed-melech, a palace eunuch, in rescuing the prophet from the mud of the cistern into which he had been placed for imprisonment and certain death through eventual suffocation. Zedekiah's respect for the prophet, set against his inabilities to resist the pressures imposed upon him by his own advisors and officials, is also brought prominently to the forefront (esp. 38:5). We must conclude that various incidents in which the prophet had been involved are brought together in the two narratives. As a whole they are slightly varied duplicates of each other, offering a reasonably detailed and coherent picture of what happened to Jeremiah at this crucial time. The treasonable nature of Jeremiah's encouragement to the population to desert to the Babylonian lines (v. 2) is quite unmistakable. It appears shocking and has aroused considerable consternation and disapproval from many commentators for its almost complete lack of patriotic feeling for Judah and Jerusalem.

To see the narrative in this light, however, is to form too hard and one-sided a judgment concerning a situation Jeremiah quite properly already regarded as militarily hopeless. In his view it was better to submit to the rigors of Babylonian captivity than to invite further widespread and inevitable bloodshed. Jeremiah must have borne in mind a firm knowledge that in the similar situation that took place more than a century earlier (when Hezekiah had surrendered to Sennacherib) such action had led to the preservation of much that was important to Jerusalem and its government (II Kings 18:13–16). Zedekiah refused to surrender in this way, although he may have been more than half convinced that it was the only reasonable course

220

of action left open to him. His advisors were clearly set against it, perhaps fearing for their own future. The separate episodes undoubtedly took place in a relatively short space of time during the second Babylonian siege, and the theological motif which dominates is that of the folly of contravening the revealed will of God. Clearly Jeremiah was advocating a highly controversial and painful policy, yet we find no stern condemnation, only a rather general recognition that it was the only sensible course left. In the eleventh hour this was the only path left open in the hope of saving lives and property. Sadly, however, even this eleventh-hour way of escape was rejected. We can note a continuing and repeated concern to present Zedekiah in as favorable a light as possible—certainly far more favorable than that echoed in the Book of Ezekiel, where he is so sharply condemned. It seems as if some room was being sought to protect the image of the office of the king and to suggest that had the king himself been free to heed the prophet's words he might have retained his throne (v. 20). This had been the case for Hezekiah when faced with the necessity to surrender to Sennacherib. Each piece of the story therefore serves to reinforce the picture of the gradual throwing away of the last opportunities for Judah to preserve something of its national identity. As each such opportunity was missed in the face of the willful and repeated rejection of the word of God through Jeremiah, so the fate of Jerusalem and of the Davidic monarchy was sealed.

On the surface reading of the situation, the ending of the reign of the line of Davidic kings and the destruction of the Jerusalem temple (with all that this implied about the presence of God with Israel) were events that could only be construed as catastrophic. A modern reading of the situation would have no difficulty in seeing it as simply one further instance of the violent conflict between Babylonian imperialism and the Judean (Israelite) national feeling and identity. However the narratives of the Book of Jeremiah are powerfully concerned to repudiate any idea of fatalism or of tragedy as the realization of an inevitably destructive destiny.

We can discern two prominent theological motifs that color the entire sequence of stories with all their incidental details. The first of these is the insistence that there was nothing inevitable about the destruction that overtook Jerusalem. Nor was the ending of the rule of the Davidic line of kings a foreordained necessity. When the city's food supply had become

221

exhausted and the Babylonian soldiers broke through the city's defenses, there still was genuine hope in a purely individual way that those who would could save themselves by fleeing to the Babylonian lines. Overshadowing the private and individual choices, however, there lay the deeper awareness of an unreasoned but still widely entertained expectation that God would miraculously intervene. For more than a century the fact that Judah had managed to survive in the face of the repeated Assyrian and Babylonian campaigns in the region had encouraged the belief that somehow God would find a way to protect Jerusalem and uphold the Davidic monarchy. Now this hope of God's guaranteed determination to protect Jerusalem and the Davidic line of kings at all costs was to be shown as false optimism. It set visible religious institutions over against the covenant law of God upon which they were intended to be based.

The narrative of these events of the final months of Jerusalem's agony in 588–587 B.C. also brings to the surface a further easily misunderstood theological nuance. Zedekiah's vacillating attitude to Jeremiah's message, half believing the truth of his warnings and yet failing to act upon them, together with Jeremiah's insistence that even to the last those who would flee to the Babylonian lines had a way of escape point to one firmly held conviction. Jerusalem's defeat, the destruction of the temple, and even the ending of the reign of the Davidic kings were not to be regarded as inevitable events. They are presented as the product of human obstinacy and of a willful disregard of the word of God. In this way these narratives skillfully reject any acceptance of a deterministic or fatalistic view of human history. So also do they reject, for all the severity of Jeremiah's preaching, any idea of an incalculable and overwhelming outburst of divine wrath against all creatures. Even to the last God had left open a door of hope for his people, limited and distasteful as fleeing to the Babylonians must have seemed. The prophetic interpretation of the calamitous events which befell Jerusalem in 587 B.C. is thereby strongly pointed to indicate the reality of human freedom and the validity and efficacious nature of human choices. It affirms the openness of human history to the will and purpose of God. Within that purpose catastrophes can and do occur, but they are not enacted as the unreasoned whim of an all-encompassing superior divine power. Rather catastrophe is viewed as the consequence of bad decisions, brought about in continued and repeated defiance of the divine warnings that had been given to Israel and Judah. So in these narratives there is an extraordinarily high valuation of humanity and the high responsibility borne by human beings who have been made in the image of God. They are presented as real participants in human history and as those who help to create this history for good or ill. The fall of Jerusalem was not a pre-written passion play which God then enacted but a genuine divine-human encounter in which disaster resulted from the refusal to heed the possibilities God had left open to his creatures.

Reading these narratives with a theological perspective in mind, we can discern a rather unexpected emphasis upon a considered doctrine of divine grace and human freedom. Moreover, in spite of the tragic situation which provides the focus of interest, it is also a remarkably optimistic portrayal of human history. God never forecloses on the possibility of hope. The importance of individual choices is highlighted by Zedekiah's uncertain wavering between hearkening to Jeremiah and hearkening to his headstrong advisors, by Jeremiah's persistent advocacy of surrender, and by Ebed-melech's rescue of Jeremiah and his subsequent survival of the disaster. However strange and at times almost doctrinaire this prophetic assumption may appear to be regarding the moral and spiritual nature of human history, we cannot ignore its intense conviction regarding the reality of human choices. Human disasters are not to be seen as hopelessly succumbing to an already determined fate but as a failure to live up to the possibility of human choosing to do the will of God. Just as it is impossible to escape the consequences of bad decisions, so also is it possible to enjoy the benefits of making right ones. Moreover there is even a certain weighting on the side of God, since the way of repentance—of human turning back to God—is set as an avenue of grace. Zedekiah chose one way and Ebed-melech another!

Jeremiah 39
Jerusalem's Fall and Jeremiah's Reprieve

223

The account in 39:1–18 narrating the fall of Jerusalem has evidently been abridged from the fuller report of these happenings given in 52:4–16 (cf. also II Kings 25:1–12). The information is set out here because this event marked the pivotal center of all Jeremiah's threats and warnings. With the fall of Jerusalem to the Babylonians these threats had been "fulfilled." The record of what happened has become in a sense as essential to the preservation of the prophecies as the actual words the prophet used, since the event demonstrated the correctness of the prophet's interpretation of God's intended action. God had indeed determined to set "all the earth" under the hand of the king of Babylon (cf. 25:9,11). Only when the time of judgment for Babylon should itself arrive (cf. 25:12) would that intention be reversed. By rebelling against the king of Babylon, Zedekiah had been guilty of rebelling against God (cf. Ezek. 17:15). He had brought about the shaping of his own destiny and that of the dynasty of kings he represented.

The grim account set out in 39:4–7 of how Zedekiah was punished for his political ineptness is therefore an inescapable part of the story of Jeremiah's prophecies. The king of Judah had sought to escape by a hasty flight, once it was clear that any further resistance to the Babylonian advance into the city was hopeless. However he reached only as far as the plains of Jericho (v. 5) before he was overtaken and captured by a Babylonian posse. He was then brought before the king of Babylon in person at Riblah in Syria. After witnessing the slaughter of his sons, he was himself blinded and taken in a cage to Babylon (cf. Ezek. 19:9). He died there, probably soon afterwards. With him, there died the last of the line of Davidic monarchs in Jerusalem, although expectations soon emerged that this royal line of kings would eventually be restored through Jehoiachin or his sons (cf. above on chap. 33). Such expectations appear firmly expressed in Isaiah 11:1–5 and may possibly be hinted at in II Kings 25:27–30. The question of the future of the kingship was to remain significant for at least half a century more. Such hopes later revived in the second and first centuries B.C. when a new outburst of speculation emerged, built up on the basis of the preserved texts of Scripture. It is at this later period that it acquired the form of a "Messianic" expectation in something like the form that is attested in the New Testament.

A number of interesting, if only partly answerable, questions are raised by the report of Zedekiah's punishment. The stark reality of this painful and ignominious end to the last of the Davidic kings reigning in Jerusalem contrasts strikingly

224

with the more hopeful tone of Jeremiah's prophecy regarding Zedekiah in 32:4–5. Although in this prophecy Zedekiah is threatened with military defeat and capture, there is no hint given concerning the frightful circumstances surrounding his own removal from the throne. There is further in 39:4–7 a strong hint of a genuine feeling of sympathy for Zedekiah and his terrible fate. This connects directly with the favorable account given of Zedekiah's intervention on behalf of Jeremiah recorded in 38:14–19. All of these accounts, clearly emanating from circles that had been close to Zedekiah in Jerusalem, stand in contrast to Ezekiel's sign-action regarding Zedekiah's flight from Jerusalem (Ezek. 12:6). There Zedekiah's fall is viewed as an inevitable punishment upon him. There is further evidence of a strong feeling of hostility towards Zedekiah expressed in Ezekiel 17:11–21, which has already been remarked upon. All of this suggests that Zedekiah, the last of Judah's kings of the Davidic line, was a figure who aroused controversy in his lifetime and whose memory also left divided opinions. He exemplified in his own person the tragedy that struck Judah in 587 B.C., and he was held, in substantial measure, responsible for bringing it about.

Against this feeling we can find in these narratives in the Book of Jeremiah a genuine sensitivity to the pain of his sufferings, which others also shared. The weight of condemnation implicit in Jeremiah's prophecies is far from heaping all the blame upon the king. He was not to be regarded as a scapegoat for the nation's sins! Nor was this to be the attitude held towards the generation of Zedekiah's contemporaries who had taken the fateful steps bringing about Judah's downfall. The perspective affirmed throughout Jeremiah's prophecies is that the entire nation of Israel must be regarded as blameworthy for its collapse. Israel is held as guilty as Judah, and those taken into exile in 598 are condemned as fully and roundly as those who were left in Judah. There is a national sharing of guilt, and the condemnation of those left in Judah after 598 (chap. 24) is aimed at denying to this group a claim to spiritual superiority over their less fortunate compatriots. All have sinned; all have shared in various ways in the punishment; but equally the same avenue of hope lies open to all—repentance and a renewal of obedience to God!

225

We must also raise a further issue in regard to the place and significance of Zedekiah as the last Davidic king to reign in

Judah. Comparing the prophecies of Jeremiah with those of Ezekiel has suggested that those left in Judah after 598 felt more warmly towards Zedekiah and his royal office than those taken to Babylon, for whom Ezekiel's prophecies give evidence. A number of scholars have suggested that this may reflect the rather complex political arrangement devised under the Babylonian administration. In this Jehoiachin would have retained some status as the official king of Judah, with Zedekiah acting as his deputy and vice-gerent in Jerusalem (cf. W. Zimmerli, 1979, pp. 114–115). Jehoiachin would then have served as a hostage in his Babylonian imprisonment and the hands of Zedekiah would have been effectively tied and any attempt to further rebellion discouraged. It is possible that this was the case, although the evidence adduced is far from conclusive.

We must bear in mind that there are other indications that the holding of the first group of exiles in Babylon in special encampments may have been intended to make use of them as a lever for ensuring continued loyalty and payment of tribute money from Judah. We can see in the arrangements enforced, first by the Assyrians and then later by the Babylonians, that real difficulties were felt by the great Mesopotamian imperialist powers in maintaining control over distant territories from which they hoped to ensure further gain. What role the native kingships in the vassal territories might continue to play in such administrative plans is not made clear. Evidently it was seen to be advantageous, in spite of many failures, to work through native ruling dynasties where this could be made practicable. The remarkable sophistication and complexity of Assyrian vassal-treaties imposed on their subject peoples bears witness to this (cf. D.J.McCarthy, pp. 106ff.).

The narrative report in 39:1–10 concerning the surrender and destruction of Jerusalem points us to the major event which colored the career of Jeremiah as a prophet. It demanded careful reflection and evaluation. It is followed by two reports of a directly personal nature (vv. 11–18). The first of these reports the prophet's release from the court of the guard after the Babylonian administration had taken control in Jerusalem (vv. 11–14). The second report deals with the particular personal fate of Ebed-melech (vv. 15–18), who had proved himself to be a saving-helper to Jeremiah at a critical moment. A difficulty arises over the first account since it does not readily match the account of Jeremiah's being rounded up for deportation to

226

Babylon and then subsequently released (40:1–6). It is not too difficult to reconcile both narratives by reconstructing a plausible picture of what may actually have happened in the critical days after the Babylonians entered the city of Jerusalem. We have no further evidence, however, by which to test such reconstructions. From the perspective adopted by the editors, the main point of both these short narratives lies elsewhere than to give a precise record of the prophet's movements. Jeremiah's survival account followed by the account of the promised survival of Ebed-melech served to corroborate a major theological point. God took an interest in the destinies of individuals who showed loyalty to him, and a way was opened by which they could share in the future hope that lay beyond the current doom. Such indications of a personal survival of disaster could be presented as tokens of a larger national hope. Nor is it difficult to recognize that the authors of the narrative have seen in these happenings further proof, if any were needed, of the rightness of Jeremiah's words: the reasons for Jerusalem's destruction and the way this might have been averted had the king and his officials heeded the warning to surrender to the Babylonians.

We cannot escape the conclusion that the narrative which contrasts Zedekiah's fate with that of Ebed-melech has intended to affirm a highly personal and individual doctrine of divine providence, which is not easy to sustain if broadened to become a universally applicable doctrine.

Jeremiah 40—41
The Aftermath of the Fall of Jerusalem

The historical narrative section of the Book of Jeremiah pivots on the fall of Jerusalem to the Babylonian armies in July 587 B.C. This catastrophe provides the center of the entire book, and clearly it marked the major turning-point in the life and career of Jeremiah as a prophet. It brought an end to the worst of Jeremiah's personal sufferings at the hands of his own people, even as it also brought about a deep measure of suffering for Judah as a whole. The events now unfolded in the narratives (40:1—44:30) are brought to a conclusion with a short

227

epilogue-like prophecy to Baruch in 45:1–5 and fall readily into two main categories. The first of these relates to events in Judah shortly after the city had fallen (chaps. 40—41), and probably extended over a period of time lasting several months. The second block of material (chaps. 42—44) concerns the decision by a large element of the people who had survived the catastrophe and had re-established themselves in Judah to seek refuge in Egypt. They took Jeremiah with them, against his personal advice and wishes and against what is affirmed to have been the prophet's explicit command from God not to pursue such a course. Jeremiah was apparently overridden on this issue. The life of this community that fled to Egypt is then illustrated with a series of sermonic addresses from Jeremiah condemning the people's continued idolatry and their apostate conduct in their land of refuge.

These accounts have been designed to demonstrate the completeness with which these erstwhile citizens of Judah had forsaken and forfeited their heritage as the People of God. The information provided by Jeremiah's sermon in Egypt together with the heavy emphasis placed upon his (and God's) opposition to the plan to seek refuge and a new life in Egypt provide the major key to a theological understanding of these particular narratives. This key is the awareness of continued rivalry and conflict between the newly emergent communities of former Judean citizens divided between Judah, Babylon, and Egypt. The People of God could no longer be identified as a nation but were becoming resident aliens in the midst of foreign host nations. It is striking that Ezekiel branded as apostate the survivors in Judah (cf. Ezek. 33:23–29), whereas a prominent feature of these chapters of Jeremiah's book is to level a similar charge against those who fled to Egypt. By such a process we can see in the Old Testament how a sharpened focus upon the small company of exiles in Babylon as the remnant from whom the new Israel was to spring emerged. Whether this should be taken to imply that the final editing and composition of the Book of Jeremiah took place in Babylon is far from certain (as E.W.Nicholson, pp. 124ff.). It is certainly possible that in Judah also there arose a progressive attitude of looking to the Babylonian exiles, among whom were both royal princes and leading priestly families, as the basis of leadership and hope for the future.

228

The first of the narratives in this section about the aftermath of Jerusalem's fall relates how Jeremiah was given the choice whether to go to Babylon or stay with the remnant in Judah and how he chose the latter course. The new political administration for Judah is then described through the account of the appointment of Gedaliah as governor. The story of how Jeremiah was rounded up after his release from imprisonment (39:11–14) and forced to join the numbers of those destined for deportation to Babylon is told in verses 1–6. Why the Babylonians released Jeremiah only to assign him for deportation is not clear. This has led some scholars to regard the two accounts as standing in contradiction to each other. However this appears an unlikely conclusion, and it is better to assume the correctness and compatability of both reports, with the experience of 40:1–6 coming after Jeremiah had been freed. As J. A. Thompson has suggested, he may have been released only to have been picked up subsequently by a body of soldiers looking for numbers of citizens to be deported. Only after establishing his identity could his freedom to stay in Judah have been confirmed. No clear indications are given by what criteria those due for deportation were selected, and this may have been solely on a numerical basis and left for minor officials to decide. In general it appears that the wealthier citizens were taken to Babylon, but other factors could also have been operative.

When we bear in mind the deep interest shown in the relative loyalty and spiritual vitality of the separate communities of erstwhile Judeans in Judah, Babylon, and Egypt, it is not difficult to see why it was important for the authors to establish the point that Jeremiah had chosen to stay in Judah. Why he should have done so is not further declared, but it almost certainly implies that Jeremiah nurtured a high personal hope for the future of the community in Judah. The central message of his word of hope (32:15) had been: "Houses and fields and vineyards shall again be bought in this land." Jeremiah cherished "the land" God had given the nation's ancestors, and he attached great importance to it. Furthermore, Jeremiah's action in choosing to stay must demonstrate that initially he had expected the renewed Israel to arise through a reawakening of spiritual life and loyalty in Judah. The prophet's editors had then to show how this hope had been frustrated by what led to a positive turning to Babylon as the place where hope was to be found through the exiles there.

We learn of the new administrative arrangements for the

229

province with the appointment of Gedaliah as governor and the setting up of his district capital in Mizpah (40:7–12). In this one act the line of Davidic kings and their close bond with Jerusalem were set aside. How far this was a deliberate move concerning a new order and how far a necessary consequence of the ruin of Jerusalem we can only guess. It seems likely that it was intended as a firm break with the past, so it is noteworthy that Jeremiah appears willing to accept this. Neither a Davidic king nor a sanctuary on Mount Zion were essential to the divine plan for the new Israel, or so the implication of the new arrangement appears.

This situation is reported with a view to drawing attention to the possibilities that lay within it, but with a full intention of leading on to show how these possibilities were frustrated by Gedaliah's murder (40:13—41:3). It held out a promise which quickly proved to be unrealizable and futile as a result of this major political crime. The course of political developments in Judah (which took place after 587 B.C.) followed by the religious apostasy of those who fled to Egypt (and to which Jeremiah was a witness [chap. 44]) eliminated first the former and then the latter as effective participants in the hope of restoring a devout and loyal people of Israel. The intention of using these narrative accounts to establish his contention that all hope of Israel's restoration had narrowed to and centered upon the community of the exiles in Babylon is amply illustrated. Why this should have been so, and why the authors of the narratives felt so keenly about this issue is more difficult to understand. Clearly Jeremiah's personal actions (choosing to stay in Judah after 587 and then reluctantly joining the community that fled to Egypt) point to a situation in which the prophet acted differently from the way the narratives show would have been preferable.

We should certainly recognize that a number of political motives, no longer fully known to us, may have influenced the editors' convictions. Gedaliah was not himself a member of the royal line, so there was no attempt to designate his position as that of king. Furthermore the removal of the administrative center from Jerusalem to Mizpah, however necessary this may have been on account of the former city's destruction, would have aroused inevitable resentment. The "city of David" was not to be so readily discounted. For those who had come to regard Jerusalem as the rightful and indispensable spiritual and political center of Israel this was an action bound to offend their sensitivities, especially when we consider priestly attachment to Jerusalem. This had undoubtedly been intensified after Josiah's action in restricting all sacrificial worship to Jerusalem (II Kings 22—23). No doubt this move to Mizpah was aimed at undermining traditional patriotic feelings in Judah on the part of those who were now committed to serve under the will of the king of Babylon. Obviously we are forced into the position of speculating over these questions, although it is not difficult to appreciate that the negative attitude adopted by these narratives to the short-lived experiment of Gedaliah's governorship from Mizpah (under overall Babylonian sovereignty) would have attracted inevitable opposition. Such opposition was linked to established concerns regarding the Davidic kingship and the unique Jerusalem traditions attached to the temple, which quickly surfaced again after the setback occasioned by what happened in 587 B.C.

There are also a number of interesting features that surround the leading personalities involved. Gedaliah's family had figured prominently in Judah's administrative life for more than half a century. His grandfather Shaphan had been secretary of state to Josiah (II Kings 22:8–10), and his father Ahikam had been responsible for intervening on Jeremiah's behalf at the time of the latter's temple sermon (26:24). Furthermore the naming of Gedaliah's supporters at Mizpah (40:8) indicates that a strong party of local leaders had joined forces to establish firm control over the province. Their ample food supplies (40:10,12) show that the effects of the siege were now being allayed and also that this had taken place with the assistance of the local population, possibly under Babylonian supervision. The author has gone into considerable detail to show the viability of the new situation under the hand of Gedaliah and to point out that this took place with the full recognition and support of the Babylonian authorities. Gedaliah's murder and the events which follow are shown to have been all the more tragic and unnecessary (40:13—41:3). Throughout there is an implied, though not overtly declared, assumption that Judah's social and economic revival under the hand of the king of Babylon was an effective political and religious possibility.

The circumstances relating to the murder of the governor Gedaliah are now presented in 40:13—41:18 at significant length and with a wealth of circumstantial detail. We need not doubt the fact that they record an authentic picture of events

231

otherwise not attested in the Old Testament. Not only was a member of the royal line of Judah directly and centrally involved, Ishmael-ben-Nethaniah (41:1), but also Baalis, king of the Ammonites, acted as his sponsor and protector (40:14; 41: 15). Age-old rivalries between leading families and national communities in the region had flared up in the wake of the confusion and weakness brought about by the Babylonian invasion. An unmistakable feature of the story is recounted with full awareness that those reading it and pondering its significance could not fail to accept its clearly implied conclusion. Those who had survived the death and destruction brought about in the siege of Jerusalem and its aftermath had tried courageously to restore normal life in Judah. They failed, not through their own personal guilt or misdeeds but through the tragic complexity of events in which the evil intentions of Baalis, king of the Ammonites, had been allied to those of a worthless and unscrupulous member of the Judean royal house. Hope of restoration from within the Judean community was ruled out and henceforth the whole focus of a restored Israel was directed to those exiled in Babylon.

This is a powerful theme coloring all future hope in the Book of Jeremiah, and in even larger compass was destined to become a major feature of the way in which prophetic hope developed in the post-exilic period. Hope came to be indissolubly related to the notion of "return," in the spiritual sense of a returning to God in obedience and in the sense of a physical returning from the lands of exile to the homeland in Judah (cf. Isa. 11:11). Meanwhile those in Judah had suffered such political reverses that the entire land had been reduced to ruin and desolation. The Chronicler later portrayed the entire aftermath of 587 B.C. in Judah as a dark age in which the land had been left desolate and virtually empty (II Chron. 36:20–21).

The story of Gedaliah's murder requires little in the way of extended comment. Its various subordinate stages become more or less self-explanatory. The report introduces us to some of the fundamental characteristics of the way in which the narratives of the Book of Jeremiah deal with the events and all that surrounded them of those years. There is no doubt at all where the sympathies of the authors are to be found, and these are assumed to relate closely to the ideals and hopes of the intended readers. Gedaliah's statesmanlike courage and good will contrast dramatically with the evil intentions of Baalis and the

232

treachery and self-seeking of Ishmael. Throughout the story the character of the Babylonian administration is presented as both fair and trustworthy. Fear of Babylonian reprisals against the general public after the assassination of Gedaliah is shown to be unfounded (esp. 41:18). The reader is expected to see in the period of Babylonian overlordship an acceptable administrative rule, though it could never be wholly desirable.

It may even have been a significant part of the editors' intention to encourage the view that Jewish existence under vassalage to the king of Babylon was both possible and reasonably acceptable (40:9–12; cf. 42:11). This was an inescapable necessity for the exiles in Babylon from whom so much was now being expected so far as a renewed Israel of the future was concerned. At a more personal level the narrative brings out that the reasons leading to the panic-stricken flight to Egypt against the declared will of God (through Jeremiah) were unworthy ones. They were the product of fear and distrust. Such a perspective sheds valuable light on the aims and future expectations of those who have given the Book of Jeremiah its present shape, at least in its narrative section. Later a more sharply hostile attitude towards Babylon has been injected into the book (chaps. 50—51). This must be regarded as a matter of immense theological importance once we consider the later view of Jewish attitudes to the Persian administration which arose in the time of Ezra, Nehemiah, and the Chronicler of their work.

One incidental feature of the story of Gedaliah's murder has given rise to a considerable amount of comment and discussion. The arrival of a party of no less than eighty pilgrims from the celebrated northern Israelite cities of Shechem, Shiloh, and Samaria with gifts to present at "the temple of the Lord" in Jerusalem is striking and unexpected (41:5). After being systematically destroyed by the Babylonians, it could readily have been supposed that the temple would have fallen entirely into disuse (cf. Lam. 2:7). The indication given from this episode is that at least the temple area and certain of the altars remained accessible for worship. Veneration for the temple site had continued to enjoy recognition, even by the citizens of those very cities with long-remembered religious traditions of their own, which had often been antipathetic towards Jerusalem. By his selection of material, by skillful sketching of the characters of the principal persons involved, and by drawing attention to the

233

issues raised by events, the implications of these happenings are effectively brought home to the readers of the book.

One further major issue needs to be noted. The land of Israel, understood in terms of a divinely given gift and closely related to questions of its ownership and use, was to become a prominent feature of controversy and deep theological reflection in the period of the exile. This is well highlighted in the narratives and prophecies of the Book of Jeremiah, offering a strong contrast to the more systematized understanding given in the Book of Deuteronomy (cf. Brueggemann, *The Land,* pp. 107ff.).

The situation of the survivors in Judah brings out the fact that not all of those who maintained a strong religious claim to this land were able to enforce their claim in the turmoil of the period. The Babylonian invasion had brought about much confusion, still further exacerbated by the emergence of exiled communities in both Babylon and Egypt. These communities by no means gave up all interest in or claim to this land. So the entire issue of the religious meaning of the land of Israel came to take on a new perspective as a consequence of what had happened in 587 B.C., which has left a profound legacy in the post-exilic literature of both the Law and the Prophets (cf. W.D. Davies, pp. 49ff.).

Jeremiah 42:1—43:7
The Flight to Egypt

An unexpectedly long and transparently clear theme runs through this narrative: 'They (i.e., the surviving remnant who went to Egypt) did not obey the voice of the LORD" (43:7). In spite of Jeremiah's presence among those who fled to Egypt after Gedaliah's murder, the account makes it plain that this was a wrong move undertaken at the behest of "insolent men" (43:2). Why such strong feelings had arisen against the Jewish community in Egypt by the time these events were recorded in this fashion is not explained. Almost certainly such a feeling had arisen among the circle that edited Jeremiah's prophecies; blaming the community in Egypt for a deep spirit of apostasy tends to offset the contrastingly high expectations concerning

234

the exiles forcibly taken to Babylon. The concluding picture in chapter 44 of the evident apostate spirit among those who had fled to Egypt forms a natural sequel to the story of how they came to seek refuge there.

When we examine the separate details of the narrative report in the light of these general observations, a number of significant features come to the forefront. The account of Gedaliah's murder sets the scene by showing the tensions that had arisen among the community in Judah; and it shows why after so much hardship and suffering had already been endured all hope had not been extinguished and why anxiety for flight from the land had arisen. Now a point appears to have been reached when a kind of despair took hold of the leaders of the community convincing them that further efforts to restore normal life in Judah were hopeless. Fear of Babylonian reprisal for the murder of Gedaliah, even upon those who had not been directly involved in the event, led to deep uncertainties about the future. A strong emphasis is achieved in the narrative through repetition, especially where the leaders seek guidance from God through Jeremiah (vv. 2–3); they disclose an attitude which they fail to maintain. These selfsame leaders declare unequivocally and entirely of their own volition: "Whether for good or ill we will obey the voice of the LORD our God . . ." (v. 6). Apparently the remark is made in full sincerity and with every intention of adhering to its spirit. The narrative emphasizes this affirmation and the freedom with which it was made only to lead up to the point later where it was not obeyed (vv. 20–21), in spite of the fact that the will of God had been made explicit. The fearful, hopeless fate which awaited them in Egypt— sword, famine, and pestilence—was therefore to be understood as wholly deserved. It was for them a self-chosen disaster: The narrative effectively "disinherits" the community that had sought refuge in Egypt from any place in the renewed Israel.

Jeremiah's prophetic prayer and his enquiry for guidance on behalf of the fear-struck community is unfolded in detail. Jeremiah accedes to the request; a full ten days elapse before the divine response becomes known (v. 7). God's firm injunction to remain in Judah and not to flee to Egypt is fully spelled out (vv. 10–17). Furthermore the reasons for the flight to Egypt— fear of reprisals by the king of Babylon—are declared groundless (vv. 11–12). In spite of their previous promises concerning

235

the genuineness of their desire to know God's will, the remnant in Judah (led by Azariah-ben-Hoshaiah and Johanan-ben-Kareah, together with other "insolent" [arrogant, headstrong] men) determined to seek refuge in Egypt. Surprisingly, in view of the sharpness of his disclosure, Jeremiah went with them. The inference is that he was taken by force, although this is not spelled out with any clarity. It is possible that in spite of everything he chose to remain with the people he felt divinely called to serve. A large company then proceeded on this journey, including more than one of the princesses of the royal line (43:6). The narrative has been concerned to show that Jeremiah's going to Egypt was entirely out of line with the guidance God had given through Jeremiah to the community.

It was evidently a matter of great importance to the authors of the narrative to show that the hope foretold by the prophet for the community of Israel in the land of Judah (32:15) had been compromised by what took place afterwards. It could be realized in only one way: by the return from Babylon of those who had been taken there. They are the standard bearers of hope and the promised remnant!

We are left to speculate why the feelings against the community that had gone to Egypt should have been so strongly expressed, especially in view of the fact that Jeremiah was of their number and must have died there.

It is noteworthy that the authors of the story were deeply concerned to show that there was nothing to fear from the action of the Babylonian authorities. It is firmly implied that this administration could have been trusted to be fair. It posed no threat to those who were merely innocent victims of the crimes of others. Possibly there were already strong indications that all was not well with those who had gone to Egypt, and this news had come to the attention of the authors. In any case, their purpose seems to have been to encourage an attitude of acceptance and trust to the Babylonian administration rather than risk further break-up of the surviving community in Judah. It is unfortunate that we know so little about the circumstances and hopes of those who did remain in Judah after 587 until Babylonian control over the region ended. The narrative that follows has been designed to show the despair of those who went to Egypt; this despair led them into ever deeper apostasy so that they lost all sense of being the People of the Lord God.

Jeremiah 43:8—44:30
Apostasy and Division in Egypt

Now the folly of the flight to Egypt by the remnant in Judah (taking Jeremiah with them) is fully and extensively spelled out. First Jeremiah declares (43:9–13) that Nebuchadnezzar, from whom the fear-struck Judeans were endeavoring to flee, would invade Egypt. So much then for their misplaced anxiety to flee from the power of the king of Babylon! This prophecy is followed by a long homiletical discourse, not unlike later Greek diatribes, rebuking those who had fled to Egypt (chap. 44). They are shown to be guilty of the most ill-founded and conventionally naïve form of apostasy. They have returned to the age-old and completely discredited worship of "the queen of heaven." Both prophecies belong in close relationship and have been set alongside each other to show that the message of assurance concerning Israel's eventual restoration, central to the Book of Jeremiah, could no longer include such people. They had forfeited their right to share in the hope of the new Israel that God had promised. This is strikingly clear and marks a point of major importance for the circles among whom the Book of Jeremiah was expected to be read.

The sermon discourse in chapter 44, which rounds off the whole sequence of narratives about what happened to the community that remained in Judah after 587 B.C., is formulated in the style and vocabulary of the Deuteronomistic circle. It brands those who fled to Egypt as unashamed apostates who had abandoned all genuine loyalty to the Lord their God. In spite of the fact that Jeremiah, whose prophecies have been so vital to understanding God's action in the defeats of 587 B.C., was among them they are totally unresponsive to his preaching. We can recognize that the broad intention of the prophecy of 43:8–13 is similar, although it is less clear how closely it relates to a direct knowledge of Jeremiah's actual words. The central point has been knowing of Nebuchadnezzar's campaigns as far as Egypt, amply demonstrating the folly of fleeing to that land. The contention that "all the world" was to remain under the

237

rule of the king of Babylon until his own time for divine removal should come is consistently substantiated (cf. 27:7).

Nebuchadnezzar invaded Egypt in his thirty-seventh regnal year (567–566 B.C.) to secure plunder and to extend his power to Africa. Almost certainly there was a desire to weaken Egypt yet further, thus removing the possibility of Egyptian support for rebellion in the states to the north. Jeremiah's prophecy takes the form of a sign-action performed at the entrance to the celebrated royal palace in Tahpanhes. The king of Babylon would set up his throne at this location, meting out to the rulers and citizens of Egypt the same cruel fate administered to other peoples further north. Memories of what had happened in Judah after 587 and to Zedekiah at Riblah in Syria may have been all too consciously present to the authors. They knew this was exactly how a Babylonian king would behave! Further punishment would take the form of plundering the richly furnished temples of the deities of Egypt (v. 13), an act of gross impiety and further proof of the powerlessness of the gods of Egypt. This is not seen in relation to the conduct and religion of the Egyptians but more directly related to the conduct of the Judeans who fled there. Egypt offered no haven from the will of the Lord, the God of all nations; God was using the king of Babylon to work out his own plan among the peoples of the earth. The same dread agencies of death and devastation—sword and captivity—which had been felt so terribly in Judah would be felt in Egypt also. There was no escape from the will and power of the Lord God! When Nebuchadnezzar marched into Egypt in 567 B.C., it was seen as proof that the decision of the survivors in Judah to flee there was a mistake.

We should not rule out a further, more speculative feature concerning the sharply critical attitude towards those who fled to Egypt, especially as it contrasts with the much more positive attitude towards Egypt and the Egyptians revealed in the Book of Isaiah (cf. Isa. 19:18–25). Those who edited the prophecies of Jeremiah have evidently gone to some trouble to inculcate an attitude of acceptance of Babylonian administrative rule, if not of positive cooperation with it. Resistance is futile and destructive. It may have been the case that those who fled to Egypt from Judea could not and would not accept such an attitude, so this prophecy has been recorded to show the mistakenness of their position. It appears likely that the whole narrative and the sermonic section of Jeremiah 41—45, dealing with the after-

math of the catastrophe of 587 B.C., has been designed to establish a pattern of behavior and political action (and inaction!) in
the small community existing still in Judah. They were urged to
look for guidance and support to the exiles in Babylon, rather
than to former compatriots in Egypt.

In chapter 44 we have an admonitory address ascribed to
Jeremiah which shows that he maintained hostility toward his
fellow Judeans for their apostasy. All was now effectively lost for
these divided Jewish people in Egypt. Having lost their foothold
on the land, they abandoned the last bonds of loyalty and faith
in the God who had given that land to their ancestors. They had
inwardly lost the power to reason aright concerning their fate
and their hopes for the future. The wordy homiletical style of
the Deuteronomistic authors of this sermon, combined with its
stereotyped and conventionalized descriptions of Israel's religious disloyalty, confirm that this is a composition from Jeremiah's prophecy made for this point in the narrative story to
provide an interpretation of the spiritual condition of those who
had sought refuge in Egypt. They are accused of returning to
the worship of "the queen of heaven" (44:18,19,25). The overall
intention is clear; recording such a Jeremianic sermon is to
demonstrate the spiritual unfitness of the Jews in Egypt for
participation in the future hope. They are accused of complete
abandonment of their ancestral faith and now they lacked the
inner motivation and spiritual insight which could have given
them new hope. Hope is seen as an aspect of religious loyalty
and faith; despair as its opposite. They had chosen despair
rather than hope.

The Elephantine Letters which derive from a Jewish colony in Egypt a century later (cf. Pritchard, pp. 491ff.) may assist
to corroborate the general picture of a compromised and poly-
theistic version of the Israelite faith among some Jews in Egypt
(cf. W. F. Albright, pp. 168ff.). However we cannot directly
identify these Jews at the military colony of Elephantine (Yeb)
in the late fifth century B.C. with those depicted in the Book of
Jeremiah. Nonetheless all comparative evidence of the effect of
living in an alien religious environment shows how strong the
pressures are for the abandonment of an older and increasingly
obsolete body of religious ideas and practices.

The authors of chapter 44 did possess some direct knowl-   239
edge of the religious practices of the Jews exiled in Egypt.
Probably Jews they were aware of in several places (Judah itself

and possibly also Babylon) were inclined to reason in the manner described in 44:16–19. The Lord had failed the nation, allowing it to be defeated and dismembered. Even his glorious sanctuary in Jerusalem had suffered destruction. It would have been tempting and superficially plausible to return to the worship of the goddess Ishtar (the queen of heaven) and the rituals celebrating the powers of life and death seen in the natural order. The counter arguments in 44:20–23 reaffirm the whole-hearted and passionate conviction of the exclusiveness and authority of the Lord as the God of Israel. He alone was worthy to receive worship from his people who had survived the disasters that had befallen Judah.

A further point requires careful reflection. The goddess described as "the queen of heaven" was a form of Astarte, also found in the Assyrian-Babylonian sphere as Ishtar. Aspects of the worship of the goddess Anat, whose name is recalled in Anathoth, Jeremiah's birthplace, also show a number of essentially similar characteristics. These are usually described as features of a "fertility" goddess, although this is really too narrow a characterization. Anat (-Astarte, Ishtar) was a goddess who brought "life," expressed most of all in her sexuality, and her power was sought to bring about safe childbirth among women, healthy offspring, and freedom from disease. Her devotees called upon her to promote the benefits of life and fertility in all their various aspects. Although her sexual power as a giver of life and children received most prominent attention by ancient worshipers and was linked to a number of licentious fertility rites, it was not this aspect which secured her such wide appeal for so many centuries. Sexuality was a part of the larger mystery of life; the dangers of childbirth, widespread infant mortality, and the many undetectable ways in which death could strike through disease all vested her with added fascination and fear.

Worship of the queen of heaven, therefore, was a continuing and almost ineradicable temptation to many generations of Israelites and Jews. Her links were with life itself, not the more abstract entities of nation, temple, and the unique national traditions of Israelite religion. It cannot be a matter of surprise therefore that after the collapse of the Jewish state there should have been a reawakening of the age-old appeal of the mother-goddess figure. Worship of this "life" goddess knew no national boundaries in the ancient Near East, and we take it as a mark

240

of the carefully thought-through apologetic of this sermonic discourse to have used the vague title "queen of heaven." Each community would know such a goddess under her particular local name and form. The apostasy that is condemned among the fugitive Jews in Egypt was thereby shown to be widespread and a temptation to communities of Jews in many locations. In a number of respects it is more readily intelligible that such a temptation remained stronger in Judah and Babylon than in Egypt.

The vigorous polemic contained within the dialogue between Jeremiah and the Jews in Egypt was, therefore, not simply intended to brand only one section of the increasingly scattered Jewish community seeking to reestablish a viable existence among alien nations. In a wider sense it was applicable to the mentality and thought processes of the many scattered groups of former Judean citizens. They sought to make a new start in an unfamiliar and unfriendly environment, but the national elements attaching to the religion of the Lord God of Israel appeared to discredit the value of continuing to worship him. Rather the appeal of the queen of heaven seemed to proffer the appeal of "life."

All such apostate thinking which implied a turning away from the Lord, the God of Israel, is firmly rejected in this sermon ascribed to Jeremiah. It represents an "up-dating" of Jeremiah's message for the newly emergent communities of Jews who would be the readers of the book. Such apostasy is presented as a counsel of cynical despair and misguided folly that could only lead to further ruin and disaster. In general the entire aim and meaning of the Book of Jeremiah is designed to oppose turning from God. It is entirely appropriate that this "last address" from the great prophet to those driven into exile was concerned with it.

Israel had from the beginning been familiar with a dual religious tradition: On the one hand there was the religion of the Lord God, with its strong national basis and high moral austerity and purposefulness. On the other side was the cult of "life," focused especially upon the god Baal and the goddess Anat; the aim of the cult was to promote fertility, blessing, and protection against death, epitomized in the figure of the god Mot. Mot is a god of total negativity, concerned only with the destruction of life wherever manifested. He was a deity no one could worship or come to terms with. In returning to this

241

worship of the false goddess who proferred life, there was an inherent temptation to return to a religion of great simplicity; it was uncluttered by the demands of morality and required only the appropriate rites and offerings: "... burn incense to the queen of heaven ... pour out libations ... then we had plenty of food and saw no evil" (v. 17).

Jeremiah's austere prophetic tradition of the worship of the Lord God demanded a more thought-provoking religion involving obedience, moral rectitude, and especially belonging to a nation: Israel. Throughout the five hundred years that ensued upon the ministry of Jeremiah, when more Jews came to be living in an alien world of the Diaspora, the temptation to return to the simple demands of the worship of the queen of heaven remained. Jews could become "like the nations round-about" by adopting a form of religion easily recognizable and readily acceptable to such gentile host nations.

We have good reason to recognize, therefore, that even though the prophecy of chapter 44 can hardly be precisely Jeremiah's own words, it represents a profound and intensely moving summary of his essential message. The disasters that had befallen Judah had left the broken and scattered remnants of the nation with a painful world to deal with and stark choices to make concerning their future. The message of the Book of Jeremiah addressed to them is passionately and penetratingly expressed in this last address to the rebellious Jews who fled to Egypt. The choice facing them was one being presented to many comparable communities of scattered Jews. They had to choose to remain loyal to the Lord as God and in doing so to choose a path of hope and restoration. The alternative was to turn back to the spurious promises offered by the seductive queen of heaven.

Jeremiah 45
The Consolation of Baruch

Baruch, Jeremiah's scribe and disciple, had been taken with the prophet to Egypt (43:6). This fact helps to explain the presence of this short consolatory prophecy to him here. If there was no hope at all for those who had fled to Egypt (42:22), then it would follow that even these two loyal worshipers taken there unwillingly could have no individual hope. Would this not then have been deeply unfair of God to deal with such loyal and righteous individuals wholly in terms of the communities to which they now belonged? Already the splitting of groups of Judeans into smaller communities was beginning to raise this question. The theme is taken up in Genesis 18:23–33, where many scholars have seen the influence of the post-exilic situation beginning to manifest itself. The prophecy addressed to Baruch by Jeremiah in 45:4–5 deals with this issue. We may feel that much of the answer the prophet gives is negative: "What I have built I am breaking down, and what I have planted I am plucking up—that is, the whole land" (cf. 1:10; 2:21; 31:5).

In such circumstances there could be only a limited prospect of hope for Baruch. He could not enjoy a private, separate salvation set apart from the community to which he now belonged. Yet on the other side there was still something precious he could receive and experience as a gift from God: "I will give you your life as a prize of war in all places to which you may go" (v. 5). This positive and reassuring message at first glance appears to be little enough. On reflection, however, we can see it has a wealth of meaning and is the product of long reflection. Life itself is a precious gift and always provides a fundamental opportunity for the knowledge and service of God.

In considering this seemingly personal and private message addressed to Baruch, we should not fail to see that it has been deliberately set down in a manner that has wider implications. The concluding phrase provides an important clue to recognizing this: "in all places to which you may go." Baruch is presented here as representative of all the loyal Jewish citizens carried unwillingly into an alien and hostile world. Baruch was an example of those who were to become the Jews of the dispersion. He is therefore presented as an archetype of "the wandering Jew." He no longer possessed a land of his own; he had no temple in which to worship. Daily he encountered neighbors who taunted him and his fellow Jews about their distinctive beliefs and forms of worship. His loyalty to God had become a potential cause of difficulty and persecution, so that normal social life would be continually affected by this. God's determination to break down and to pluck up the whole land had brought these inevitable and unenviable social limitations upon the dispersed. However Baruch is given firm and full assurance

243

that he remained a child of God's election and heir of a great religious tradition. Daily he continued to receive the greatest of all gifts—life itself! This then was to be enjoyed and savored in all its many facets.

In reflecting upon the distinctive fate that had befallen Baruch, taken against his will to Egypt, the Book of Jeremiah contemplates along with him the destiny of many others compelled to share his experience. The Babylonian imperial expansion to the borders of Egypt had brought about a great upheaval in the entire region of the Levant. Whole populations had been broken up, and the little kingdom of Judah had been broken apart in the new political alignments forced upon the country. Out of this experience a new dimension of Israel had been brought to life: scattering into a number of small communities which no longer comprised separate nations. Jeremiah's message to Baruch is also intended to address these people, that they might find in their straitened circumstances a basis for hope. They, like Baruch (cf. v. 3), would have good cause to bemoan their fate; yet they could learn to find within it a basis of hope for the conquering of despair and for a continued experience of God. They could share the consolations promised Baruch until the time when God determined once again to build up and plant his people afresh in their own land. Meanwhile Baruch, and fellow exiles like him, had to learn to be content with their meagre destiny, which was not what he would have chosen for himself. For the readers of the Book of Jeremiah who could almost echo the fears, anxieties, and disappointment experienced by Baruch, they could learn to find beyond these fears and anxieties and disappointments the continued providence of God's gracious purpose.

PART SIX

The Testing of the Nations
JEREMIAH 46—52

With chapter 46 we begin a new section of the book continuing through chapter 51 which deals with prophecies against foreign nations and peoples. To these there has been appended in chapter 52 a summarizing review of the major events which formed the political background to Jeremiah's prophecies. The other major prophetic collections of the Old Testament contain similar series of prophecies against foreign nations (Amos 1:3—2:16; Isa. 13—23; Ezek. 25—31) confirming the importance of this type of prophetic speech to the religious and political world of ancient Israel. It comes as no surprise therefore to learn that at his call Jeremiah was designated "a prophet to the nations" (1:5). From a textual and literary point of view the foreign nation prophecies of Jeremiah have elicited considerable attention because they are placed differently in the ancient Greek text of the book. They appear after the title in 25:13*a* in this Greek version, so that 25:15–38 of the Hebrew text forms their conclusion (this is then chapter 32 in the Greek). Furthermore the order of the prophecies is different in the two versions and the Hebrew text is substantially longer (see above, Introduction).

The literary and textual distinctiveness of these prophecies simply represent one aspect of their special interest. A whole range of significant issues is connected with the differences that exist between the Hebrew and Greek versions of the book. Such differences reflect directly the extended process of composition and editing which brought the book to its extant form. Not all the questions can yet be regarded as having been resolved to the satisfaction of a majority of scholars. From the theological

245

and historical perspectives they reveal how the prophetic understanding that God was at work in and through the events of the Babylonian campaigns in Judah necessarily occasioned a wider questioning of the divine purpose with respect to other nations. If these close neighbors of Judah were caught up in the same events, was not the same divine purpose that related to Judah also operational for them? Inevitable questions relating to the interpretation of the divine purpose for all nations arose out of the conviction that historical events manifested in some way a divine purpose. A number of general questions relating to the meaning and significance of the prophecies addressed to foreign nations and cities are dealt with in my book *Prophecy and Tradition* (pp. 58ff.).

There is an element of necessary reasoning implicit in the prophetic concern with the fate of the nations close to Judah similarly made victims of Babylonian domination during the sixth century B.C. If, as Jeremiah declared, Yahweh the God of Israel was controlling and using Babylon to punish Judah, then what was God's purpose with respect of these other nations who did not worship him as the Lord? Was the same Lord God punishing them also, although they did not know him by name? If so, what were their sins? Were they perhaps simply to be regarded as purely innocent victims of events which concerned them only indirectly? Major questions regarding the morality of God's actions and of the theological implications of monotheism are involved with the answers presented or implied regarding these issues.

We may deal initially and briefly with certain literary questions which cannot be left out of consideration. The possibility that the whole unit of Jeremianic foreign nation prophecies at one time circulated as an independent block and came to be incorporated in dissimilar ways into the Book of Jeremiah (as suggested by Thompson, pp. 686ff.) is improbable and is too simple an explanation of the complex textual and structural distinctions which appear. The process of the book's composition has certainly taken place in successive stages (cf. W.McKane's hypothesis of a "rolling corpus") and it would appear that the location of these prophecies in the Septuagint represents an earlier literary situation than does their position in the Hebrew Masoretic text. Later proto-apocalyptic interests of Jewish interpreters and scribes has led to the foreign nations prophecies being transposed to form the end of the Jeremiah literary collection. To regard Jeremiah as the author of the entire collection is almost certainly mistaken, although it is highly probable that at least some of the prophecies emanate from him and that he was truly "a prophet to the nations." It has been widely concluded among scholars that Jeremiah was the author of 46:2–12 and 14–24, since both these prophecies relate to events occurring in the period of the prophet's ministry. It should also be considered that certain other prophecies in the collection may also have originated with Jeremiah. However there are so many contacts in certain of them with earlier passages and themes from the Old Testament, and so stereotyped a pattern of formulation, that in general Jeremiah's authorship appears unlikely. The primary reason for locating a collection of such prophecies at this point has been the historical fact that all these nations along with Judah were profoundly affected by the same military and political impact of Babylonian expansion. If God was at work in these events, then the divine purpose must also incorporate these other peoples in its range. Furthermore there are marked indications, most notably in the long prophecy against Moab in Jeremiah 48, that extensive expansions and additions have been made over a period of time to the original prophecy or prophecies.

The prophecies against Babylon in chapters 50—51, which show several literary connections with similar prophetic materials in Isaiah, reveal a different character and purpose from the rest of Jeremiah 46—52. They almost certainly have had a later origin and serve a different purpose in the collection as a whole.

Why a prophet such as Jeremiah should have felt moved to proclaim prophecies against foreign nations and cities is not susceptible of any uniform explanation. Probably most prophets did concern themselves with the destinies of neighboring nations, so that Jeremiah would have been no exception. However the major reason for their inclusion in Jeremiah's book must lie in the fact that the events relating to what Jeremiah had to say about Judah embraced a great many other nations also. It is also important to note that there is no single emotional tone evident throughout the prophecies, whether of shared grief, vengeful recriminations, or a naïve "I told you so!" sense of satisfaction. There are many moods expressed in them, and only in the prophecies against Babylon is there a consistent affirmation that this empire's downfall is a well-deserved punishment from God.

247

Jeremiah 46
Against Egypt

The first two prophecies are addressed to Egypt and are to be found in 46:1–12 and verses 14–24. The first of these is related to the defeat of the Egyptian army at Carchemish, which took place in 605 B.C. This was a city on the Upper Euphrates in Mesopotamia, and the defeat of Pharaoh Necho's army there left the entire Fertile Crescent open to the domination of Nebuchadnezzar. As a result of this defeat, Judah, which had been under Egyptian control since 609 B.C., came under the hand of the king of Babylon. Egypt's defeat therefore marked a turning-point for Judah and brought king Jehoiakim under the power of a new master. That Jeremiah should have had a message to declare about Egypt at this time comes as no surprise, since what was taking place had the most direct bearing on the internal situation in Judah. All the more is this likely if the politics of the kingdom had been divided over whether to look for an accord with Egypt or with Mesopotamia once Assyrian power had collapsed.

The second prophecy in verses 14–24 comes as a direct sequel to this and may well have been proclaimed by Jeremiah at about the same time. At this period Nebuchadnezzar was making preparations for an advance into Egypt, since the way lay open to him and the lure of Egypt's famed riches must have been great. With her army defeated Egypt lay helpless before the ambitions of Nebuchadnezzar (cf. v. 19): "For Memphis shall become a waste, a ruin, without inhabitant." Compare also verse 24: ". . . she (Egypt) shall be delivered into the hand of a people from the north." The prophecy is of interest on a number of counts. It clearly offered a kind of news forecast concerning the military advance of Babylon, which would have been of great significance to all who had listened to Jeremiah's warning concerning "a foe from the north." It is also noteworthy that it contains no note of bitterness or hostility towards Egypt, and this in its own way is remarkable. This absence of any word of bitter ill-feeling or reproach towards Egypt has called forth from a later writer the comment of verses 25–26. This seeks to identify the culpable figures in Egyptian society as "Pharaoh and those who trust in him," and so to point out that the events were a deserved punishment for the tyrannical behavior of Egypt's ruler and her idolatrous religion.

So far as the book's readers were concerned, Egypt's defeat at Carchemish and its powerlessness to halt the further advance of Nebuchadnezzar into Egypt were part of the mysterious divine purpose behind the rise of Babylon to become a world-conquering power (cf. 25:8–11; 27:6–7). Egypt's defeat and suffering were closely allied to and broadly contemporary with the sufferings and defeat of Judah. There could therefore be no misplaced satisfaction over Egypt's downfall that did not also relate directly, and even more forcibly, to Judah's helplessness before the power of Nebuchadnezzar. The significance of Egypt's defeat was that it rendered impossible any hope of Egyptian assistance for Judah against Babylon.

Verses 25–26 can be seen then as a later scribal addition supplying some indication of why Egypt needed to be punished. It positively explains Egypt's defeat as a punishment for the worship of the false gods of Egypt, especially Amon of Thebes and the offense occasioned by Egypt's Pharaoh who encouraged such false worship. The tradition of Israel's ancestors suffering oppression in Egypt (Exod. 1—12) has served to highlight the condemnation of Pharaoh, together with all his claims to power, both political and religious.

It is noteworthy that in the narrative tradition of Exodus 1—12 as well as in the short addition here a clear distinction is made between the Egyptians and Pharaoh; Pharaoh receives strong condemnation without this being fastened upon the people of Egypt more generally. On this account special attention is given here to the assurance that "afterward Egypt shall be inhabited as in the days of old" (v. 26). The Egyptian people were then to share happily in the richness of their land. The tone of this assurance points to a warm feeling of tolerance towards the Egyptian people without any expectation that this would eventually lead to their turning to worship the Lord as God (cf. similarly Isa. 19:23–25).

The precise date the addition of verses 25–26 was made cannot be determined, although it is likely that it points us to the period of expanding Jewish settlements in Egypt during the later years of Babylonian rule over Judah. A yet later editor has then added further comment in verses 27–28 concerned with the future destiny of Israel over against all nations. It is one of the few fully apocalyptic type interpretations of prophecy found in the Book of Jeremiah promising the final destruction of gentile nations and the glorification of Israel. A key theme is that of the "full end" (Heb. *kalah*) decreed by God upon the nations (cf. above on 30:11). Israel too must be punished, but this will take the form of a chastening which will not result in Israel's final demise. The short unit undoubtedly interrupts the overall sequence of prophecies concerning foreign nations, but is clearly intended to be directly related to them. The question of the ultimate fate of the nations that were Israel's neighbors when Babylonian power dominated the entire Fertile Crescent as far as the border with Egypt has raised the more theoretical question concerning the final destiny of all the peoples of the world. The continued tension felt among Jews after the exile between the threatening and promissory elements contained in the prophetic tradition are here reconciled in the portrayal of a terrifying *dénouement* to all history, which would serve as a theodicy for the reality that the Lord is God and would also explain the historical experience of Israel's weakness and sufferings.

Jeremiah 47
Against the Philistines

Like Judah, the Philistines were caught up between the larger powers of Egypt and Mesopotamia. Since the whole period that extended from the middle of the eighth century B.C. down to the fourth century, Judah had been trapped between Mesopotamia (Assyria and Babylon) and Egypt. Philistia had found itself locked between the same external powers. Situated at the northern border of Egypt this cluster of cities had been used by Egypt to serve as a buffer against incursions from the north. The possibility of an Egyptian attack upon Gaza therefore, which is mentioned in 47:1 (although this is absent in the Greek text!), is readily intelligible. The precise date of this attack is not known and suggestions have ranged between possible Egyptian attacks upon the Philistine cities in either 609 or

601 B.C. or a Babylonian attack upon Philistia after 605 B.C. We certainly ought not to rule out the possibility that a yet later event is envisaged. The reference to "waters rising out of the north" would certainly point us to a Mesopotamian source of danger.

In spite of these uncertainties the intent of the prophecy is clear: the Philistine cities are to experience fearful destruction in which the northern enemy is understood to be acting as God's agent. No reason is given as to why this must happen, nor in what way the Philistines had offended God. All is seen as part of the same comprehensive divine purpose to bring about the submission of all nations to the king of Babylon. The significance of the prophecy is considerably enhanced by the lack of any simple moralistic condemnation of the Philistine cities for their traditional reputation as enemies of Judah. By its retention and inclusion with others which deal with fellow-sufferers of Babylonian imperial power, it is clear the prophecy is intended to point to a larger divine purpose at work in historical events, involving many nations.

When we press further to ask the cause of such a major political transformation of the ancient Near Eastern world, we are faced with a somewhat muted reply. The biblical prophetic tradition has sought to affirm that there are reasons bringing about such changes and that at every turning-point the Lord God has remained in control. In certain cases clear explanations are offered why some nations must suffer, and undoubtedly Judah and Jerusalem are to be set at the head of such a list. Yet they are not alone in such world-transforming events, so attention must be given to the sufferings and miseries inflicted upon the entire region. History is leading to a changed world-order and the prophetic tradition expressed in the oracles against foreign nations affirms that this change is the working out of a divine purpose. In making this affirmation there is a firm rejection of older mythological ideas concerning the divine apportionment of the boundaries of all nations as part of the act of creation itself (cf. Deut. 32:8).

Over against such a mythological conception of world order we find instead a historical order elevated to reveal a process of re-creating of the world under the hand of God. The simple insistence upon moral principles discernible in what was taking place among the nations, such as in certain prophecies addressed to Moab (48:11, 26–27), provides some explanation of

251

why God was acting in this way. Beyond it however there is more than a hint that some "grand design" is operative and that it is important for prophecy to provide a basis for understanding this. Real significance would seem to lie in such prophecies, like that here directed towards the Philistines, where no such moralistic explanation is offered. To pretend to supply it on the assumption of Israelite nationalistic fervor would appear to be mistaken. A genuine element of questioning the nature of historical reality appears to have motivated the complex structure of the prophetic literature of the Old Testament. That the Philistines should suffer defeat and destruction, as this prophecy declares, is viewed not as the opportunity for gloating over the downfall of a traditional enemy but as an important pointer to a larger and still mysterious purpose of God in re-creating the human universe.

Jeremiah 48
Against Moab

Jeremiah 48 is made up of a series of prophetic utterances against Moab which can conveniently be divided into a number of smaller units (J. Bright, followed by J.A. Thompson and R.P. Carroll, formulates these as vv. 1–10, 11–17, 18–28, 29–39, 40–47; see their *Jeremiah* commentaries). However this division is more than a little artificial and can be regarded only as a provisional assessment. Undoubtedly a singularly complex literary history and structuring underlies the chapter as it now stands. The Septuagint omits a number of verses (including most of vv. 40–42, 45–46) and clearly verse 47 has been added later. There are prose insertions in verses 12–13, 21–24, 26–27 and 34–39, besides some positive borrowings from Isaiah 15—16. That any of the chapter originates with Jeremiah must be regarded as highly unlikely, although some of the material appears to be from the period of Babylonian power in the region. It is the fact that Moab, as a close neighbor and traditional rival of Judah, was heavily caught up in the events surrounding Babylonian domination of the region in the period 605–538 B.C. that has occasioned its inclusion at this point. Like Judah and Philistia, Moab after initially succumbing to Nebuchadnezzar's demands re-

252

belled and suffered severe devastation. As a result it progressively lost its national identity, never to regain it.

The territory of Moab was situated to the east and south of Judah, bordering the Jordan Valley and the Dead Sea. After the sixth century B.C. it became prey to incursions by tribes from Arabia, which came eventually to dominate the territory. Moabite identity disappeared. Chapter 48 is intended to present a comprehensive overview of the divine purpose for Moab.

In ethical and theological content we find a considerable shift of tone and outlook in these sayings addressed to Moab. The final unit portraying Moab as helpless and defeated has a strong feeling of pity for the victims and shares in their fear and confusion (vv. 40–46). The sayings that precede this, however, sharply condemn the traditional pride of Moab (vv. 29–30 condemn Moab for rejoicing over Israel's misfortunes and v. 27 develops an accusation of complacency against Moab based on its fame for good wine). A more theological note has been struck in verses 12–13 by introducing a denunciation of the worship of Chemosh, the name under which the Moabites worshiped God. Verse 10 adds a touch of brutality by its comment "cursed is he who keeps back his sword from bloodshed," but the precise context for this is not made clear. This too may be a later addition to reinforce the sense that Moab's downfall was just punishment for her offenses against Judah (cf. Amos 2:1–3). All told, however, there is a mixture of emotions displayed against Moab throughout the chapter and virtually nothing by way of direct allusion to identifiable military actions. We should not therefore rule out the possibility that more explicit historical allusions have been deliberately suppressed in building up the whole composite poem. In a number of places heavy use is made of place-names of Moabite territory, with extensive wordplays upon their significance.

In spite of the sharper note of hostility to be found in these verses, when compared with the prophecies against Egypt and Philistia which have preceded them, it is evidently the quest for an understanding of the meaning and significance of Moab's downfall that is uppermost in the prophecy. Israel has not been alone in her sufferings since others, even age-old rivals and enemies like Moab, have been overtaken by the same world-changing events in which the rise and fall of entire nations had been manifested. The reaction to these changes displayed in this prophecy embraces the fundamental search for meaning in

253

history and for the justification of the ways of God towards humankind that we sense still remain with us in the present. It is one thing to recognize and to grasp the nature of what has happened in such major world events, but it requires a much deeper level of understanding to reflect upon their meaning. It may be legitimate to respond that such prophecies as are preserved here in the Book of Jeremiah offer only a partial answer to such questions, and this appears to have been consciously recognized even in the period of the formation of the book. Nevertheless, by the manner in which the poems have been composed, often out of earlier fragments and on the basis of very limited acquaintance with the affairs of the nation concerned, there is a careful attempt to bring together the framework in which a fuller understanding is to be sought. In the process of piecing together a historical "map" of the range and savagery of Babylonian conquests among Israel's neighbors, there is a concern to mark out its pattern, to relinquish old grievances and enmities, and to search out in the character and conduct of the nations dealt with some basic clues to understanding the nature of the historical order. Not least is the concern to draw attention to the powerful currents of historical and political change as a part of the creating and re-creating work of God.

In our attempts to grasp the theological value of this long and complex prophecy addressed to Moab, several factors forcibly present themselves to our attention. In the first place the desire to be comprehensive, as evidenced by the range across the full extent of Moabite territory and with this an overview of the entire history of the Moabite people, should be regarded as a feature of religious importance. Traditional and deeply felt attitudes towards the Moabite people are expressed through the characterization of Moab's pride (vv. 29–30), there is bitter anger expressed against the worship of Chemosh (v. 7), and even Moab's high reputation for its good vintage is turned against it (v. 11). Nevertheless, all such negative attitudes are totally swallowed up in the larger recognition of the tragedy and horror of Moab's sufferings in the wars against Babylon. The sense is that Moab has suffered far more than it or any people deserve, so that although Moab has been punished for her faults (v. 44) the onward sweep of Babylonian power points to a deeper purpose in history than a simple pattern of retribution. By the richness and variety of its poetry, the prophecy as a whole displays a genuine sense of grief shared with Moab in her sufferings (vv. 45–46). A later editor has developed this still further by expressing a hope of Moab's ultimate restoration to a place among the nations of the earth (v. 47). By such a complex range of emotions and images the author of the finished poem has endeavored to see mirrored in Moab's fate a key to understanding the destructive element in human history. Wrapped in the fabric of the historical process an ineradicable element of tragedy is seen and an awareness that all human pride in achievement can be made futile and devoid of lasting greatness. Great triumphs and understandable pride and self-esteem may lead on to an eventual unexplained and terrifying downfall. Even so, hope of renewal and a new beginning is never wholly lost (v. 47).

Jeremiah 49
Against Other Nations

The series of prophecies against foreign nations is now enlarged with threats directed against an additional five nations: Ammon (vv. 1–6); Edom (vv. 7–22); Damascus (vv. 23–27); Arabia (vv. 28–33); Elam (vv. 34–39). Four of these were close neighbors of Judah and were caught up in the Babylonian conquests, but the last of them, Elam, was more distant and appears to have been included for a different purpose. In any case it prepares for the transition to the long sequence of prophecies against Babylon in chapters 50—51, which bring the collection to a conclusion.

The disparity in the length of the various prophecies suggests that they are not all from a single source and have simply been brought into the overall scheme. This is further borne out by the presence of short sayings drawn from earlier prophecies (vv. 9–10 are closely parallel to Obad. 5–6 and vv. 14–16 correspond to Obad. 1–4). There have also been some additions made in prose (vv. 12–13, 20, 34, 39). It seems then that the individual sections of the prophecy have been put together on the basis of traditional sayings so as to make a single rounded whole. Further additions to this already long series of prophecies have then been made.

INTERPRETATION

It is unlikely that any of the prophecies derive directly from Jeremiah since it is once again the direct involvement of these peoples in Nebuchadnezzar's campaigns of conquest that have prompted their inclusion in Jeremiah's book. Ammon, Edom, and Moab had all been involved in the plan for a concerted withdrawal of allegiance to Nebuchadnezzar in 594 B.C., which came to nothing. More adversely felt was the willingness of Edom to join forces with the Babylonians in the campaign against Judah in 598–597 B.C. (cf. Obad.; Lam. 4:21). Ammon too had undoubtedly taken advantage of the Babylonian defeat of Judah in 598 to make territorial gains in the southern Jordan valley, and we must remember that Baalis, king of Ammon, had played a major role in sponsoring the assassination of Gedaliah (40:13—41:15). In the traditional attitude felt by Israel, Ammon was regarded as a rival for territory and as a dangerous political enemy. Similarly Edom, which occupied most of the region east of the Rift Valley from the Dead Sea to the Gulf of Aqaba, was a constant threat. Periodic alliances between these peoples and Judah appear to have been short lived and largely forced by political necessity.

In the prophecy against Ammon the promise is that Israel would repossess territory taken from her by Ammon. Whether this refers to action of the recent past or to gains made by Ammon in the eighth century when Assyrian power swept across the region is not made clear (cf. Amos 1:13–15). In either case this assurance that Israel would restore the situation is most probably a later addition to the text. For the rest the prophecy offers little explanation why Ammon was doomed to suffer so violently at the hands of Nebuchadnezzar. It had boasted of its strength as a people (v. 4), which suggests that a people proud of its fierce warlike tradition could not now complain when a more fierce and militarily skilled nation brought desolation upon it. Unlike some of the prophecies concerning Moab, there is little sympathy expressed for Ammon's fate.

The words of assurance concerning eventual restoration of Ammon (v. 6) are certainly a later addition pointing to a more generous feeling that in the coming eschatological age even Israel's most traditional enemies would experience the saving health of God's grace (cf. also 48:47 and 49:39). In fact, once Babylonian domination had passed, Ammon, like Moab, suffered incursions from Arab tribespeople which left them powerless to re-establish their national identity.

256

The prophecy against Edom in verses 7–22 has undergone considerable expansion, as is evident from the prose units in verses 12–13, 17–22. The alleviating word of comfort for Edom's children in verse 11 contrasts with the surrounding context and may itself have been added later. There is a torrential outpouring of bitterness and anger towards Edom, with no effort spared to bring home in vivid poetic imagery the full horror of the fate that was shortly to befall the people. There is no hint of sympathy for those who were to suffer the same fate that had so deeply wounded Judah. However this renders all the more surprising the absence of any explicit sins which had called forth Edom's fate. Nor is there any indication of the circumstances and political conflicts which had served to bring it about. Surprisingly the downfall of Edom, as of the other nations made the subject of these prophecies, hangs in the air as a fate decreed by God with virtually no explanation, either moral or historical. Only the mood of the poem reveals a sense that this fate is fully deserved. Those who have lived by the sword are about to perish by it. The words concerning national renewal for Moab, Ammon, and Elam are designed to present this work as a mark of God's grace, who desires to maintain national boundaries as part of a world order.

The next prophecy is addressed to Damascus (vv. 23–27), the city which effectively represents the Syrian people. Since the neighboring small kingdoms of Hamath and Arpad are mentioned in verse 23 there is a possible intention of affirming that all these kingdoms are to be taken together. The prophecy is brief and does no more than describe the sufferings and defeat of the people of Damascus in battle. No explanation is offered why this punishment has to come, or by whom it will be inflicted. Only the general context implies that this too will be a consequence of the advance of Nebuchadnezzar westwards from Babylon. The poetic images throughout portray the violence and carnage of battle. Since it is probable that one of the earliest roles fulfilled by a prophet in biblical times was to hurl threats and denunciations against enemies in time of war, we can deduce that such pictures of the aftermath of a battle were an established element within certain categories of prophecy. There is a hint, at times more than a hint, that war is a supreme manifestation of human folly and sinfulness. In rejecting the order and peace of God's rule, human beings have left themselves open to the ruinous consequences of their own greed and

257

love of violence. In boasting of their power and strength these neighbors of Israel had left themselves open to prey by a more powerful conqueror. Nebuchadnezzar of Babylon was such a conqueror.

If such is the intended message, then more than a purely nationalistic message in favor of Judah was conveyed. On the basis of a tradition in which local and nationalistic loyalties were given expression through prophecy, there has emerged here a sense of moral order and human destiny that stretched across national boundaries and had universal meaning. This succession of vivid pictures of nation after nation watching the slaughter of its finest young men in battle and witnessing the ruin and devastation left in the streets of its once beautiful towns and cities, gives a firm hint that war itself is a major evil that offends the reign of God. It is pictured as a flagrant consequence of human pride and self-assertion, set over against the acceptance of the righteous and just order of God for all nations.

The fourth in this group of shorter prophecies concerned with nations involved in Nebuchadnezzar's campaigns is addressed to Kedar (vv. 28–33). This is representative of the Arab tribes which dwelt in the Syrian desert region, to the south and east of Judah. They too had suffered defeat at the hands of Nebuchadnezzar (v. 28). The city of Hazor that is mentioned (vv. 28,30,33) can hardly be the well-known city of that name to the north of Galilee. It appears to have been a settled oasis town in the desert to the east of Judah. The people are pictured as the familiar distrusted and feared tent-dwelling bedouin. They harried and plundered the settled peoples to the west and took great pride in their hardiness. They subsequently proved to be a thorn in the side of the Babylonians, who undertook a punitive raid against them in 599–598 B.C. In the prophecy here nothing suggests that the defeats inflicted by Babylon were retribution for offenses perpetrated against Judah. Rather, as in the other related prophecies, there is a desire to draw attention to the larger, divinely ordained purpose operative in the Babylonian conquests.

The last of the short prophecies (vv. 34–39) is addressed to Elam and is precisely dated to the beginning of Zedekiah's reign (ca. 597 B.C.; v. 34). A substantial distinction relates to the presence of this prophecy, since Elam lay to the east of Babylon and was in no way to be regarded as a close neighbor to Judah, as were the other nations named. The date of the prophecy in verse 34 may provide some clue for its inclusion here. Zedekiah's reign in Judah marked the commencement of Babylonian exile for king Jehoiachin and those deported with him from Judah. As a powerful people domiciled close to Babylon itself, it is possible that some quarters in Judah had nursed hopes that Babylon would quickly find itself caught up in a military campaign in the east. It would then be too preoccupied to trouble Judah further, a calculation which must have weighed heavily with those who urged Zedekiah into further rebellion. Portrayal of forthcoming defeat for Elam would then have been intended to remove any thought by Judeans that Babylonian power was in imminent danger of collapse through troubles in the east. Relevance to the situation in Judah can then be clearly inferred.

Jeremiah 50—51
Against Babylon

The message of the extremely long prophecy of chapters 50—51 is simple and direct: Babylon will itself eventually suffer military defeat and be left a desolate ruin. For all this simplicity in the basic content of the prophecy, its structure and wider significance raise issues of considerable complexity. Its literary structure shows it to have been composed from a number of shorter prophecies and its message about Babylon's fall raises major questions concerning the attitude towards Babylon displayed in Jeremiah's earlier prophecies in Judah. The shorter prophetic units are readily identifiable, so that J.A. Thompson identifies no less than thirteen sections (50:1–10, 11–16, 17–20, 21–40, 41–46; 51:1–14, 15–19, 20–26, 27–33, 34–40, 41–48, 49–53, 54–58). The concluding prose report (51:59–64) of a sign-action commissioned by Jeremiah, dated to Zedekiah's fourth year (594–593 B.C.), has a separate origin and character, despite its obvious connection with what precedes on account of its message concerning the doom of Babylon.

The fundamental stratum of the prophecies describes in vivid poetic imagery the downfall of Babylon, firmly understood to be a yet future event. The most forceful of such word-pictures are seen in 50:1–3, 11–16, 21–40, 41–46; 51:1–14,

259

41–48, 54–58. They describe the all too familiar horrors of war. This time, however, they are consistently colored by a sense that this will satisfy a deep longing for vengeance on the part of peoples who have suffered long and that Babylon's ruination will be a richly deserved doom. This power had brought war and destruction to many nations; now war and death had entered into her very heart with all its pitiless savagery. Death and devastation would be found on all sides, leaving the city of Babylon a perpetual ruin.

These prophecies, typical of the type found in the Old Testament addressed to foreign nations, must go back to the oldest levels of prophesying in biblical times. The themes and word-pictures show a stereotyped character, fully borne out by the fact that the prophecy of 50:44–46 represents an adaptation with only slight change of wording of the prophecy addressed to Edom in 49:19–21. Only the name of the nation-victim is changed. Onto the larger compilation of the units into a single prophecy a number of identifiable additions have been made. Since Babylon's downfall affected the future hope of Israel as a nation, there have been introduced certain appeals to Judean exiles to flee from the doomed city (51:6,9). This is coupled with a promise that the defeat of Babylon will make possible a return of such exiles to their homeland and to Zion (50:4–5, 17–20).

A didactic hymn of praise in 51:15–19 signifies that all of this will be a result of the providential rule of God, who wields unlimited power and impartial justice in determining the rise and fall of nations. This is a straightforward repetition of 10:12–16. Babylon as the metaphorical "hammer" of God to hammer the nations (50:23) is elaborated upon in 51:20–23, emphasizing that sovereignty over all nations and peoples belongs exclusively to God. The hammer itself must suffer a violent blow, thereby utilizing a conventional theme of the circle of retribution which completes a pattern of moral order. Such pieces have been developed secondarily to bring further comment upon and to provide fuller interpretation of the world-wide significance of Babylon's coming downfall. Though this event still lies in the future of the prophetic author, it is presented as wholly assured. God's justice demands it.

260

The date of composition of the basic anti-Babylonian prophecies is not indicated directly, but it must lie somewhere between 598 and 538 B.C. This can be narrowed further if we take into the reckoning that the destruction of the Jerusalem temple is twice referred to (50:28; 51:11), which would point to some time after 587, although the separate prophetic compositions may not have originated at the same time. It is significant that the circumstances surrounding the rise of Cyrus and the Medo-Persian empire, which eventually brought about the overthrow of Babylonian power in 538 B.C., are not spelled out and clearly lay in the future. The basic prophecies should then be assumed to have arisen between 570 and 550 B.C., almost certainly as separate units, and only subsequently brought together to form a single collection. They have been further supplemented to adapt them more fully into the Book of Jeremiah. It must be regarded as highly unlikely that any of them derive directly from Jeremiah (see further below on the narrative of 51:59–64). They form a coherent whole which appropriately rounds off the book of the prophecies of Jeremiah, all of which have been concerned, either directly or indirectly, with the period of Judah's submission to Babylonian rule (605–538 B.C.). While there is a *prima facie* case for supposing that such prophecies originated in Judah, the use of the cipher "Sheshak" for "Babylon" in 51:41 indicates a need for secretiveness and subversiveness in the prophecies, which would not be incompatible with an origin of some of them among the Babylonian exiles.

The theological significance of these prophecies requires fuller and deeper reflection than has often been accorded, since they reflect upon a number of central issues regarding biblical prophecy as a whole. Their intensely political nature is obvious, as is their undoubted delight in the strong conviction that retribution will soon be inflicted upon Babylon for all the misery and suffering it heaped on other nations. Vengeance belongs to God, and there is obvious delight in the expectation that he will repay Babylon in full for its violent exercise of power. A sense of purpose strongly animates these prophecies and is the outworking of the belief that God's power is ultimately assured to achieve its purpose in human history. No hint of sympathy for Babylon is expressed, but rather the reverse. No suggestion is found here that in the passing of Babylon a great civilization with immense achievements to its credit will have passed from the scene of world history. There is even a simple outburst of thanksgiving and praise to God that Babylon's days are soon to be finished (51:15–19)!

The emergence of this attitude to Babylon and its eventual

261

dominance of the entire prophetic literature of the Old Testament must undoubtedly have been part of a complex process of political and religious thinking. Originally it must have been less uniform and complete. It is noteworthy that Ezekiel, in his prophecies against foreign nations, nowhere breathes a word about an eventual downfall of Babylon. He leaves unexplained how Israel's restoration is to be brought about, except that it will be the work of the spirit of God acting graciously and for the honor of God's own name (Ezek. 36:22–32). The Book of Isaiah, conversely, is effectively dominated by the awareness that Babylon had succeeded Assyria as the oppressor of the nations (as also here in 50:17–20) and that it in turn would be punished. The prophecies of Babylon's downfall now preserved in Isaiah 13—14, 40—55 constitute a central and vitally important part of the message of the book. The Book of Jeremiah too, by the inclusion of this many-sided prophecy in chapters 50—51, conforms with this message concerning Babylon's forthcoming defeat and removal from the throne of world power. How it relates historically to Jeremiah's actual prophesying is far less clear.

Chapter 29 refers to two Judean prophets among the exiles in Babylonia, Ahab and Zedekiah; they had prophesied lies in God's name and were executed by burning as a result of this fact coming to the knowledge of the Babylonian authorities (29:21–23). Although what they prophesied is not, to our knowledge, now preserved, the context leaves no doubt that the message concerned Babylon's imminent downfall and the speedy return of the Judean exiles to their homeland. This is shown by the nature of the Babylonian retribution and by Jeremiah's counter-message that those who had gone into exile would stay there for the rest of their normal life-span (seventy years, 29:10). How are we to understand the message of chapters 50—51 as being in any significant way different from the "lies" condemned by Jeremiah with respect to these two unfortunate prophets?

We must also take into account the fact that the detailed accounts of the aftermath of Jerusalem's destruction in 587 B.C. preserved in chapters 40—42 present very forthrightly a message concerning the necessity for Judah's continued submission to Babylonian rule, at least for the foreseeable future (cf. esp. 27:11–12; 40:9; 42:11–12). Such rule is presented as being trustworthy and fair. Babylon's downfall is regarded as inevitable but left to an undefined future, namely, "until the time of his

262

own land comes" (25:12; 27:7). Even then it is outlined in brief affirmations. It could be argued that this has been precisely because a much fuller declaration concerning retribution upon Babylon has been left to the series of prophetic sayings at the end of the book. Yet this does not seem to have been the case. Clearly, tension exists between Jeremiah's advocacy of submission to Babylon for the present and his sharp condemnation of promises of its imminent downfall, with the presence in the book of the most forthright declarations that Babylon was doomed.

This difference must obviously be accounted for as part of a changed perspective that has come about through the passage of time. Nevertheless it is a changed perspective and is very important both for the structure of the book and for the impact of prophetic eschatology upon the political outlook of emergent Judaism in an age of diaspora. Recognition of this change of perspective has probably brought about the evident care with which the period of "seventy years" has been utilized in the book to define the period of Babylonian domination. The issue has become major precisely because of the necessity to accommodate Jeremiah's message of submission to Babylon with the more radical eschatological vision of its eventual downfall. Seen in this light we must conclude that the powerful declaration concerning Babylon's fall in chapters 50—51 should be regarded as a relatively late appendage to the book of Jeremiah's prophecies. This lateness, however, should certainly not be taken to suggest that it is not very important.

We may note in particular two deeply significant aspects of this message for the theology of Old Testament prophecy as a whole. In the first place it is evident from the prophecies addressed to Zedekiah at the time of the second Judean rebellion against Babylon (cf. 37:6–10), as well as from Jeremiah's advocacy of surrender to the Babylonian armies at the time when Jerusalem was under siege, that Jeremiah fully accepted the inevitability of a substantial period of Babylonian control, with all that this implied by way of economic loss. Resistance was useless and would only promote needless bloodshed. So the report of Jeremiah's message is quite accurately given: "Do not listen to the words of the prophets who are saying to you, 'You shall not serve the king of Babylon,' for it is a lie which they are prophesying to you" (27:14)! In line with this the label of "false prophets" is raised against those who were prophesying

263

"Behold, the vessels of the Lord's house will now shortly be brought back from Babylon" (27:16). Jeremiah's message could be summarized in simple political injunctions: ". . . serve the king of Babylon and live. Why should this city become a desolation?" (27:17).

It might appear that the fundamental prophecies of chapters 50—51 were just such false prophecies, offering assurance that divine justice would bring about the downfall of Babylon. Presumably for such a message Ahab and Zedekiah had paid with their lives (29:21-22). It is impossible that Jeremiah could have maintained this political stance and at the same time been declaring the certainty of Babylon's downfall. This would have been confusing to his hearers and inconsistent in its purpose. By bringing fully into the understanding of the message concerning retribution upon Babylon a sense of the time that must elapse before this could take place, both positions can be reconciled. With this change in perspective, we can understand not simply that the two positions can be held together but that they can be used to support each other. The expectation of divine eschatological judgment upon Babylon at an undefined point in the future can inculcate a political stance which enjoins acceptance of the unwelcome conditions of the present.

The certainty of Babylon's fall as a demonstration of the sovereign rule of God over the world has made an acceptance of the hurtful necessity of submission to Babylon tolerable in the present. This divine sovereign rule, however, has become part of a more absolute eschatological scheme of hope. Tension between the here and now of an imperfect order of submission to the authority of the king of Babylon and the future eschatological hope of Babylon's ultimate downfall emerges. When this downfall will occur is left open to the mystery of an as yet undisclosed aspect of the divine plan. That the prophetic Book of Jeremiah should include both a condemnation of the "false" prophets who have foretold Babylon's imminent collapse and at the same time include elaborate and full-blooded prophecies of that empire's ultimate downfall may at first appear to be inconsistent, but a deeper perspective shows their compatibility. Taken together they bear witness to what was to become a major feature of the prophetic understanding of divine providence, and they offer a basis for the openness of post-exilic Judaism's attitude to the experience of foreign rule. The message of the Book of Jeremiah is that Babylon was divinely des-

264

tined for ultimate judgment and collapse, but it would be the hand of God that delivered the fatal blow. Meanwhile the People of God, whether in Judah or among the exiles in Babylon, were bound to await God's time. The eschatological reality would emerge from the historical process, and it would achieve a full and complete realization. Nevertheless it demanded patience, faith, and painful submission to a less than satisfactory present experience before this divine purpose achieved its end.

A second feature is no less significant for an understanding of the impact of the book of Jeremiah's prophecies upon the way prophecy subsequently came to be understood. Perhaps the most remarkable features of Judaism which ensured its survival in the ancient world and characterized Jewish life for centuries afterwards has been its practical resilience and flexibility combined with a rigid theological absolutism. One God, one People of God, and one purpose of God embracing all nations have been combined with a Jewish way of life that adapted to living under the sovereign control of foreign powers: first Babylon, then Persia, followed by Greece and Rome. After the close of the Old Testament canon an even greater variety of social forms and political loyalties came to color and control Jewish life.

A key to understanding this flexibility and resilience is found in the fact that the future hope expressed through prophecy had come to be interpreted within an eschatological framework. Hope in the present learned to accept imperfections and temporary accommodation to the demands of changing political control without abandoning the prophetic vision of a free, triumphant, and peaceful Israel, exalted and at the head of all nations.

Within this prophetic vision the downfall of Israel's enemies occupied a prominent place, as exemplified in these prophecies declaring the certainty and inevitability of Babylon's downfall. In this fashion a flexible *realpolitik* could be developed. Judaism was able to cope with its present world while at the same time a more absolute form of faith looked for the ultimate triumph of justice over oppression. Israel's divine election came to be viewed as poised within a historical timescale which had not yet reached its full and necessary goal. Inconsistencies inevitably remained and the balance between the polarities of contemporary submission to a hostile world order and the affirmation of eschatological triumph could undergo considerable changes. Nevertheless the ambivalence and tension of such an outlook upon world order was important for the subsequent survival of Judaism. Had the Book of Jeremiah contained only the memory of this prophet's advocacy of submission and surrender to Babylon in Jerusalem's years of peril, it would have turned Jeremiah into a most dangerous prophetic figure—the despairing herald of doom and defeat, as he has sometimes mistakenly been portrayed. Such despairing submissiveness could have become only surrender to the dominance of unbridled power and the lust for plunder. Instead we are given a more balanced and tolerable picture, which affirms that the savage conqueror must ultimately suffer the ignominy of defeat, the humiliation of powerlessness, and being rendered a vanquished nonentity. So Babylon must fall if prophecy is to present a full message concerning the nature of God's providential government of history. It is not surprising therefore that as the elaborate process of prophetic interpretation and reinterpretation passed over into the world of apocalyptic thought the very name "Babylon" came to be used as a code-word for the oppressive temporary world power that ruled over the nations (cf. Rev. 18:2–3, 10, 21–24).

We should recognize the significance that attaches to the deep sense of divinely ordained vindication expressed in the prophecies of Babylon's fall. No longer is it simply Israel's cry for vengeance against a power that had so cruelly abused her that is expressed in these prophecies. Rather there emerges a deeper awareness that wrongs have been perpetrated against many nations, some of whom are dealt with in the foreign nation prophecies. These wrongs too are avenged and justice vindicated by Babylon's downfall. Had the prophecy been merely historical pronouncement regarding the rise of Cyrus and the triumph of the Medo-Persian empire over Babylon, it would have lacked the element which is now so important, that of divine vindication of a righteous world order. As it stands, it points beyond the overthrow of one major world power by another to an ultimate assertion of the overthrow of oppression and exploitation in all its many forms.

The concluding section of the prophecy against Babylon comprises a prose narrative message purportedly sent by Jeremiah to Babylon through the agency of Seraiah, the son of Keraiah, in the fourth year of Zedekiah's reign. Since Zedekiah is said to have gone to Babylon at that time, this would have been the year the abortive plan for rebellion against Babylon had been hatched in Jerusalem (cf. 27—28); most likely Zedekiah had been summoned to appear before Nebuchadnezzar to demonstrate his loyalty. That Jeremiah sent a secret message announcing that great misfortune would befall Babylon—"Jeremiah wrote in a book all the evil that should come upon Babylon, all these words that are written concerning Babylon" (51:60)—is startling and unexpected. At a time when Jeremiah was so vehemently denouncing as false the prophets foretelling Babylon's fall and urging Zedekiah not to join the rebellion against Nebuchadnezzar, it is scarcely credible as a factual statement. Clearly it has been composed as a narrative to defend the authenticity of Jeremiah's prophecies concerning Babylon's eventual downfall, which are now in chapters 50—51. On the surface these appear to stand in marked contrast to the message of Jeremiah during the years of Zedekiah's reign. Nevertheless we can readily see the importance of the inclusion of this narrative episode with its implications regarding Jeremiah's conviction of Babylon's eventual downfall. Its presence in the collection points to the larger context given to the word about Babylon's fall and the manner in which this is made compatible with Jeremiah's advocacy of continued Judean submission to Nebuchadnezzar. Rebellion was not the way to achieve God's purpose, nor was the time yet ripe for the hour of judgment upon Babylon to strike.

We cannot, of course, rule out the possibility that Jeremiah did nurture the expectation that Babylon would eventually lose its powerful position as ruler and oppressor of the nations. On the contrary, with the example of Assyria already fresh in the mind of the prophet and many of his contemporaries, it is highly probable that this was expected, even if the time was postponed for an indeterminate future. Clearly earthly powers did not last forever!

In the light of such reflections and the undoubted fact that this narrative must have been composed to round off the collection of prophetic sayings regarding Babylon, the distinctive eschatological nature of what that message conveyed is demonstrated. This is also in line with the rather strange character of affirming by a sign-action the totality of the overthrow that awaited Babylon: ". . . nothing shall dwell in it, neither man nor beast, and it shall be desolate for ever" (v. 62). Its absolutist theological boldness lifts it above the normal historically

267

conditioned words addressed to particular situations. There is even an element of detectable contrast with the promises afforded the victims of Babylonian power-hunger which assured these nations of eventual restoration (cf. Moab, 48:47; Ammon, 49:6; and Elam, 49:39). Babylon's savagery had been such that its return to power among the nations could never be contemplated. In this sense the eschatological element in this message ascribed to Jeremiah at a time when Judah had been so recently involved in plans to join a rebellion against Babylon points us to its distinctive nature as a message concerning a future action of God. Far from encouraging rebellion, it was intended to show why such rebellion was not necessary. Babylon's downfall had to be left to the hand of God; it could not be prematurely brought about by hasty and futile attempts on Zedekiah's part. Similarly the Jewish exiles in Babylon, who alone could have been thought to know of Jeremiah's commissioning such a prophetic sign-action and who alone could have welcomed its meaning, had to learn to accept their life-time (seventy year) fate. In their suffering and misery in exile they could hold on to a certain word of hope concerning Babylon's eventual end. Their trust in God would be rewarded, however painful the necessity for accepting the present might become.

Jeremiah 52
A Historical Summary with Signs of Hope

This concluding section of the Book of Jeremiah is clearly the work of editors who have striven to provide the book with an appendix relating it to specific historical events. This appendix served to show how the major warnings given by Jeremiah from the beginning about a "foe from the north" had been fulfilled and how there were, hidden within even the most painful realities, signs of hope for the future. Much of the material has been taken from the record of II Kings 24:18—25:30, omitting any repetition of the details concerning the period of Gedaliah's governorship and assassination. These have already been narrated in chapters 40—41, but more importantly, they no longer mark the avenue of hope for Israel's future. The basic factual details reported serve as a reminder of the major events which had occurred during Jeremiah's prophetic ministry. They also establish a groundwork of guidance and assurance for understanding how the words of hope declared by Jeremiah were beginning to move towards their fulfillment.

First of all, however, a significant literary feature is worthy of consideration. The narrative reports spread through chapters 26—44 show a close affinity to ideas, language, and dominant characteristics of the Deuteronomic movement. This is further borne out by an analysis of the literary contacts that abound between the Book of Jeremiah and the Deuteronomistic historical work (Josh.—II Kings). This becomes especially evident in the reporting of the last days of Judah, so that it appears quite natural that a brief survey of the sad events pertaining to Judah's collapse in 587 B.C. should be used to round off the story given in Second Kings and that these same events should bring the Book of Jeremiah to its conclusion.

It is noteworthy, however, that the Book of Jeremiah adds a significant dimension of hope to the otherwise hopeless end to Israel's story as set out in First and Second Kings. This element of hope and the events having a direct bearing upon it have been given the major emphasis in chapter 52. A comparison between the outline of events in II Kings 23—24 and those narrated in Jeremiah 52 is therefore particularly instructive. Both are appended summaries added to bring a literary work to a conclusion, and there are several close literary contacts between them. At the same time it appears that the episodes recounted at the close of the Book of Jeremiah have been chosen deliberately to provide a pointer towards the future.

There are four historical episodes recounted in Jeremiah 52 (vv. 1–16, 17–23, 24–30, 31–34), and it is immediately noticeable that the first two draw special attention to those institutions—the kingship of the house of David and the temple—of central interest to the composition of the history of First and Second Kings and also of major concern to the editing of the Book of Jeremiah. So far as Israel's traditional faith was concerned the seemingly impossible had happened, in that these two institutional assurances of God's election of Israel and of his presence with her as a nation had been removed.

The second two episodes concerning the numbers taken to Babylon and the release of king Jehoiachin from prison are clearly signs of hope. God had left his people sorely wounded and chastened, but he had not destroyed them nor had he

269

abandoned them altogether. By his providential care a remnant survived in Babylon and among them was a prince of the royal house. These were clearly intended to be pathways towards a better future.

Of the four specific events that are covered, the first, concerning Zedekiah's tragic reign and culminating in his fateful rebellion against Nebuchadnezzar, is set at the head (vv. 1–16). The story is self-explanatory and stands as effectively complete within itself. In rebelling against the king of Babylon, Zedekiah had rebelled against the purpose of God for his people and against his own solemn oath of allegiance sworn to the Babylonian ruler (cf. Ezek. 17:15–21). Jeremiah had continually presented a warning that Judah was threatened by a "foe from the north" (i.e., Mesopotamia). Zedekiah had left that warning unheeded and had paid the terrible price with the loss of his throne, the lives of his sons and potential heirs, and had suffered the loss of his own sight. Having been spiritually and politically blind, he had been made so physically.

The second incident reported concerns the desecration of God's temple in Jerusalem (vv. 17–23). The holy vessels made of gold and silver had been removed to Babylon as part of the spoils of war. The larger castings of bronze, including the great water container known as "the Sea" and the massive pillars given the names Jachin and Boaz (I Kings 6:15–22), had been broken and melted down. The raw metal had then been taken to Babylon. It was an act of desecration, deliberately defiling the house of God to demonstrate the powerlessness of the Lord God to defend his people and sanctuary. So it seemed to the popular mind to mark God's disowning of his sanctuary (cf. Lam. 2:6–7). The hope of eventual return of the precious temple vessels to Jerusalem is taken in the Book of Jeremiah to be a prominent indication of God's reassertion of power, so premature promises of this could be condemned as "false" prophecy (27:16–22). Later on, return of these vessels was developed as a theme demonstrating the continuity of the old temple with the one rebuilt and restored in the age of Zerubbabel (Ezra 1:5–11). This theme of the fate of the temple vessels was one of outstanding importance in upholding the claim that God had taken steps to care for his temple and to make possible its restoration. The idea is expressed that the temple had not been wholly rejected but had simply been taken out of commission for a period.

The third episode in this summary concerns the rounding

270

up of many prominent citizens, including the most senior priests and those of military and civil importance (vv. 24–30). These were taken to Riblah in Syria and after presentation before Nebuchadnezzar were executed. Whether all of them were implicated in the rebellion or were merely singled out to be made an example of is not clear. A list of the number of those deported to Babylon in three separate acts of punishment by the Babylonians is added in verses 28–30 (598, 587, and 582 B.C.).

The relative smallness of the numbers given for those taken has frequently occasioned comment. This is true even if, as is usually allowed, the numbers list only male heads of families and not their immediate dependents who accompanied them. Clearly there can have been no intention on the part of the Babylonian authorities to depopulate Judah and remove all able-bodied citizens to Babylon. The case of Jeremiah's personal experience (cf. 40:1–6) shows that some form of selectivity was exercised. There can be no question of the exiled community in Babylon representing the majority of all Judeans who had survived the disasters of 598 and 587 B.C. (cf. what is later said in II Chron. 36:20–21). It appears instead that the Babylonians deported a significant number of the most influential citizens from Judah, especially from the city of Jerusalem and almost certainly including the major land-owning families. This leaves many uncertainties about the precise intention behind the Babylonian action; at this distance in time it appears to have been more a concern to retain a body of "hostages" in Babylon than to have left Judah without an effective population to work the land. No doubt it was this exiled community in Babylon, who appear for the most part to have been kept together in large settlements (which facilitated Jeremiah's correspondence with them and their own eventual survival), who formed the basis of hope for the future (cf. 24:4–7). They are the "remnant" from which the new Israel can emerge.

The final episode recounted in verses 31–34 is taken directly from II Kings 25:27–30 and concerns the release of Jehoiachin from prison in Babylon in the year 561 B.C. This was the year Amel-Marduk assumed the Babylonian throne and the precise intention of his action in releasing the ex-king of Judah has been variously interpreted. It may well have been no more than an act of clemency to a long-term prisoner, made in celebration of a royal accession. However it is also possible that

271

Amel-Marduk's intention was to bolster his own position. His throne was decidedly insecure, and he may well have sought to gain support by an act of clemency towards a notable royal person held in Babylon. In any event, he signally failed to do so, since Amel-Marduk was assassinated in little more than a year. Nonetheless the important question concerns not what the Babylonian king intended by this action in releasing Jehoiachin but what the suffering citizens of Judah, especially those held in exile in Babylon, saw in it. Both in II Kings 25:27–30 as well as here it appears to have been an action viewed as a definite sign of hope (cf. G. von Rad, *Theology*, I, 343).

The release of the scion of the Davidic line from his wretched imprisonment in Babylon demonstrated that God had not forgotten to be gracious to this royal house, that great importance still attached to the ancient divine promise made to the ancestor of this royal line of Israel (II Sam. 7:13; cf. Jer. 33:19–22). The promise seemed to have kept its significance in spite of the negative import of the message given earlier by Jeremiah when Jehoiachin had first been taken to Babylon (22: 28–30). Clearly we can see how a few decades later the descendants of Jehoiachin (of whom Zerubbabel was one) were eagerly looked to with the expectation that they would lead to the restoration of the Davidic monarchy in the new Israel (cf. Hagg. 2:23; I Chron. 3:17–24).

By drawing attention to the presence in Babylon of an important body of exiles from Judah, including the royal figure of Jehoiachin, the Book of Jeremiah comes to a close on a theme of hope. Judgment had fallen upon Judah and Jerusalem, as Jeremiah had repeatedly affirmed that it would. The nation had not been annihilated, however, and even in judgment God had carefully preserved for his people a remnant to provide a basis of hope for the future.

Bibliography

1. For further study

ACKROYD, P.R. "The Temple Vessels—A Continuity Theme," *Supplements to Vetus Testamentum* 23 (1972) 166–81.

BOGAERT, P.- M. (ed.). *Le livre de Jeremie. Le prophete et son milieu. Les oracles et leur transmission.* BIBLIOTHECA EPHEMERIDUM THEOLOGICARUM LOVANIENSIUM LIV (Leuven: University Press/ Peeters, 1981).

BRIGHT, J. *Jeremiah.* ANCHOR BIBLE 20 (Garden City: Doubleday, 1965).

CLEMENTS, R. E. *Prophecy and Tradition.* GROWING POINTS IN THEOLOGY (Oxford: B. H. Blackwell, 1975).

COGGINS, R. J., A. Phillips and M. A. Knibb. *Israel's Prophetic Tradition. Essays in Honour of P. R. Ackroyd* (Cambridge: University Press, 1982).

GERSTENBERGER, E. "Jeremiah's Complaints: Observations on Jer. 15:10–21," *Journal of Biblical Literature* 82 (1963) 393–403.

HOLLADAY, W. L. *The Architecture of Jeremiah 1—20* (Lewisberg, PA: Bucknell University, 1976).

HYATT, J. P. *Jeremiah. Prophet of Courage and Hope* (New York/ Nashville: Abingdon Press, 1958).

MOWINCKEL, S. *Zur Komposition des Buches Jeremia* (Oslo, Dybwad, 1914).

NICHOLSON, E. W. *The Book of the Prophet Jeremiah.* 2 Vols. CAMBRIDGE COMMENTARIES ON THE NEW ENGLISH BIBLE (Cambridge: University Press, 1963/1965).

OVERHOLT, T. W. *The Threat of Falsehood. A Study in the Theology of the Book of Jeremiah.* STUDIES IN BIBLICAL THEOLOGY. SECOND SERIES 16 (Naperville, IL: Allenson, 1970).

PERDUE, L. G., and B. W. Kovacs. *A Prophet to the Nations. Essays in Jeremiah Studies* (Winona Lake: Eisenbrauns, 1984).

POLK, T. *The Prophetic Persona. Jeremiah and the Language of the Self.* JOURNAL FOR THE STUDY OF THE OLD TESTAMENT. SUPPLEMENT SERIES 32 (Sheffield: Sheffield Academic Press, 1984).

RUDOLPH, W. *Jeremia.* HANDBUCH ZUM ALTEN TESTAMENT I,12 (Tübingen: Mohr, 1968 [3rd ed.]).

SODERLUND, S. *The Greek Text of Jeremiah. A Revised Hypothesis.* JOURNAL FOR THE STUDY OF THE OLD TESTAMENT. SUPPLEMENT SERIES 47 (Sheffield: Sheffield Academic Press, 1985).

WEIPPERT, H. *Die Prosareden des Jeremiabuches.* BEIHEFT ZUR ZEITSCHRIFT FUR DIE ALTTESTAMENTLICHE WISSENSCHAFT 132 (Berlin: de Gruyter, 1973).

WEISER, A. *Das Buch des Propheten Jeremia.* DAS ALTE TESTAMENT DEUTSCH 20–21 (Göttingen: Vandenhoeck & Ruprecht, 1960 [4th ed.]).

273

WELCH, A. C. *Jeremiah. His Time and His Work* (Oxford: B. H. Blackwell, 1955).

2. Literature cited

ACKROYD, P. R. *Exile and Restoration. A Study of Hebrew Thought of the Sixth Century B.C.* OLD TESTAMENT LIBRARY (London: SCM Press, 1968).

————. "The Temple Vessels" (see Bibliography 1).

ALBRIGHT, W. F. *Archaeology and the Religion of Israel* (Baltimore: Johns Hopkins, 1953 [3rd ed.]).

BAILEY, L. R., Sr. *Biblical Perspectives on Death.* OVERTURES TO BIBLICAL THEOLOGY (Philadelphia: Fortress Press, 1979).

BLENKINSOPP, J. *Prophecy and Canon. A Contribution to the Study of Jewish Origins* (Notre Dame: University of Notre Dame Press, 1977).

BRIGHT, J. *Covenant and Promise. The Future in the Preaching of the Pre-exilic Prophets* (Philadelphia: Fortress Press, 1977).

————. *Jeremiah* (see Bibliography 1).

BRUEGGEMANN, WALTER. *The Land. Place as Gift, Promise and Challenge in Biblical Faith.* OVERTURES TO BIBLICAL THEOLOGY (Philadelphia: Fortress Press, 1977).

———— "The Epistemological Crisis of Israel's Two Histories (Jer. 9:22–23)," *Israelite Wisdom. Theological and Literary Essays in Honor of Samuel Terrien,* in J. G. Gammie et al., eds. (Missoula: Scholars Press, 1978), pp. 85–105.

CARROLL, R. P. *Jeremiah. A Commentary.* OLD TESTAMENT LIBRARY (London: SCM Press, 1986).

———— *From Chaos to Covenant* (London: SCM Press, 1981).

CLEMENTS, R. E. *Prophecy and Tradition.* GROWING POINTS IN THEOLOGY (Oxford: B. H. Blackwell, 1975).

———— "Patterns in the Prophetic Canon," *Canon and Authority,* in G. W. Coats and B. O. Long, eds. (Philadelphia: Fortress Press, 1977), pp. 42–55.

———— *Isaiah and the Deliverance of Jerusalem.* JOURNAL FOR THE STUDY OF THE OLD TESTAMENT. SUPPLEMENTS SERIES 13 (Sheffield: Sheffield Academic Press, 1980).

———— *Isaiah 1—39.* NEW CENTURY BIBLE (Grand Rapids: Eerdmans, 1980).

———— "Jeremiah. Prophet of Hope," *Review and Expositor* 78 (1981) 345–63.

———— "Prophecy as Literature. A Re-appraisal," *The Hermeneutical Quest. Essays in Honor of J. L. Mays for His 65th Birthday,* in D. G. Miller, ed., PRINCETON THEOLOGICAL MONOGRAPHS 4 (Allison Park, PA: Pickwick, 1986), pp. 59–76.

DAVIES, W. D. *The Gospel and the Land. Early Christianity and Jewish Territorial Doctrine* (Berkeley: University of California, 1974).

DIEPOLD, P. *Israels Land. Beitrage zur Wissenschaft vom Alten und Neuen Testament;* 95 (Stuttgart: Kohlhammer, 1972).

GERSTENBERGER, E. (see Bibliography 1).

GILBERT, M. "Jeremie en conflit avec les sages?" in P. -M. Bogaert, ed., *Le livre de Jeremie* (Leuven: University Press, 1981), pp. 105–18.

HERRMANN, S. "Die konstruktive Restauration. Das Deuteronomium als Mitte biblischer Theologie," in H. W. Wolff, ed., *Probleme biblischer Theologie. G. von Rad Festschrift zum 70 Geburtstag* (Munich: Kaiser Verlag, 1971), pp. 155–70.

HILLERS, D. R. *Covenant: The History of a Biblical Idea* (Baltimore: Johns Hopkins Press, 1969).

HOLLADAY, W. L. *Jeremiah I.* HERMENEIA (Philadelphia: Fortress Press, 1986).

HYATT, J. P. "The Beginning of Jeremiah's Prophecy," *Jeremiah*. THE INTERPRETER'S BIBLE (New York/Nashville: Abingdon Press, 1956).

JANZEN, J. G. *Studies in the Text of Jeremiah.* HARVARD SEMITIC MONOGRAPHS 6 (Cambridge: Harvard University Press, 1973).

KIERKEGAARD, S. *The Sickness Unto Death.* H. V. and E. H. Hong, English translation (Princeton: Princeton University Press, 1980).

McCARTHY, D. J. *Treaty and Covenant.* ANALECTA BIBLICA 21A (Rome: Biblical Institute Press, 1978).

McKANE. W. *Jeremiah I–XXV.* INTERNATIONAL CRITICAL COMMENTARY (Edinburgh: T. & T. Clark, 1986).

METTINGER, T.N.D. *Solomonic State Officials. A Study of the Civil Government of the Israelite Monarchy.* CONIECTA BIBLICA. OLD TESTAMENT SERIES 5 (Lund: CWK Gleerup, 1971).

NICHOLSON, E. W. *Preaching to the Exiles. A Study of the Prose Tradition in the Book of Jeremiah* (Oxford: B. H. Blackwell, 1970).

PERLITT, L. *Bundestheologie im Alten Testament.* WISSENSCHAFTLICHE MONOGRAPHIEN ZUM ALTEN UND NEUEN TESTAMENT 36 (Neukirchen-Vluyn: Neukirchener Verlag, 1969).

POLK, T. (see Bibliography 1).

PORTEOUS, N. W. "Jerusalem-Zion: The Growth of a Symbol," *Living The Mystery. Collected Essays* (Oxford: B. H. Blackwell, 1967), pp. 93–112.

PRITCHARD, J. B. *Ancient Near Eastern Texts Relating to the Old Testament* (Princeton: Princeton University Press, 1969 [3rd ed.]).

RAD, G. von. *Studies in Deuteronomy.* David Stalker, English translation, STUDIES IN BIBLICAL THEOLOGY 9 (Naperville: Allenson, 1953).

——— *Old Testament Theology,* Vols. 1 & 2. David Stalker, English translation (Edinburgh: Oliver & Boyd, 1962, 1965).

RIETZSCHEL, C. *Das Problem der Urrolle. Ein Beitrag zur Redaktionsgeschichte des Jeremiahbuches* (Gütersloh: Gerd Mohn, 1966).

ROWLEY, H. H. "The Prophet Jeremiah and the Book of Deuteronomy," *Studies in Old Testament Prophecy. T. H. Robinson Festschrift* (Edinburgh: T. & T. Clark, 1946), pp. 157–74.

SCHARBERT, J. "brk," *Theological Dictionary of the Old Testament,* Vol. 2. G. J. Botterweck and H. Ringgren, eds. J. T. Willis, English translation (pp. 279–308).

SKINNER, J. *Prophecy and Religion. Studies in the Life of Jeremiah* (Cambridge: University Press, 1922).

STULMAN, L. *The Other Text of Jeremiah. A Reconstruction of the Hebrew Text Underlying the Greek Version of the Prose Sections of Jeremiah with English Translation* (Lanham, MD: University Press of America, 1985).

THIEL, W. *Die deuteronomistische Redaktion von Jeremia 1—25, 26—45.* WISSENSCHAFTLICHE MONOGRAPHIEN ZUM ALTEN UND NEUEN TESTAMENTS 41, 52 (Neukirchen-Vluyn: Neukirchener Verlag, 1973, 1981).

THOMPSON, J. A. *The Book of Jeremiah.* THE NEW INTERNATIONAL CRITICAL COMMENTARY ON THE OLD TESTAMENT (Grand Rapids: Eerdmans, 1980).

VAUX, R. de. *Studies in Old Testament Sacrifice* (Cardiff: University of Wales Press, 1964).

WILSON, R. R. *Prophecy and Society in Ancient Israel* (Philadelphia: Fortress Press, 1980).

WISEMAN, D. J. *Chronicles of Chaldean Kings* (626–556 B.C.) *in the British Museum* (London: The British Museum, 1956).